Nine Men of Power

BY THE SAME AUTHOR

Mr Attlee: an Interim Biography
Pursuit of Progress
Sir Charles Dilke: a Victorian Tragedy
The Labour Case
Asquith

ROY JENKINS

Nine Men of Power

HAMISH HAMILTON

LONDON

First published in Great Britain 1974
by Hamish Hamilton Ltd
90 Great Russell Street, London WC1B 3PT

Copyright © 1974 by Roy Jenkins

SBN 241 89138 8

Printed in Great Britain by
Alden & Mowbray Ltd at the Alden Press, Oxford

Contents

INTRODUCTION	ix
J. M. Keynes	1
Léon Blum	27
Ernest Bevin	61
Stafford Cripps	81
Joseph R. McCarthy	107
Lord Halifax	133
Hugh Gaitskell	159
Adlai Stevenson	181
Robert Kennedy	205
INDEX	225

Illustrations

Between pages 144 and 145

1. Keynes in the Second World War
   Keynes at Garsington, circa 1917
2. Blum at a Popular Front demonstration, 1936
   Blum on the witness stand, 1948
3. Bevin as a trade unionist, 1920
   Bevin as world statesman, 1946
4. Cripps at his country house in the thirties
   Cripps as a sparse and austere Chancellor
5. Joseph R. McCarthy with David Schine
   Adlai Stevenson
6. Halifax as Viceroy
   Halifax greets Chamberlain, 1938
7. Hugh Gaitskell with his family, 1951
   Hugh Gaitskell with an audience, 1959
8. Robert Kennedy in London, 1967
   Robert Kennedy campaigning in Philadelphia, 1968

Introduction

I wrote these nine essays between the autumn of 1970 and the last days of 1973. They were published in *The Times*, mostly within two or three months of completion. The idea of biographical writing within such a scope—generous enough to permit a fair ration of fact as well as of opinion, yet sufficiently economical to make possible newspaper publication *in full*—was new to me, but I found it an interesting and rewarding formula.

Looking back I see that the formula went through a greater process of mutation than I appreciated at the time. The first two essays which I wrote were those on Robert Kennedy and Ernest Bevin. They are shorter than the others, and that on Kennedy appears to me to be the slightest of the nine. In terms of achievement he was, inevitably and tragically, the slightest figure. He was shortest-lived, the only one younger than myself, and one of the three I knew best. None of these considerations applied to Bevin. He lived to seventy, his achievements were massive, he was a full generation older than I, and although I watched him and heard him on many occasions, I had few conversations with him, and never one with an approach to intimacy. What separates these two essays from the others is that they were more impressionistic, less chronological, and contained a stronger blend of my own recollections and views as opposed to objective fact. They were more 'journalistic'. In the later essays, notably Halifax and Blum, I was more concerned to maintain a consecutive thread of biographical narrative, to obey Lewis Carroll's instructions about how to tell a story: 'begin at the beginning, and go on until you come to the end; then stop'. They also endeavour to give more of the background history—especially when as with the Raj of the 'twenties or the France of the Third Republic it has grown unfamiliar to most English readers. These essays are less personal, partly for the very good reason that I had no personal acquaintance with either of the subjects. I heard them speak, but no more.

Keynes, to my great regret, I knew not at all. He was the only one of the nine whom I never saw. It is a great deficiency which I wish I could retrospectively repair. There is no figure of the past generation (with the possible exception of Roosevelt) with whom I would more like to have talked. Yet I do not think this has made the Keynes essay into an impersonal 'life and times' study. He was too idiosyncratic a character for that. He is the only non-politician in the series. He has to be written about partly as a theoretician (which imposed a considerable strain upon my economics, rusty even for an ex-Chancellor) and partly as an individual; his life could not possibly be made part of a mere chronicle of public events.

Much though I would like to have known Keynes, it is an illusion to believe that acquaintanceship or even close friendship makes for easy biographical writing. The essay I found most difficult (and not merely most testing: that was the Blum biography), was the one on Gaitskell, whom I knew incomparably the best. This may have been because I had written about him before, although I think there were also special problems of striking the right balance between objectivity and identification.

Stafford Cripps and Adlai Stevenson are intermediate cases. With Cripps I knew most of the background well—both the Labour Party arguments of my youth and a Treasury struggle against balance of payments weakness—and the individual somewhat more than Bevin, but never as a friend, although as a young MP in the late 'forties I greatly admired him. Stevenson as a person I knew much better, but his field of activity was clearly less familiar. These two essays are more historical and detached than those on Gaitskell or Kennedy, but less so than the Blum or Halifax ones.

There remains McCarthy, the black joker in the pack, the anti-hero, the one man of the nine in whom (starting admittedly with a good deal of prejudice) I could find nothing of substance to admire. His selection inhibited me from introducing any possible laudatory note into the collective title. Otherwise I did not regret it. I would never wish to write a full-length biography of a figure whom I found repugnant. Several years of writing with distaste would be a warping exercise. But a few weeks of such activity is not open to the same objection, and in other ways McCarthy was an intriguing phenomenon, even though lacking the light and shade, the variety of interests and the varied careers which made, say, Blum and Keynes such rewarding subjects.

What determined the choice of the nine? There were four or five criteria, some positive, some negative, which I had in mind and tried to meet. First, although I wanted their careers to be within the recollection and not merely the historical knowledge of myself and most readers, they had to be dead. Biographical studies of the living are too inhibiting. There are enough problems in dealing with the susceptibilities of relations, without taking on those of the subjects themselves! Second, they had to be of sufficient fame, for the newspaper reader to consider working through three long articles on the subject, and of sufficient interest (not necessarily the same thing) that, once started, at any rate a proportion of those readers might continue to the end.

Third, they had closely to engage my own interest, and give me at the least the illusion that, even though I was clearly not writing from a basis of original research, I had something fresh to say about them. This made me loath to choose people who had recently attracted a great deal of attention from others. Largely for this reason I discarded Beaverbrook, who had originally been on my list. Had I been an American I might have done the same with Robert Kennedy.

Fourth, while I wanted a certain spread, across parties as well as the Atlantic and the Channel, I wanted to avoid either British Prime Ministers or American Presidents. This presented a peculiar problem of British political balance. The Labour Party seems much richer in recent deceased major figures who did not reach the highest office. Apart from the three I have included, there were three other possible candidates (Aneurin Bevan, Herbert Morrison, Hugh Dalton). The Conservative Party (although stronger in living ex-Prime Ministers) offered no one except Halifax, who was a late addition to my list, who passed the other tests. Lord Butler, save for the happy fact that he falls at the first fence, would have been a clear exception.

I had originally intended that the nine should be ten. But the General Election and the change of Government intervened. This relieved me of an awkward choice, for I was finding the tenth candidate much the most difficult to settle upon. The nine gradually chose themselves, although only five had been on my original list. The tenth stubbornly refused to do so, and the reasons further illustrate the parameters within which the book is cast. Should there not be another non-British European? Adenauer or De Gasperi? Who else apart from the over-formidable and over-written-about peak of de Gaulle had the stature? But could I write about either without being able properly to read German or Italian? Or a non-Western politician? Nehru was the obvious candidate here. But how rash and presumptuous to write about Indian politics having paid only one visit to that vastly complicated country. Or perhaps another non-politician to match Keynes? The other British figure of comparable fame would have been Bertrand Russell. But could one possibly manage the mathematics and the philosophy? Or perhaps a woman, despite the disadvantage of appearing, rather like the selector of an old-style government committee, to be including a statutory one. Again who? Mrs Roosevelt? Beatrice Webb? The first has recently exhaustively been covered by a full two-volume biography. The second was perhaps too much her own chronicler.

So there were advantages in electoral fortune restricting the list to nine. The choice, as I have indicated, was neither wholly planned nor wholly haphazard. Probably the main unifying factor was that each of them, and the events in which they were involved, seized and held my attention and imagination for three or four weeks, mostly over holiday periods, against the distractions of contemporary politics.

The collection is not intended to propound a general theory of men or politics, but merely to pass on to the reader some of my own interest in the events and individuals of the days before yesterday.

East Hendred, Easter, 1974   ROY JENKINS

Acknowledgements

To thank all those who gave me assistance in publishing essays on nine separate individuals would produce a list of excessive length. I therefore confine myself to mentioning Mr William Rees-Mogg, who suggested to me the idea of biographical studies in this form; Mrs Bess Church, who as my principal secretary was concerned with the production of each one, as well as with the compilation of the whole; Mr Matthew Oakeshott, who rescued the book from delay; and M. Daniel Norman, London correspondent of *Le Figaro*, who gave me exceptional help with sources for the essay—that on Blum—where the bibliography was most unfamiliar to me. There are many others to whom my debt is remembered even if unexpressed.

R.H.J.

Thanks are also due to the Society of Authors as agents for the Strachey Trust for permission to quote the lines by Lytton Strachey which appear on page 6.

J. M. KEYNES

J. M. Keynes

Maynard Keynes died in 1946. On the evening of the Saturday before Easter, in that first post-war spring, he was driven to Firle Beacon, above his South Down farm, and looked at the sea, the Weald and the valley of the Sussex Ouse, around which were the houses of his Bloomsbury friends, from whom he had latterly become more remote. He decided to take the unusual course of walking down. Early the next morning he was dead.

He was only 62, but his heart had given him persistent trouble since a nearly fatal illness nine years before. It had restricted the framework of his life and curbed his sense of limitless intellectual power. But it had not destroyed the force of his central activity. The last two years of his life, judged by his impact on public affairs, although not by his contribution to the advance of ideas, had been the most productive of his life. He had been a parent of the Bretton Woods agreement, and he had negotiated the American loan which enabled Britain to enter the post-war world in a position of relatively stable austerity rather than of economic collapse.

His fame, which probably makes him in the curious company of Churchill and Bertrand Russell one of the three most world renowned Englishmen of this century, does not rest primarily upon these achievements of statecraft. Much more it depends upon his position as a principal station on the line of great economists which starts with Adam Smith and extends through Ricardo and Marshall to himself, but not yet, according to the generality of judgment, to any further point of comparable importance; and also upon the fact that his writings struck such a balance between theoretical elegance and practical application that, being also lucky in their timing, they profoundly influenced the whole climate of policy-making, extending in their impact to many who, despite the lucidity of his style, have never read a single paragraph of his original words. In addition, he had a personality and range of friends and interests which, had he written no word of note, would still have made him a figure of continuing interest from the England of the first half of this century.

Nevertheless, the nature of his final work makes the present time, when the sun of Bretton Woods, having warmed world trade and world prosperity for a generation, has recently and precipitously set, a peculiarly appropriate moment from which to assess his life and his achievement.

He came from the Victorian core of the university and town of Cambridge. His father was a fellow of Pembroke College, a lecturer in logic and political economy, and later for many years Registrary of the University. His mother was the daughter of a leading and scholarly Congregationalist minister, and herself an early student of Newnham, a writer of some note and later mayor of the town. Keynes was born in one of the substantial but unbeautiful houses which had recently sprung up on the edge of the university to meet the needs of the new race of married dons. It remained his parents' home throughout his life.

He was taught at home and at a local preparatory school, and then at 14 went to Eton. He was a King's Scholar, eleventh out of 20 at his election, and Eton was in no way an inevitable school for him. His father had been at Amersham Hall, and his younger brother went to Rugby. Nevertheless he had a highly successful Eton career, studded with a great number of friendships and a wide range of intellectual and other activities. He was primarily a mathematician, but far from narrowly specialized. He was on the fringe of the highest level of academic achievement. In 1902 he went back to Cambridge, to King's with a closed Eton scholarship in the unusual combination of mathematics and classics.

If Eton was not an inevitable school for him, Cambridge was certainly an inevitable university. It thought of itself as very different from Oxford. When Keynes was a small child there was a rumour that his father might become Professor of Political Economy at that other university.

'Pray don't go', Professor Foxwell wrote in half-serious horror. '. . . Think of the effect your move may have on your son. He may grow up flippantly epigrammatical and end by becoming the proprietor of a Gutter Gazette, or the hero of a popular party; instead of emulating his father's noble example, becoming an accurate, clear-headed Cambridge man, spending his life in the valuable and unpretentious service of his kind, dying beloved of his friends, venerated by the wise and unknown to the masses, as true merit and worth mostly are.'

The elder Keynes did not go, and his son was protected from the superficial worldliness of an Oxford education which Foxwell rather oddly thought would necessarily follow from such a translation. Maynard Keynes remained faithful to Cambridge, although not to any extreme version of its intellectual austerity. He eschewed neither epigram nor fame. And from the beginning of his time at King's, he appeared as a rather worldly figure. This impression was marred only by his enthusiasm. He did almost everything that an undergraduate could do. He joined all sorts of societies and delivered as well as listened to papers on subjects from Abelard to the nature of time. He pursued his mathematics but only to the extent of becoming twelfth wrangler. He diluted them by winning an English essay prize. He played golf at Royston. He bought rare books. He became President of the Union and a leading if cool Liberal. As a scholar he read the lesson in King's Chapel, and took great pleasure in doing so, until the Dean stopped him because, as a disbeliever, he would not promise regular attendance when he was not performing. For his first year he even continued to row.

Although he had 'never enjoyed himself so much before', as he wrote to an Eton friend, he was not swept away by King's to the extent of suppressing his critical spirit. The view that any institution which he surveyed was run in a fairly muddled way and that he could do it a great deal better was a constant ingredient of his life. 'I have had a good look round the place', he said in his first term, 'and come to the conclusion that it's pretty inefficient.'

He had to wait 17 years before he could make King's more efficient, but in the meantime he was full of other occupations. In that same first term he began his tumultuous friendship with Lytton Strachey, which led on both to the main pattern of his early Cambridge relationships and to his Bloomsbury life. Towards the end of 1902 Strachey and Leonard Woolf, both at Trinity, visited him in his rooms in King's Lane. They had come to inspect him as a possible member of a self-consciously select university club known alternatively as 'the Society' or 'the Apostles'. It had existed since the 1820s, when it was founded by F. D. Maurice. Tennyson and Hallam had been early members. Later Sidgwick was the dominant figure.

At the time when Keynes was invited to join the influence of the philosopher G. E. Moore was supreme. A few months later he was to publish *Principia Ethica*. Keynes read it at once, and wrote: '. . . a stupendous and entrancing work, *the greatest* on the subject'. Strachey, usually at least equally critical as Keynes, was even more carried away. 'I think your book has not only wrecked and shattered all writers on Ethics from Aristotle and Christ to Herbert Spencer and Mr Bradley', he wrote to the author, 'it has not only laid the true foundations of Ethics, it has not only left all modern philosophy *bafouée*—these seem to me small achievements compared to the establishment of that Method which shines like a sword between the lines ... I date from Oct. 1903. The beginning of the Age of Reason.'

It is a little difficult now to understand the state of excitement produced by Moore. But that it existed, and embraced Keynes, cannot be doubted. Moore was in some ways a naive man, which was far from true of either Keynes or Strachey. Indeed the end of the *Principia* had an unworldliness which once led Keynes to say that, by comparison, the New Testament was a handbook for politicians. But Moore had a shining clarity of thought and language, as well as a message which was extremely welcome to the recipients. In the crudest terms it was that conduct should be determined by the obligation to select the course which, by a rational prediction of probable consequences, was likely to achieve more good than any practicable alternative. This of course begged the question of what was 'good'. Moore's answer was that 'By far the most valuable things, which we can know or can imagine, are certain states of consciousness which may be roughly described as the pleasures of human intercourse and the enjoyment of beautiful objects.' Strachey paraphrased this, according to Mr Michael Holroyd, by forgetting the puritanical element in Moore's teaching and forming an equation of 'aesthetic experience + personal relations = the good life'.

In spite of his sophistication, Keynes found the Apostles a heady experience. Apart from Moore, McTaggert, Whitehead, Bertrand Russell and Lowes Dickinson were among the senior members. There were only six undergraduate members at the time, who, in addition to Keynes's two sponsors, included Desmond MacCarthy and J. T. Sheppard, later Provost of King's. The make-up perfectly suited his main intellectual interest which was then in the borderland between mathematics and philosophy, with the support of a wide range of reading, embracing much general literature, but centring upon the development of ideas. Whether its central outlook, with its elevation of abstract thought above action in the world, was ever fully acceptable to him is more doubtful. Certainly his later life did not meet this standard. Perhaps, in spite of Professor Foxwell's attempted inoculation, he was always something of an Oxford Trojan horse in Cambridge. He soon became too fond of the trains to London to be a strict Cambridge man.

The Strachey connexion also led him deep into the pre-1914 world of Cambridge homosexuality. No doubt this proclivity had been there before, and was the basis of at least some of his intense Eton friendships. It may indeed be the case that the recent revelations about Strachey's life and, as a side effect, about Keynes's give Strachey, by accident, too central a role in this. But what is certainly true is that homosexual relations played a great although not necessarily a direct role in the fluctuating course of the Keynes-Strachey friendship. The exact nature of the relationships is not very clear, particularly as it was the practice of the group to use rather extreme language to describe rather mild activities. But what is certain is that there was a great deal of emotional entanglement and upheaval, some of it appearing, in retrospect and from the outside at least, as verging upon the farcical.

First Strachey and then Keynes became involved with a young man called Duckworth. They vied with each other to secure his election to the Apostles, apparently being both equally willing on this occasion to subordinate intellectual to personal tests. Keynes, being the more subtle and determined, succeeded in acting as sponsor and Strachey was cast into despair and bitterness. But soon Duckworth drifted away from Keynes, which at least had the effect of bringing a sympathetic Strachey back to Keynes.

A few years later, after an interlude with B. W. Swithinbank, Keynes's principal Eton friend and later a distinguished Indian administrator, Strachey became deeply embroiled with Duncan Grant the painter, who was his first cousin. Then, after a time, he discovered with immense shock that Keynes had again replaced him. And in the midst of it all Duncan Grant had for a time been swept away by the ubiquitous Duckworth, and *vice versa!*

It was all very involved, and the chief interest is perhaps that in periods of jealousy it brought out, no doubt in an exaggerated form, some of Strachey's latent criticisms of Keynes. Keynes's brilliance was not in doubt. Bertrand Russell thought his intellect was 'the sharpest and clearest' he had ever known, but doubted, although then dismissed the doubt, whether it was compatible with depth. Professor J. D. Beazley, the great interpreter of Greek ceramic art, recalled after a gap of 50 years a visit to Cambridge at the time and he thought then that 'Keynes and Strachey were the two cleverest men I had ever met'; and added, 'looking back over the years I still think they were the two cleverest men I ever met.' Sir Steven Runciman, of a different generation, saw them together many years later and thought much the same thing, although he put Keynes first: 'But I have to admit that, brilliant as Lytton was, Maynard was the more brilliant.'

Behind this association of peers there was a view, not confined to Strachey, that Keynes lacked feeling and imagination, that his intellect was too brittle and mechanical, his purposes too worldly, and his aesthetic appreciation too contrived. Desmond MacCarthy said that his object in life was to impress men of forty. Strachey went much further. 'His sense of values, and indeed all his feelings', he announced under stress to a meeting of the Society, 'offer the spectacle of a complete paradox. He is a hedonist and a follower of Moore; he is lascivious without lust; he is an Apostle without tears.'

More calmly and many years later he referred to 'his curious typewriter intellect'. He gave him the nickname of 'Pozzo', after Pozzo di Borgo, the devious Corsican diplomat, which Keynes much disliked but which continued to be used for several decades. Yet he was fascinated by him throughout all the vicissitudes of their relationship and despite his conviction that Keynes 'possessed no aesthetic sense whatsoever'. Perhaps the median point of Strachey's attitude to Keynes and something too of the latter's early character is best expressed by some satirical lines which Strachey wrote and presented to the subject when Keynes passed second into the Home Civil Service:

> *In Memoriam J.M.K. 06 Sept., 1906.*
> Here lies the last remains of one
> Who always did what should be done.
> Who never misbehaved at table
> And loved as much as he was able.
> Who couldn't fail to make a joke
> And, though he stammered, always spoke;
> Both penetrating and polite,
> A liberal and a sodomite,
> An atheist and a statistician,
> A man of sense, without ambition.
> A man of business, without bustle.
> A follower of Moore and Russell,
> One who in fact, in every way,
> Combined the features of the day.
> By curses blest, by blessings cursed.
> He didn't merely get a first.
> A first he got on that he reckoned;
> But then he also got a second.
> He got a first with modest pride;
> He got a second, and he died.

But here, again, there was a tinge of envy—Strachey never got a first at all—and still more of disapproval of Keynes for passing into the service, if not of Mammon, at least of the state.

This first phase of Keynes's public career was not an outstanding success. He embarked on it with some hesitation. After his moderate achievement in the Mathematical Tripos he went back to King's for a further year. He devoted his time partly to economics, taught by Marshall and seeing a good deal of Pigou, and to preparing for the Civil Service examination. Marshall was anxious that he should do the Economics Tripos, and G. M. Trevelyan wrote urging that he should not rush 'into the tomb of the civil service', but should go to the Bar and prepare himself for politics. But politics were too alien to his Cambridge friends, and at the same time he wished to escape a little, but not too much, from their cocoon. By April he had decided in favour of the Civil Service examination.

Its results rather exasperated him: 'I have done worst in the only subjects of which I possessed a solid knowledge—Mathematics and Economics ... I evidently knew more about Economics than my examiners', he added, probably correctly.

However, in October, 1906, the Treasury having been pre-empted by the first successful candidate, he entered the India Office. From the beginning he was under-employed, and devoted many of his office hours to writing a fellowship dissertation on Probability. He did not form a high view of the India Office, he thought it 'pretty inefficient', like King's. He resigned in June, 1908. This was in spite of the rejection of his Probability thesis. After long discussion, and a rather doubtful report from Whitehead, another mathematician and a classical scholar were elected to the two available Prize Fellowships.

For three years Keynes's academic sun had not shone as brightly as it might have done. His position as twelfth wrangler had been good but not magnificent. So had his performance in the Civil Service examination. And now there was this distinct set-back.

Nevertheless he decided to return to Cambridge. He accepted one of two £100-a-year lectureships in economics for which the new professor, Pigou, following the example of his predecessor Marshall, paid for from his own pocket. The post was not a glorious one, and, despite another £100 a year from his father and the prospect of some supplementary earnings, the financial prospect it offered was exiguous. However the gamble came off. In the following spring, with the re-submission of his somewhat amended thesis, Keynes got his King's Fellowship.

He held it for the rest of his life, adding the bursarship after the First War, but never seeking a chair or even a doctorate. Until he received an honorary LLD in 1942, he acquired no degree beyond that following from his Mathematical Tripos. Until he became a peer in the same year, he remained 'Mr' Keynes. As his academic eminence grew this caused some confusion, particularly among Americans. They found it difficult not to add at least an honorary 'Professor' to his name. He rejected it with disdain. 'Least of all do I want the indignity without the emoluments', was his favourite reply.

Keynes's brief India Office excursion was not entirely profitless. In 1912 he wrote *Indian Currency and Finance*, his first published book. The subject often exercised a fascination for English economists, principally because it allowed them to play with a sand-model, uninhibited by the entrenched rigidities of the British system. Keynes's work, combined with his having left a better impression on the India Office than *vice versa*, led to his membership of a Royal Commission on the subject. As he was still only 29, it was an unexpected appointment. The chairman was Austen Chamberlain, to whom Keynes reacted typically. 'Austen came out of the ordeal very well', he wrote towards the end, 'and I believe he may yet be Prime Minister—I don't suppose on the purely intellectual score that he is any stupider than Campbell-Bannerman . . .' On the Commission, Keynes was dominating and astringent, but not to the extent of alienating himself from the other members.

This work brought him within the official orbit. In August, 1914, he was asked to assist the Treasury. At first he was only an outside adviser, and fought a successful but not wholly characteristic battle against the suspension of gold payments by the Bank of England. He joined the Treasury full-time at the beginning of 1915, worked on the overseas side, and by 1917 was in charge of the division dealing with the external finance of the war effort. He developed and applied the system of inter-allied loans, planned our payments of foreign currency, and played the primary part in managing the exchange rate in New York. It was his one experience of major, direct, executive responsibility.

On the whole he performed his role with calm, cool competence, although there are a number of stories of rash unorthodoxy. One highly successful example was his handling of a sudden shortage of Spanish pesetas. With difficulty a small supply was obtained. The Permanent Secretary was greatly relieved, until he discovered that Keynes had immediately sold them in an attempt to break the market. Then he was still more relieved, for the market behaved as it was intended to, and dutifully broke.

There was some ambiguity about Keynes's general position on the war. Nearly all his close friends were conscientious objectors. He never claimed to be one, although he was strong in his opposition to conscription, and suggested that if a Bill were introduced McKenna, his ministerial chief, would resign, and that he would do so too. Neither did. Keynes contented himself with the gesture of refusing either to attest or to seek exemption, but merely writing on Treasury paper to say he was too busy. For a year or so this worked, but eventually he had to claim exemption. He also appeared before Military Tribunals to give support to the scruples of Duncan Grant, James Strachey and David Garnett. Neither this nor the Café Royal dinners at which he cosseted them on the evenings of their ordeals were entirely appeasing. There was some complaint, mainly from Lytton Strachey, about his 'quibbling, sophistry and vacillation'. But they remained his friends.

By the end of the war Keynes's position in the Treasury was such that he went to the Paris Peace Conference as deputy to the Chancellor on the Supreme Economic Council. He spent much of the first half of 1919 in Paris. But this visit was less satisfactory than a brief one which he had paid in the spring of 1918. Then he obtained the permission of Bonar Law—of all people—to take £20,000 and spend it on buying pictures for the National Gallery at the sale of Degas's private collection. The market was depressed, and Keynes secured 13 paintings, including a Corot, two Monets, a Gauguin and five Ingres, as well as 11 drawings, for his money. He also bought Cézanne's *Apples* and an Ingres drawing for himself. He took careful counsel from Duncan Grant. It was one of the best conducted Treasury purchasing missions.

In 1919 he was less able to do what he wanted. He brought off one or two minor coups, including the famous incident when he switched Lloyd George's brief after the Prime Minister had started addressing the Council of Four, and watched him elide with complete success and apparent continuity from the presentation of one case to the still more persuasive presentation of its opposite. Such pyrotechnics gave him a certain reluctant admiration for the Prime Minister, of whom he had not previously thought much. But his general experience in Paris filled him with growing despair. He was not on the Reparation Commission, where he believed that the worst disasters were perpetrated, but he became increasingly opposed to the whole shape of the Treaty. Clemenceau was a constant villain. Lloyd George sowed many of the seeds of the disaster, but towards the end, so Keynes believed, might have wished to repent. But by then Woodrow Wilson's stubbornness had become a major force for error.

At the end of May Keynes resigned. He had been seriously ill for a few weeks—a not unusual event with him at the end of any period of sustained effort. But this was not the reason for his going. He had to get away from 'this scene of nightmare'. He went back to Cambridge for a rest. After three weeks he began to write one of the most famous polemics of the twentieth century. By the end of September the 70,000 word book was complete. *The Economic Consequences of the Peace* was published in December. It immediately brought him world fame and made him a figure of major controversy. Its main theme was obviously economic: the reparation clauses of the treaty would disrupt European trade and lead to chaos, suffering, and a future of doom wrought by folly. But the statistics by which this was demonstrated rode easily on a narrative of passion, illuminated by devastating portraits of the main participants of the Conference.

Clemenceau 'felt about France what Pericles felt of Athens—unique value in her, nothing else mattering; but his theory of politics was Bismarck's. He had one illusion—France; and one disillusion—mankind, including Frenchmen, and his colleagues not least.' Wilson was 'like a nonconformist minister, perhaps a Presbyterian. His thought and his temperament were essentially theological not intellectual . . .' But 'at the crisis of his fortunes' he was a lonely man: 'Caught up in the toils of the Old World, he stood in great need of sympathy, of moral support, of the enthusiasm of the masses. But buried in the Conference, stifled in the hot and poisoned atmosphere of Paris, no echo reached him from the outer world, and no throb of passion, sympathy, or encouragement from his silent constituents in all countries . . . And in this drought the flower of the President's faith withered and dried up.' As a result there 'began the weaving of that web of sophistry and Jesuitical exegesis that was finally to clothe with insincerity the language and substance of the whole Treaty'.

The dominant figure of whom there was no major portrait was Lloyd George. Keynes wrote it and then cut it out. He had shown it to Asquith, not perhaps the most impartial of witnesses on this subject, who had pronounced it fair. But the author decided that he ought not to write in such a way of someone he had so recently served. It appeared fourteen years later in *Essays in Biography*:

But it is not appropriate to apply to him the ordinary standards. How can I convey to the reader, who does not know him, any impression of this extraordinary figure of our time, this syren, this goat-footed bard, this half-human visitor to our age from the hag-ridden magic and enchanted woods of Celtic antiquity? One catches in his company that flavour of final purposelessness, inner irresponsibility, existence outside or away from our Saxon good or evil, mixed with cunning remorselessness, love of power, that lend fascination, enthralment, and terror to the fair-seeming magicians of North European folklore . . . Lloyd George is rooted in nothing; he is void and without content;

he lives and feeds on his immediate surroundings; he is an instrument and a player at the same time which plays on the company and is played on by them too: he is a prism . . . which collects light and distorts it and is most brilliant if the light comes from many quarters at once; a vampire and a medium in one.

The Economic Consequences therefore belongs to a very rare category of books. Not only did it achieve world renown almost as much for its phraseology as for its argument. It did so after the excision of the most striking passage of all. It also has another singular claim to fame. It attracted a refutation, *The Carthaginian Peace, or the Economic Consequences of Mr Keynes,* by Etienne Mantoux, written no less than 25 years later. It was a measure of the continuing influence of the original work.

Some saw this as a highly baneful influence. In their view it was partly responsible for the refusal of the American Senate to ratify the Treaty, and thus for the retreat into isolation; it weakened our will to resist the later resurgence of Germany; it damaged our relations with France. The first point is fanciful; the key Senate vote took place before the book was published. The second is muddled; a successful resistence to Hitler could hardly be held to depend upon creating the conditions which helped him to emerge. The third was probably inevitable if any sensible policy was to be advocated and pursued.

What is the case, however, is that the book ruptured Keynes's relations with Whitehall. There was to be no significant renewal for two decades. The accepted official view came to be that his brilliance was fatally marred by inconsistency and irresponsibility. Even before his resignation, Sir Eyre Crowe, the Foreign Office Permanent Under-Secretary, had included the following words in a description of him: 'Many of us who had frequent contact with him during the War have learnt to our cost that he only sees, for the time being, the point he has set himself to prove, and regardless of the fact that he had proved something very different yesterday, and is likely to prove something different still tomorrow.'

Thereafter this view became magnified and more widely disseminated. Keynes was certainly inconsistent in the sense that he often tried one idea and then, if it was unacceptable or did not work, quickly discarded it in favour of another; and sometimes he pursued two contradictory ones at the same time. And whatever idea he was pursuing he advocated with trenchancy and even virulence. He was irresponsible only in believing that many accepted ideas and institutions were based upon muddle and folly, and that he could run things a great deal better than those who were in charge. The performance of Britain and Europe in the inter-war years does not suggest that this was an unreasonable position, but it was enough to cut him off for the whole of this period from official action. He became an independent pundit, and one whose ideas were on the whole much more acceptable to the left than to the right.

Earlier he had begun to move on the fringe of the Liberal political world. His prewar London life had been centred on Bloomsbury, both geographically and socially. Pre-1914 'Bloomsbury' was an extension and development of the Cambridge society in which he had lived so intensively as an undergraduate. It was the ideas of G. E. Moore and the sparkling erudition and cliquish conversation of Lytton Strachey transferred to London, and there blended, somewhat surprisingly, with a strong feminine re-inforcement. The core members of 'Bloomsbury' were Strachey himself and the two Stephen sisters, Vanessa Bell and Virginia Woolf. Immediately around the core were Keynes, Duncan Grant, Clive Bell, Leonard Woolf, Thoby and Adrian Stephen, Roger Fry, Desmond MacCarthy and Oliver, Marjorie and James Strachey. A little more peripheral, and also in some cases a little later on the scene, were E. M. Forster, Gerald Shove, David Garnett, Raymond Mortimer, Dadie Rylands, Ralph Partridge, and perhaps ten or twelve others.

It was a tight-knit group, somewhat frayed at the edges as with all coteries, well enough off in most cases, although, where there was any interest, mildly leftward inclined in politics, suspicious of established values in the arts and in private behaviour, but substituting a rigid and exclusive set of its own, cultivating a pattern of intense personal relations, high aesthetic appreciation, and irreverent but inquiring conversation.

Geographically the centre was 46 Gordon Square. The Stephen family had lived there since 1904. Then it became the home of Clive and Vanessa Bell. Keynes lived from 1911 at 38 Brunswick Square, sharing it with Duncan Grant and Adrian and Virginia Stephen. In 1916, the Bells having removed to Sussex, he took over 46 Gordon Square, which remained his London house for the rest of his life, with the later addition of the next door house, mainly for the accommodation of his growing collection of books.

Well before this, however, Keynes's social life had developed, not away from, but outside Bloomsbury. Lady Ottoline Morrell was probably the main catalyst. He began to go often to her house at Garsington, near Oxford. He was there for Christmas, 1915, and so too were the Bells and Lytton Strachey. From there his circuit extended to the Asquiths' house at Sutton Courtenay.

He was frequently at the Wharf, both before and after Asquith ceased to be Prime Minister. In March, 1916, he dined twice at 10 Downing

Street within a week. Margot was his friend more than Asquith himself, although she once told him, with remarkable lack of percipience, that he would never get on in the world if he did not get up early in the mornings —he habitually stayed in bed until he had settled a good part of the day's work. Asquith was reported as having said of Keynes: 'Not much juice in *him*'; 'So superficial we all thought it', was the rejoinder of Bloomsbury. But this may have been after an incident at Garsington when the Prime Minister and Keynes arrived together and were announced by the butler as 'Mr Keynes and another gentleman'.

Keynes had rather a high continuing view of Asquith, partly because he so much preferred him to Lloyd George. As late as 1926, when Asquith's star was certainly not burning at its brightest, he went out of his way to refer with approval to Lord Oxford's quality of 'a certain coolness of temper', which 'seems to me at the same time peculiarly *Liberal* in flavour, and also a much bolder and more desirable and more valuable political possession and endowment than sentimental ardours'.

This passage was from one of two talks which Keynes gave in 1925-26 (and published in 1931) which come nearest to defining his own view of his inter-war political position. He defined it negatively rather than positively:

How could I bring myself to be a Conservative? They offer me neither food nor drink—neither intellectual nor spiritual consolation. I should not be amused or excited or edified. That which is common to the atmosphere, the mentality, the view of life of—well, I will not mention names—promotes neither my self-interest nor the public good. It leads nowhere; it satisfies no ideal; it conforms to no intellectual standard; it is not even safe, or calculated to preserve from spoilers that degree of civilization which we have already attained.

He contemplated the Labour Party of the 'twenties with little more enthusiasm, and gave his reasons against adherence with a characteristic lack of euphemism:

Ought I, then, to join the Labour Party? Superficially that is more attractive. But looked at closer, there are great difficulties. To begin with it is a class party and the class is not my class. If I am going to pursue sectional interests at all, I shall pursue my own . . . I can be influenced by what seems to me Justice and good sense, but the *Class* war will find me on the side of the educated *bourgeoisie*.

He therefore decided that he was probably a Liberal, although one by elimination and without great faith in the ability of the Liberal Party to regain its former political power. Furthermore, he thought that those who believed 'with Mr Winston Churchill and Sir Alfred Mond that the coming struggle was Capitalism versus Socialism and that their duty was to fight for Capitalism, ought to get out of the Liberal Party'. Yet he uttered an only too realistic *cri de coeur:* 'I do not wish to live under a Conservative Government for the next twenty years.' His recipe, not deployed with his usual certainty, was Liberal-Labour co-operation and a rejuvenated and radicalized Liberalism providing most of the ideas.

Keynes in the twenties became a *bourgeois*, not merely by heredity and occupation, but in the full Marxist sense of the word too. He became a man of substantial property. In August, 1919, in the midst of writing *The Economic Consequences*, he began a policy of intensive forward foreign exchange speculation. He had always been a natural gambler, much attracted by the green baize tables whenever on a foreign visit. But he did not begin this new policy for the excitement. He wanted to make money, to give himself full financial independence and to make possible the moderate indulgence of a wide range of tastes. The risk-taking was considerable, for he operated on very narrow margins and plunged deeply. He dealt in dollars, francs, marks, lire, rupees and Dutch florins. At first most things went well. By the following Easter he had made £22,000 on francs against an £8,000 dollar loss. Then he got into serious trouble. The mark would not depreciate, as it should, and the dollar would not rise. He lost well over £20,000 that spring. He had to close positions disadvantageously, which made matters worse. He was fairly near to bankruptcy, which as Sir Roy Harrod rightly points out, would have been intellectually as well as financially destructive: 'It would indeed have been a disaster if the man who had so recently set world opinion agog by claiming to know better than the mighty of the land had himself become involved in bankruptcy.' At the expense of his £6,000 of savings, the profits of *The Economic Consequences*, and some borrowing, he avoided this.

He then immediately started again, and more successfully. Gradually he extended his interests, first to commodities, and then to general Stock Exchange investment. He became a director of several insurance companies, and the chairman of one, as well as a member of a number of syndicates. He invested a good deal on behalf of his friends, as well as of King's, of which he became First Bursar in 1924. His policies, particularly on behalf of others, became more orthodox and long-term. There were occasional hazards, as when he once bought wheat forward for King's, got caught, and was found looking ruminatively at the Chapel and murmering '*I think* we could use it as a granary if necessary.' In the end even this deal came out well. He made King's richer than it had been since Henry VI was deposed and the Yorkists took much of the endowment.

Apart from the inevitable setback of the slump years he also did well for his friends and himself. At the end of 1924 he was worth nearly £60,000, not counting books and pictures. By 1937 the sum had grown to £506,000.

In addition he earned a lot. In September, 1925, Lytton Strachey went to stay with him at the farm he had bought near Charleston in Sussex, and wrote: 'Would you believe it? Not one drop of alcohol appeared. The Charlestonians declare that *il gran Pozzo* is now immensely rich — probably £10,000 a year. I can believe it—and water, water everywhere! Such is the result of wealth.' The austerity was not wholly characteristic although Keynes was often 'close' with money. But the rumours of wealth were well founded.

The 'Bloomsburyites' were in any case in somewhat bad humour with him at that stage. This was because of his marriage. His wife was Lydia Lopokova, prima ballerina in the Diaghilev company, formerly of the Imperial Company in St. Petersburg. He had first met her on Armistice Night, at a Bloomsbury party. Since the first Diaghilev London presentations in 1912 he had been a ballet devotee—and was to remain one for the rest of his life. Since 1921 he had seen Mlle Lopokova frequently. Bloomsbury and Cambridge were both a little doubtful, but when the marriage took place, Cambridge accepted it the more easily. Strachey screeched at Keynes's marrying such 'a half-witted canary'. He even appeared to be in love with her. They might even have children. And she was so plain! Vanessa Bell behaved even more extraordinarily, virtually stealing a Duncan Grant picture from Keynes's London house as a *riposte*. After a time a calmer atmosphere began to prevail. Nevertheless, despite the location of Tilton, Keynes's Sussex farm, within easy range of a group of other Bloomsbury dwellings, there was never a return to quite the full previous intimacy. But there were no complete ruptures.

Keynes's life then settled into the rhythm which he was to maintain until his illness in 1937. In term time he spent Friday to Tuesday in Cambridge, the middle of the week in London. He used Tilton for holidays and for weekends out of term. In Cambridge he lectured once a week on Money to a ruthlessly restricted group, he founded and ran the Political Economy Club, he reorganized the finances of King's, and almost single-handed sponsored the building and launching of the new Arts Theatre. He was a very considerable figure in the Combination Room, although, perhaps not quite to the extent that he was in some circles in London, and among a chosen group of undergraduates.

In or from London he edited the *Economic Journal*, chaired the board of the *Nation and Athenaeum* until by an amalgamation which he never ceased to regret it became the *New Statesman and Nation*, wrote numerous articles on the politico-economic questions of the day, always ensuring that they were as well paid as possible, inspired the Tuesday Club of critical economists, wrote substantial parts of the Liberal Party's Yellow Book, maintained a wide range of acquaintances, and conducted his financial affairs.

Between the two, or at Tilton, he wrote his books. In 1921 he had published his *Treatise on Probability*, much of which had been written before the first war. It was more a logician's than a mathematician's work. In 1923 he published his *Tract on Monetary Reform*. In 1927 he followed up *The Economic Consequences* with *A Revision of the Treaty*, which was more strictly economic and did not attract such a wide audience. In 1930 he published his first major work of economic theory, the two-volume *Treatise on Money*, which contained much of the work which he had been doing with D. H. Robertson on the nature of saving and investment, and their relationship to price movements.

Then, in January, 1936, came the *General Theory of Employment Interest and Money*. It is the work upon which his claim to lasting renown as a theoretical economist must rest. Without it, he would be remembered as an outstanding international financial negotiator, as a coruscating pamphleteer and polemicist, as a man of strong and original views on the questions of the day, as well as a writer of some interesting but transient books and articles. His reputation would be roughly equivalent to that of a Harold Laski, reinforced by that of a Lord Cherwell, if an amalgam of the two can be imagined. But he could not conceivably be put in the category of Adam Smith, Ricardo and Marshall.

The General Theory did not come out of a vacuum. In the first place it was a direct response to the major economic problem of the time—the exacerbation by the worst slump in a history of already unacceptable unemployment levels. This accounted for much of its impact. It was an elegant work of academic theory, but it was also urgent. Second, it had been presaged by a good deal of writing and talking by Keynes himself, as well as others. One of the basic ideas, that of under-consumption or 'excess of thrift', had indeed been propounded by J. A. Hobson nearly 40 years before. Keynes had been critical of Hobson in some of his earlier writings, but made fairly handsome amends in *The General Theory*. Again, some of the other ideas, particularly the absence of any causal connexion between savings and investment, had been developed in the *Treatise on Money*, although there was a confusing and doubtfully necessary conceptual change between the two works. In addition Keynes made substantial use of tools fashioned and announced by others, most notably of R. F. Kahn's 'multiplier', which had been outlined in an *Economic Journal* article of June, 1931.

In general, however, there could be no question of Keynes's work being derivative; he was much more open to the charge of having been too busy with his other concerns to read enough of the works of others, and being inadequately aware, for example, of the works of European economists such as Wicksell. But if he did not read a lot, he wrote a lot, and there had been a substantial outpouring of articles from his pen on the subject of unemployment and the under-use of resources, both in England and America, in the few years before publication. Furthermore, the book had been in typescript, and much discussed among his associates, from the end of 1934.

The General Theory did not therefore arrive unheralded. But it was a complete reshaping of the doctrines of macro-economics in terms which were directly relevant to the major problems of the time. It was not just a torpedo fired at the hull of neo-classical economics; many of these had previously been let loose by Keynes and others. It was a new model ship to set alongside the old, a new model incorporating admittedly many of the features of the old, and not perfectly finished either. There had been a good deal of rush to get it into the water—that was always Keynes's way —and there were some faults of erudition and some arguments which were not wholly water-tight. But it was recognizably different, and it was complete.

It was also sufficiently theoretically sophisticated to demand the full notice of the old navigators. Even though cheaply priced by Keynes himself at 5s for 384 pages (he had his own 'profits basis' arrangement with Macmillans, by which *he* paid *them* the costs and a royalty and then took the remainder of the proceeds), it was primarily aimed at an academic audience, and is in parts a fairly difficult book. A good number of the audience, including Keynes's old teacher Pigou and his old collaborator Robertson, did not like it much. They veered between claiming that it was not really a new design, but merely used new and confusing terminology, and alleging that it was so remote from and ill-grounded in the old rules as to make it unseaworthy. Keynes, it must be said, had not gone out of his way to make it acceptable. He probably understated his debt to the neo-classicists, and his attacks on them, notably on Pigou, were in typically astringent terms.

But *The General Theory* was new. Previous general theoretical works had assumed that supply created its own demand. The unspoken premise, except in special studies of the trade cycle, was full employment. If it did not exist, it was because wages were temporarily too high, or because some other avoidable rigidity had temporarily intervened. The real issues of economics were the effective allocation of resources so that they would yield the largest returns; and, with the development of welfare economics, the distribution of the rewards. Equally, in the field of international trade, the object was to maximize the availability of resources: its effect on employment in domestic economies was hardly considered.

Keynes completely changed the angle of view. He looked from a new direction. To an excessive extent he regarded the allocation and use of resources as a solved problem, and he was prepared to leave the problems of supply to businessmen and production managers, which meant that he regarded them as very minor. He was concerned with demand, which, contrary to accepted doctrine, had no natural tendency to settle at a full employment level. Stable equilibrium could easily be achieved in a state of gross waste of resources, with no natural forces working to change this. The classical theory held that the rate of interest combined with the wage level would perform the necessary correction.

Keynes argued that neither of these mechanisms would work. Indeed, he dismissed the traditional view of the rate of interest as not merely inadequate but as nonsense. He developed this by means of a new concept, 'liquidity preference'. There might well be decisions to save without subsequent decisions to invest. No manipulation of the rate of interest or the money supply alone could deal with this. There would be no increase in the 'propensity to invest' to offset the decreased level of consumption. The economy would merely settle down at a lower rate of activity.

A lowering of wages, either in money or real terms, might also be ineffective as an adjustment to full employment. It was easy to draw a false analogy between the behaviour of an individual firm and the behaviour of the economy as a whole. Of course, if with total demand remaining constant, the wages of one firm fell, it would tend to employ more labour. But this would not necessarily happen in the economy as a whole. The decline in total demand might cancel any beneficial employment tendency.

Investment was the key. It was the element of demand which fluctuated most, and which was in greatest need of stimulus from outside. In his best-remembered passage Keynes set out the case for public works in an ironically extreme form:

If the Treasury were to fill old bottles with bank-notes, bury them at suitable depths in disused coal-mines which are then filled up to the surface with town rubbish, and leave it to private enterprise on well-tried principles of laisser faire to dig the notes up again (the right to do so being obtained, of course, by tendering for leases of the note-bearing territory), there need be no more unemployment and, with the help of the repercussions, the real income of the community, and its capital wealth also, would probably become a good deal greater than it actually is. It would, indeed, be more sensible to build houses and the like; but if there are political and practical difficulties in the way of this, the above would be better than nothing.

This led Keynes on both to advocating an active role for the state in investment policy ('When the capital development of a country becomes the by-product of the activities of a casino, the job is likely to be ill-done.') and to deficit financing. Balanced budgets when resources were underused were a mark not of virtue but of stupidity. As a result he became fastened with an inflationary tag, although in fact his approach and methods, as he showed four years later when he came to write *How to Pay for the War*, were easily adaptable to circumstances of excessive pressure on resources. But in 1934-36 it was deflation with which he was concerned. He therefore spoke in appropriate terms for that situation. It did not mean that he would say the same thing in a totally different one. As he had written in a riposte to the charge of inconsistency in 1931: 'I seem to see the elder parrots sitting round and saying: "You can *rely* on us. Every day for thirty years, we have said 'What a lovely morning!' But this is a bad bird. He says one thing one day, and something else the next."'

Keynes was at pains to point out that *The General Theory* was not a politically extreme book. He called it 'moderately conservative in its implications'. It was conservationist of the existing system. 'Keynes's mission in life', Professor Seymour Harris, his most devoted American exponent, has written, 'was to save capitalism, not destroy it.' But at the same time Keynes believed and desired that *The General Theory* should be revolutionary in its impact on economic thought. He wrote to Bernard Shaw on January 1, 1935:

To understand my state of mind, however, you have to know that I believe myself to be writing a book on economic theory which will largely revolutionize —not, I suppose, at once, but in the course of the next ten years—the way the world thinks about economic problems. When my new theory has been duly assimilated and mixed with politics and feelings and passions, I can't predict what the final upshot will be in its effect on actions and affairs. But there will be a great change, and in particular the Ricardian foundations of Marxism will be knocked away.

It was a bold claim to make in advance for a book, but it is one which has been abundantly justified, although not in exactly the way which

Keynes predicted. It was not 'the Ricardian foundations of Marxism' which have been the main victim. It was much more the framework of traditional 'capitalist' economics in England and America which was first shattered and then put together again in another mould. Even those who disagreed found that in due course their thought had been profoundly affected. Pigou, sceptical and maligned though he had been, made this clear after Keynes's death:

We were pedestrian, perhaps a little complacent . . . [He] broke resoundingly that dogmatic slumber . . . Economics and economists came alive. The period of tranquillity was ended. A period of active, and, so far as might be, creative thought was born. For this the credit was almost wholly due to Keynes.

Another achievement of *The General Theory*, apart from its central message, was that it re-unified economics. Previously the study of demand and the factors of production had been sharply divorced from the study of banking and monetary policy. As Keynes himself put it: 'We have all of us become used to finding ourselves sometimes on one side of the moon and sometimes on the other, without knowing what route or journey connects them . . . ' He provided the connexion. It was indeed a *general* theory.

So far as influence upon practical policy-making is concerned, the interest was in the 'thirties more concentrated upon America than upon Britain. Across the Atlantic there was an experimenting Government, which in Britain there was not. And there has always appeared to be a link between Keynes's words and Roosevelt's actions. How real this was is open to some doubt. In the first place, of course, much of Roosevelt's pump-priming took place before 1936. But that is not a fatal objection, for Keynes was propagating many of his ideas well before he gave them full theoretical backing. Indeed, in the spring of 1934 he wrote a *New York Times* article entitled 'Agenda for the President', and followed this up with a visit to the White House. It was the only time that he saw Roosevelt until the problems had shifted to those of war mobilization.

The visit was not a great success. Perhaps neither was a good enough listener. Keynes was disappointed in the President's hands—a feature to which he always attached great importance in determining character. They were 'firm and fairly strong, but not clever or with finesse'. They reminded him of Sir Edward Grey's. Roosevelt found Keynes too mathematical and abstruse. He referred to him afterwards as 'the gent', not a very obvious term of approval. Keynes's earlier attacks on Woodrow Wilson may have been a cause.

What is certain is that Roosevelt never read a word of Keynes's main works. But, of course, some members of his entourage did, and there may have been an indirect influence. Keynes approved of many of Roosevelt's actions, but thought that his pump-priming failed to secure adequate results because it was too pragmatic. It lacked the follow-through which clear theoretical thinking would have shown to be necessary.

The main policy-making influence of *The General Theory* and associated writings came not before but after the war. By then his central doctrine had achieved most powerful practical vindication. The principal economy which was stimulated but not ravaged by war was that of the United States. As a result the increase in national output was so great that it made possible not only a vast outpouring of war material but a substantial increase in private consumption as well. Munitions production proved a good substitute for bottles in disused coal-mines.

Thereafter there was a long period with no return, either in the United States or in the other principal industrial countries, to the massive, debilitating unemployment of the inter-war years. How much this was due to Keynes is difficult to judge. What is undoubtedly true is that his analytical methods, combined with the greatly improved provision of national income statistics, a process which in Britain he had done a lot to prod along, deeply affected the whole postwar practice and discussion of demand management in the Finance Ministries and even the Central Banks of the world. No one in 1951 or 1961 could have spoken in the terms used by Montagu Norman before the Macmillan Committee in 1931 and escaped public ridicule. 'Crude Keynesianism', as it is now fashionable to describe some applications of his doctrine, has its limitations, but it is a great advance on crude pre-Keynesianism, and is in any event not where Keynes's thought would have stopped had he been alive today.

In the meantime Keynes had turned from his full employment proselytizing to the last phase of his career. Eighteen months after the publication of *The General Theory*, he became dangerously ill with a coronary thrombosis. For most of the time between then and the outbreak of war he was a semi-invalid. For the rest of his life he had to husband his strength very carefully, and was subject to mild recurrent attacks. His wife, with whom he had enjoyed a highly successful marriage for the preceding twelve years, became a more dominating figure. She was constantly with him, and constantly conserving his energies.

Nevertheless he was fairly active in 1939-40, spending more time in Cambridge than had been his habit, and working hard on war finance. This time he was whole-heartedly in favour of the war. In 1938 he had given money to Cripps's Popular Front campaign, but when hostilities began he was impatient of niggling on the left, particularly in the columns of his disappointing child, the *New Statesman*. In October, 1939, he wrote to them:

The intelligentsia of the Left were the loudest in demanding that the Nazi aggression should be resisted at all costs. When it comes to a showdown scarce four weeks have passed before they remember that they are pacifists and write defeatist letters to your columns, leaving the defence of freedom and of civilization to Colonel Blimp and the Old School Tie, for whom Three Cheers.

This was the beginning of a perceptible move to the right, both socially and politically, which lasted for the rest of his life. Occasionally his old radicalism could flare up, as in his protest against the 'stupidity and callousness' of the policy of interning enemy aliens, but he became increasingly attached to established values and institutions.

In the late summer of 1940 he again moved into the Treasury. He had a room, but, this time, no executive responsibility. He saw everything which went on and poured out a stream of provocative, critical and occasionally inaccurate memoranda. His main work, however, lay in the field of negotiation with the Americans. He went there in May, 1941, and remained for several months. Curiously, it was only the fourth visit of his life. He expounded Britain's economic needs with exceptional persuasiveness, and established a circle of admiring official friends, although his astringency and intolerance of slowness in others also made him some enemies, a store on which he built in subsequent years.

In late 1941 he began serious work on the economic shape of the postwar world and the way in which Britain could hope to survive within it without resort to the closed citadel methods associated with the name of Dr Schacht. Within a few months he produced a detailed scheme for an international 'Clearing Union' with 'Bancor' as its unit of exchange; with big initial credits; with unlimited liability in the sense that like any banking concern it could build up its assets without a ceiling as it went along; with substantial obligations upon creditor as well as upon debtor countries; with a leadership role for America and Britain; and with the right of any country to devalue its currency by up to 5 per cent a year without prior permission.

There followed a process of intensive discussion, first within the Whitehall machine and then, mostly at long range, with the Americans, which lasted throughout 1942 and into 1943. A roughly parallel scheme, for a 'Stabilisation Fund', emerged from Washington in July, 1942. Its principal author was Harry Dexter White, under-secretary of the United States Treasury, who ended his life in the early 'fifties under the shadow of an unproven but unwithdrawn charge that he was a Communist agent. He counted himself a 'Keynesian' in economics, but he was also a rough and abrasive upholder of the power of the United States. Over the following two years he and Keynes engaged in a number of notable encounters. It was a battle between the rasp and the rapier. But it was the rasp that won. Keynes's intellect was a match for most things, but not for the power of the United States in wartime. Between them, however, he and White managed to be the parents at the somewhat laborious birth of both the International Monetary Fund and the World Bank. The latter, in a somewhat different form, had been part of the original American scheme. Keynes held—with a lot of justice—that they were wrongly named, that the Fund was a bank and the Bank a fund.

The first series of encounters took place in Washington in the autumn of 1943. Keynes was there on another extended visit. It was then that the Clearing Union died. The Americans, with moderate but not complete foresight, saw themselves as the perpetual creditor nation. They did not therefore want heavy obligations on creditor countries; nor did they want unlimited liability; nor easy devaluation; nor a special joint leadership role for Britain. 'Bancor' was no more popular, although at one stage they had a unit of their own called 'Unitas'. But essentially they thought that the dollar, linked to gold, could perform the pivotal role. The main concession which they offered in return was the 'scarce currency' clause, by which debtor nations could discriminate against persistent creditors. Ironically it was never used. The Americans avoided it by a combination of generosity and diplomatic pressure while they were in surplus, and then, imprisoned by their previous attitude, leant against it being applied to the Germans or the Japanese.

In Washington, therefore, although he won some tactical victories, Keynes suffered a strategic defeat. The following year the same pattern was followed at Bretton Woods, the New Hampshire mountain resort, where the representatives of 44 nations assembled to put the finishing touches to the arrangements for both the Bank and the Fund. The meeting lasted three weeks. Keynes, although he suffered one heart attack there, was personally and intellectually dominant throughout. Lord Robbins has given a striking impression of his qualities at this time:

Keynes was in his most lucid and persuasive mood; and the effect was irresistible. At such moments I often find myself thinking that Keynes must be one of the most remarkable men that have ever lived—the quick logic, the birdlike swoop of intuition, the vivid fancy, the wide vision, above all the incomparable sense of the fitness of words, all combine to make something several degrees beyond the limit of ordinary human achievement. Certainly, in our own age, only [Churchill] is of comparable stature.

But, in spite of it all, it was the American scheme which prevailed. As recent events have shown, they were perhaps foolish, in the long run, to make it so. They and the world might have been better off with Keynes's Clearing Union. Nevertheless, by the standards of human institutions, their scheme was a relatively good one. It worked well for a long time. And Keynes, even if he did not get his own way, had played a decisive part in persuading the world to adopt a workable system. It was a great advance on the twenties and thirties.

Keynes paid three more visits to America. Almost immediately after Bretton Woods he was back for two months of hard negotiation on the final stages of Lend-Lease. Then, in the late summer of 1945, with that beneficent arrangement abruptly terminated and the new Labour Government in power in Britain, he went again to try to secure massive but necessary post-war assistance. Before he left he was highly optimistic. The Americans could usually be persuaded. He thought he could get $6 billion as a free gift, or at least an interest-free loan. Ernest Bevin was more realistic. 'When I listen to Lord Keynes talking', he said, 'I seem to hear those coins jingling in my pocket; but I am not so sure they are really there.'

In Washington Keynes found a harder atmosphere than he had been used to. He deployed the British case over three continuous days of masterly exposition in the Federal Reserve building. But he did not get his $6 billion. He got 3\frac{3}{4}$ billion, with a rate of interest of 4 per cent. Convertibility of sterling by 1947 was a required string. He had some difficulty in persuading the British Government that he had got the best available terms, and they, when convinced, had some further difficulty in persuading Parliament and public. Keynes contributed to the advocacy by a beautifully argued, semi-impromptu speech in the House of Lords. It was the last of his few speeches there. It was also the culmination of his final public service.

In early 1946 he presided over the gala opening of a reborn Covent Garden, and watched Margot Fonteyn dance the *Sleeping Beauty*. He had been chairman of the Council for the Encouragement of Music and the Arts during the war, which led to his taking the chairmanship of the Arts Council and of the new Covent Garden trust. He spent some time in Cambridge, and told Noël Annan at a King's Feast that one of the few regrets of his life was that he had not drunk more champagne. (Lytton Strachey, with memories of Charleston in the twenties, would have agreed.) In March he went again to America for the first meeting of the Fund and the Bank, but the visit was not a success. He offended Fred Vinson, the new United States Secretary of the Treasury, by the imagery of his speech, and he nearly died on the train back from Savannah to Washington.

He recovered, and at the beginning of April he did a full week's work in London. Then he went to Sussex and to Firle Beacon; and then came the further and final attack.

At his memorial service in Westminster Abbey his 94-year-old father and 85-year-old mother walked together up the aisle. It must have been an unprecedented event. Rarely if ever before can a man have earned an Abbey memorial service by the distinction of his achievement, and died while both his parents were still alive to attend it. It was not his only claim to be almost unique.

LÉON BLUM

Léon Blum

In the summer of 1936 Léon Blum held in his hands the hopes of the humane forces of Europe. The head of the electorally triumphant *Front Populaire*, he was the first Socialist and the first Jew to become Prime Minister of France. He was the one man who, from a dismal continent, with Hitler creating a new barbarism in Germany, with Mussolini grooming Italy for the role of predatory auxiliary, with Spain on the verge of eruption into the cruellest and most international of civil wars, with power in England about to pass from the fading benignity of Baldwin to the harsher defeatism of Chamberlain, might have sent back an answering light to the uncertain signals of encouragement which came across the Atlantic from Roosevelt.

He did not for long hold those hopes. Perhaps the vessel was too fragile, perhaps the hands were too fastidious. Blum had many qualities, but a sure instinct for the retention of power was not among them. He was better at fortitude in adversity, as he had shown before and as he was to show again, at the Riom trials and at Buchenwald, than at the skilful and self-confident exploitation of victory. None the less in a few brief months he made a greater impact upon the social balance in France than has been done by anyone else in the past fifty years.

What was far more extraordinary than that the flicker of radical hope should have been so quickly extinguished was that it should have been concentrated, however briefly, upon the person of Blum. That he was intellectually distinguished goes without saying. He combined subtle sophistication and simple integrity to an unique degree. He was a child of the nascent Third Republic and an acolyte of the *Belle Époque*. As a young man, known in the salons as *le petit Bob*, he could have been a minor character in Proust's imaginary world, as indeed he was a close acquaintance in his real life. As an old man—he was 64 when he first became Prime Minister—with his walrus moustache, his white spats and his double-breasted suits, neither comfortable nor elegant, he looked like a good member of the *République des Camarades*. But he pricked its conscience more than he accepted its prizes. He held French socialism together against the depredations both of the communists and of a vicious right, the malice of which he was peculiarly adept at arousing, for 30 difficult years, although at the end he left less emotional legacy than his own mentor, Jaurès, had bequeathed. But it was remarkable that he did it at all.

He had nothing of the earthiness of Jaurès himself, or of a great radical politician like Édouard Herriot. He was not rooted in the soil of France, although he was imbued with the spirit of its capital. He was a Parisian of the Parisians, but of alien race. There is nothing exceptional about a *grand bourgeois* leading a proletarian movement. From Lassalle to Gaitskell this has been so. But it would have been surprising if Attlee had spent his youth, not at Toynbee Hall, but in the company of Oscar Wilde, and his early middle age, not in the trenches or as Mayor of Stepney, but deep in the bosom of Bloomsbury, cosseted by Lytton Strachey and Virginia Woolf.

Blum was born on April 9, 1872, in the Rue St Denis, in the third *arrondissement* of Paris, almost in the shadow of the forbidding Church of Saint Eustache, where the first Revolution celebrated the Feast of Reason, and half-way between those temples of finance, the *Bourse* and the *Banque de France*, and the great working class eastern *carrefours* of the Place de la République and the Place de la Bastille. It was a modest apartment, above a grocer's shop in a mixed and crowded part of Paris, but an appropriate location for his parents. His father was the son of a not very successful lawyer whose forebears were probably of Frankfurt origin, and who had come from Alsace to Paris by way of Holland and had arrived in the capital in 1845.

Auguste (formerly Abraham) Blum, the father, had stepped down by way of occupation but up by way of reward. He had gone into the silk business and in 1865 had established himself, under the name of Blum Frères, as a wholesale purveyor of ribbons, tulles, lace and velours, mainly to the millinery trade. At the time of Léon Blum's birth, he was still in a fairly small way, but he had chosen his trade well for the Paris of the late nineteenth century, and with the remarkable recovery of French prosperity in the middle and late seventies, he became the proprietor of one of the foremost houses of its sort. He also invented the collapsible silk-hat, a great adjunct to the life of the theatres and the boulevards. He soon moved his business to three floors in the Rue du Quatre Septembre, where it outlived the Third Republic, and his residence to a spacious apartment in the Boulevard de Sébastopol. He prospered, but he remained rooted in east central Paris, in what was then, as now, the most Jewish quarter.

Auguste Blum had five sons. Léon was the second. The eldest, the third and the fourth all went into the family business. The fifth directed the ballet at the Monte Carlo Opera. When Auguste Blum died in 1921 he left substantial patrimonies to all five. Léon Blum was rich only for a short time. He spent a lot on *Le Populaire* and later, with fashion changes and the slump, had to put money back into rescuing the declining business from bankruptcy. The family was close-knit and rigidly orthodox. Léon Blum ceased his Jewish observances as soon as he left home, but remained filial. He visited his father every day until his death. (His mother, whose own mother kept a bookshop of note on the Île de la Cité, had died earlier.)

Over Paris, and particularly over the quarter in which Léon Blum grew up, there hung the violent memory of the Prussian siege and the Commune. Crushing defeat followed by internecine butchery was not the most obvious recipe for the spectacular flowering which France achieved under the unwanted, unloved, scandal-ridden, crisis-prone, but curiously successful and long-lasting Third Republican régime. There was bitterness, both towards the enemy across the Rhine and between the supporters of those who had burned the monuments and property of Paris and of those who, in the Bloody Week, only 10 months before Blum's birth, had shot down nearly 20,000 Communards, and created a new proletarian shrine at the *Mur des Fedérés* in the cemetery of Père Lachaise. But it was febrile rather than sullen bitterness. It did not inhibit either the intellectual renaissance of the end of the century or the growth of the material splendours of the *Ville Lumière*. Blum was a minor participant in the former, and a close onlooker, tolerant when his instinctive hatred of injustice was not aroused, at the latter.

He received the most élite of Parisian educations and, with one stumble which did not agitate him, became one of the brightest ornaments of the most stringent and selective system in the world. He went at the age of 11 to the Lycée Charlemagne, close to the Bastille. Its fame was not diminished by its unprepossessing premises or its unfashionable location. It was the school of Victor Hugo, of Sainte-Beuve, of Gautier, of Blanqui and of Marshal Joffre. He stayed there for five years, gaining almost every possible prize, in classics, in German, in mathematics, in natural science, in French composition, in history, in declamation. He then transferred for two years to the Lycée Henry IV which, from its position in the heart of the *quartier Latin*, specialized in preparation for entrance to the physical austerities and intellectual rigour of the École Normale Supérieure. At the Henry IV, Blum shared a bench with André Gide, and successfully and easily secured his entrance.

He was not, however, a good *normalien*. He did not much like the dedicated atmosphere of that august institution in the Rue d'Ulm. He twice failed his preliminary examinations and after a year was asked to leave. He transferred, his intellectual confidence unshaken, to the Faculté de Droit of Paris. He decided that his earlier ambition, to which the École Normale naturally led, of passing through a period of schoolmastership (at a very high level) to become a professor of philosophy, was misplaced. He preferred a wider ranging life. At the Faculté de Droit, he studied literature and philosophy as well as law, and emerged, in 1894, at the age of 22, with the highest honours. He then applied himself to the highly competitive examination for admission to a career in the *Conseil d'État*.

The functions of this Napoleonic institution are part administrative and part judicial. It does much of the work carried out in Britain by the Law Officers of the Crown and the parliamentary draftsmen, as well as acting as the final judicial arbiter in matters of civil dispute between the individual and the State. Blum passed at the second attempt. He entered the service of the *Conseil* in 1895, and remained with it until 1919, rising to a senior rank and retiring (at 47) with a pension, a high decoration, and the life-title of Honorary State Counsellor. It provided him for 24 years with an exacting but not heavily time-consuming occupation. It was the base of his life, but hardly more its purpose than the same *Conseil* had been to Stendhal, or the British Post Office to Trollope.

From 1892 to 1912, from his 20th to his 40th year, a large part of the purpose of Blum's life was literature. His writing was critical rather than creative. It was prolific and ranged wide. He always had great fluency with his pen and in his later days of heavy political involvement found little difficulty in combining with his other commitments the production of a daily article for the *Populaire*. In these earlier years, however, it was mostly the aesthetic rather than the political to which he applied his fluency. He was an inveterate inhabitant of the world of small, often transient, avant-garde periodicals. The most important of these was the *Revue Blanche* of which he was literary editor for the latter half of the 'nineties. It was a magazine of anarchism and symbolism. Amongst his fellow contributors were Mallarmé and Debussy, Verlaine and Proust. Gide followed him as literary editor. Apart from his numerous reviews, he also used its columns for the first publication of a work of remarkable presumption. Seventy years earlier, J. P. Eckermann had published his

Gespräche mit Goethe. Blum decided to imagine the continued life of the German humanist and to bring his thought up to date, even including a re-writing of Faust. Goethe's reactions to modern authors and modern politics were all intrepidly dealt with. He was made to journey to Paris to attend a socialist conference, and was escorted by Verlaine to a Montmartre *cabaret*. Blum hesitated about putting his name to the work. 'Why not'? Jules Renard told him, 'the arrogance lies not in signing it, but in having the idea of writing it.' It remained anonymous until the 1909 edition.

In the first decade of the new century, Blum turned his main literary attention to dramatic criticism. Writing for a variety of journals, but principally for Jaurès's new paper *Humanité*, and afterwards, when his articles proved a little too elegant even for such a distinguished organ of proletarian propaganda, for *Le Matin*, he attended almost every first night of the then prolific Paris theatre. He not only wrote about what he saw. He also talked a great deal about it, in the intervals and at the end of the piece. In 1912, as a semi-comical apotheosis of his career as a *boulevardier*, his sharp and undisciplined tongue involved him in a duel with an enraged playwright. The choice of weapons lay with the future Socialist leader. He chose rapiers. He was seconded by the editor of *Le Matin* and a more friendly dramatist, the then famous and splendidly named de Porto-Riche. Blum was slightly wounded in the hand, his opponent in the temple and the chest. Both recovered, Blum without difficulty. His subsequent battles were more dangerous and less in the nature of a Palais-Royal farce.

In his early middle age, Blum published two substantial and important books. The first caused him a lot of trouble, both at the time and subsequently. It was an essay, part sociological treatise and part novel, on marriage. *Du Mariage* came out in 1907. It did not attack marriage as such, but saw it as badly regulated, because, as practised in the bourgeois society of the time, it failed to harmonize custom with natural law. Human beings, in Blum's view, started polygamous and gradually evolved towards monogamy. To some extent society allowed for this in its attitude towards male, but not towards female behaviour. The virginity of girls should not be protected beyond the age of 15. The thesis provided a rich hunting-ground for those who wished then and still more later, to impugn Blum's own morality. *La Pornographie au Conseil d'État: Un Libre Ignoble*, was the title of a contemporary attack. *Action Française* devoted continuing time and money to unrewarding investigations of Blum's private life. Passages such as his prediction that, in the future, 'young girls will return home from their lovers as naturally as they return at present from a walk, or from having tea with a friend', were undoubtedly a little rash, in the France of 70 years ago, for a future political leader. The book, which contained some fairly hackneyed views about the differences between the intellectual qualities of men and women, had its sententious side, and was mocked, together with its author, in Anatole France's description of the lucubrations of 'Professor Haddock'.

The second work, published in 1914, only three weeks before the guns of August began their slaughter, was a literary and philosophical study of Stendhal (Henri Beyle), the romantic yet logical novelist who most attracted Blum's admiration and constant re-reading. *Stendhal et le Beylisme* was his most mature literary work. He was fascinated by the paradox of Stendhal's position. Men must always seek an unattainable ideal. Happiness must be pursued methodically, yet with the knowledge that this is not really accessible. There was a great deal of Blum's own character and philosophy in this last swallow of his literary summer.

In 1896, just after his admission to the *Conseil d'État*, Blum had married Lise Bloch, a Parisian Jewess whose family were high in the public service and deep in the musical world of Fauré and Ravel. She was his wife until her death in 1931. It appears to have been a happy and successful marriage, even though contracted at an age younger than Blum's later treatise indicated to be desirable, and despite a determined lack of political involvement on the part of Mme Blum. *Du Mariage* was dedicated to her. They had one son, who graduated from the École Polytechnique and became an engineer with the Hispano-Suiza Company.

For 12 years after their marriage the Blums lived in a small but well-placed ground-floor apartment alongside the Luxembourg Gardens. They then removed to a much larger one recessed behind two courtyards in a new building on the Boulevard Montparnasse. Here he assembled a large library. In both apartments they maintained a table of high bourgeois quality and entertained a good deal, although on an informal basis. They did not live in society, but had a wide circle of friends, mostly artistic and intellectual, but with an increasing political admixture.

The date of Blum's political initiation is not easy to place. From his earliest days he was a natural man of the left. Despite a strong early friendship with Maurice Barrès, whose writing he greatly admired and who was already a right-wing deputy from Nancy, it never occurred to him to ally himself with the forces of tradition and authority. What is certain is that there were two men and one event which, between them, decisively impelled him into socialist belief and political commitment.

The men were Lucien Herr and Jean Jaurès. The event, if its rolling reverberations can be so concentrated, was the Dreyfus Affair.

Herr was the Marxist librarian of the École Normale. His influence upon Blum did not date from the latter's brief and unsuccessful sojourn at that institution. Herr, if he noticed him at all, then thought him insufficiently serious to be worthy of much attention. They met again, by chance, in 1893, and Herr then applied his great private proselytizing qualities to Blum's mind. It was ripe for such attention. How far Blum ever became a complete Marxist is open to doubt. The French tradition has been to claim that you were when you were not, to use the language of class warfare to cloak the politics of collaboration and opportunism, just as the English tradition has been the reverse, that of giving Marx a lower place than he deserves in the thinking of some members of the Labour Party. Blum was never an 'opportunist' (a word which became a label and not merely a description in French politics of the late nineteenth and early twentieth century and which was exemplified by the careers of those former socialists, Millerand, Viviani and Briand), but although he used much of the language of Marxism, the habits of his mind were too legalistic (the influence of the *Conseil d'État*) and the springs of his feeling were too idealistic, even optimistic, for him ever to be a full follower of the German master. He was more a Hegelian than a complete Marxist, with the dialectic superimposed on an elemental, Rousseau-like attachment to natural justice.

In 1896 Herr took Blum to meet Jaurès. He had converted them both to socialism. By bringing them together he secured one of the great confluences of French politics. Jaurès was 13 years older than Blum. In a most unusual combination for close political associates they were half alike and half in sharp contrast with each other. Jaurès was at least as much of an intellectual as Blum. So far from leaving the École Normale after one year, he had emerged as one of its most distinguished alumni, had quickly moved from the Lycée at Albi to the philosophy department of Toulouse University, and had produced a highly sophisticated work of metaphysics as his doctoral thesis. His interests were wide and his intellect remained supple throughout his middle age of full political commitment. He could write with vast fluency and without much sacrifice of standards, as was illustrated by the five large volumes of 'socialist history' of the French Revolution which he poured out between 1898 and 1902. Nor was there much difference between the political outlook of Jaurès and Blum. Both claimed to be Marxists, but both clothed the harsh angularities of the doctrine with an optimistic humanism which, although international in purpose, was essentially French in spirit.

But there the similarities ended. Blum was an aesthete and looked like one. Jaurès was not. He looked like a prosperous peasant or a small town tradesman. He was thick-set, inelegant, healthy and rough. The soil of the Tarn and the market place of Castres were to him what the theatres and literary salons of Paris were to Blum. He had a great melodious voice, which wrapped itself instinctively round phrases of imaginative oratory. On the platform he was a mixture of John Bright, Gladstone and Lloyd George, a combination of erudition, flashing eye, high-flown metaphor, warming cadence, and close relationship with his audience. Blum had none of these qualities. He had a weak, high-pitched and rather squeaky voice. The structure of his oratory was good, but he rarely illuminated a landscape with a single phrase. In later life he could command great audiences, but more because of the respect in which he was held than because of his inherent power of oratory.

Jaurès and Blum were therefore a strangely assorted couple, neither similar nor opposite. But for 18 years from their meeting in 1896, and particularly after 1900, they were very close. They lunched together several times a week. Blum's apartment was freely available to Jaurès, 'for use as a restaurant, a library, a laundry and a public bath'. It could not be a wholly equal partnership. Jaurès was the most famous politician in France, perhaps in Europe. Blum was still unknown outside a narrow circle. While Jaurès lived, Blum refused to become completely committed to politics. He twice declined to stand for election as a deputy. Yet he was much more than an acolyte. He was inspired by Jaurès. But Jaurès sought not merely support and friendship but information and even instruction from him. Blum was the more intellectually certain and had a great deal of influence upon Jaurès, as well as *vice versa*.

This began with the Dreyfus Affair. Captain Alfred Dreyfus, officer of artillery, Alsatian and Jew, seconded to duty with the General Staff, had been convicted in 1894 of betraying military secrets to the Germans. At the beginning of 1895 he was militarily degraded on the Champ-de-Mars and sent to serve a life sentence on Devil's Island. Few people greatly minded. Dreyfus was not a man to inspire widespread affection. As Blum was later to remark, Dreyfus would almost certainly, had he not been himself, have been an anti-Dreyfusard. Jaurès at first thought he ought to have been shot.

Doubts about Dreyfus's guilt began to percolate from the État-Major in 1896-7. In the autumn of the latter year *Le Figaro* took up the issue and lost half its circulation as a result. But it was not until January 13, 1898, when Zola published his memorable *J'Accuse*, a reverberating denunciation of the dissimulations of those in high military places, that the issue was thrown into the centre, not merely of French politics, but of almost every aspect of French life. Parties, families and friendships were sundered by the issue, which quickly became something much wider than the guilt or innocence of a rather dreary captain of artillery. The Dreyfusards, of course, believed that justice for a single individual was important. But even more strongly did they believe in contesting the claims of the military authorities to be a State within a State, to be specially protected, in the alleged interests of the nation's safety, from the critical spirit, from the presumptuousness of rationalism. Equally, those who wished to keep the affair under the carpet were not wholly indifferent to justice. They hoped Dreyfus was guilty. They made great efforts to persuade themselves that he must be so. But what was still more important was the authority of France, and the prestige and self-confidence of her sword and shield. To one side it appeared as a battle between truth and chicanery, to the other as one between order and iconoclasm. Oddly enough, the leaders of French socialism had some difficulty in deciding where they stood. To the right of Jaurès, Millerand and Viviani were for avoiding trouble. To his left, Jules Guesde and Édouard Vaillant were equally disinclined to get involved. Guesde, the uncompromising Marxist from the Nord, had no doubt that Dreyfus was innocent. But, man of the strictest personal honour though he was, he thought this rather irrelevant. To become excited about the misfortunes of a rich Jew, who had compounded his sins of origin by seeking a career in the casteridden officer corps, was to divert the energies of the working-class movement. It might also be needlessly unpopular.

Jaurès's position, strongly influenced by Blum, was different in almost every respect. First, he took a long time to be convinced of the fact of innocence. Then he threw himself into the battle like a tornado. Blum was with him throughout. For 18 months, in their different ways, they were swept along by a tide of inspired indignation. By comparison, nothing else counted. Jaurès delivered speeches, both in the Chamber and in the country, of unparalleled verve and passion. Blum analysed, advised and wrote. To both the issue was clear. Socialism meant justice. It also meant the true spirit of Republican France. The affair gave them the chance to proclaim alliances of principle as opposed to those of opportunism. This was what they both wanted. They were indifferent to office, but they were not indifferent to the impotence of arid isolation. They enjoyed the campaign and the victory. Jaurès thought it would bring heavy gains for the Socialist Party. Blum was more sceptical, and in the short term was certainly right. Jaurès achieved vast fame but lost his seat in the election of 1898.

In 1902, he came back to the Chamber as leader of a substantial socialist group, and played a notable role in sustaining the government of Émile Combes, which carried through a rigorous secularization of the French State. But the *Bloc des Gauches* was bourgeois as well as *laique*. Jaurès was under constant attack from the Guesdists for sustaining it. Within France itself, Guesde could not defeat Jaurès. They co-existed at the head of two separate parties. Guesde won by taking Jaurès to the tribunal of the Second International, the only higher court which Jaurès recognized and one to which he was almost unique in paying practical attention. There, fortified by the votes of the German Social Democrats, who were against participation in a government for the simple but adequate reason that there was no danger of anyone asking them to participate, Guesde won. At the Amsterdam conference of 1904, the vote went overwhelmingly against collaboration in capitalist governments. Jaurès had to decide whether to submit or resist. He decided to submit, and by so doing destroyed the *Bloc des Gauches*, but created for the first time a unified French socialist party, cumbersomely but descriptively named the *Section Française de l'Internationale Ouvrière* (SFIO). The name but not the unity was to persist throughout Blum's life-time.

For his remaining nine years, Jaurès (and Blum with him) was to live increasingly under the shadow of approaching war. Jaurès saw the menace of Armageddon far more vividly than most. He devoted much of his energy to trying to achieve a synthesis between the needs of democratic defence and the hopes of international socialism. He sank a great deal of political capital into relations with the German Social Democrats. His last political journey was to Brussels for a meeting of the International. Blum saw him off at the Gare du Nord on the night of Tuesday, July 28, 1914. Jaurès returned two days later with a rather unsatisfactory declaration. He made the best of it in his article for Friday's *Humanité*. In the next issue of the paper he would have to be more clear-cut. He could no longer merely urge goodwill and restraint. He had either to oppose or support French mobilization. While contemplating this question, he went out for dinner at a restaurant in the Rue Montmarte. On a hot July night, he sat with his back to an open window. An hour later he was assassinated by a demented youth. It was a crime without organization or rational motive.

His death was high tragedy at a moment of the utmost tension. There was ambiguity about his immediate legacy. For the mantle of the martyr there was a good deal of competition. The government, with Viviani as Prime Minister, appropriated his funeral for a patriotic demonstration. Other socialists, both at home and abroad, less renegade and flamboyant than Viviani, kept some relic for themselves. But the guardianship of the main garment passed primarily to Blum. He reproached himself for his lack of public involvement while Jaurès lived. He must expiate the fault by changing his life to one of full political commitment. If he was not exactly Jaurès's heir, he soon began to appear to many as his political executor, the keeper of the bones of the saint, the best interpreter of the true faith.

The French socialists were stunned and disorganized by the death of Jaurès. As soon as they could pull themselves together, they decided that it was their duty to give full support to the national war effort. The war was not the fault of France. She was not merely entitled but obliged to defend herself. This was wholly the view of Blum. Indeed it remained his view through to 1918, after first a minority and then a majority of his fellow militants had defected to a semi-pacifist position. But in 1914 there was no such division. Two socialists were invited to join Viviani's government of national unity—the *Union Sacrée*—and their identity symbolized the unanimity both of the nation and of the party. The intransigent Guesde became a Minister without Portfolio, and Marcel Sembat, an erstwhile Blanquist who had gradually moved into a 'centrist', Jaurès-like position, became Minister of Public Works.

Blum, aged 42 and far too short-sighted ever to have been a candidate for military service, became Sembat's *chef de cabinet*. For three years the the job commanded his energies and enthusiasm. Blum was a good administrator, and the department was more important than it sounds. It was responsible for a good part of the French wartime economy, including railways, and at first, the production of munitions.

By late 1917, however, a month after the October Revolution had taken Russia out of the war and fortified the far left, the French Socialist Party, which had been edging in this direction for the previous 18 months, refused authority for further participation in government. Sembat reluctantly declined membership of the Clemenceau Cabinet, and Blum left with him. He returned to the *Conseil d'État*, occasional articles for *Humanité*, and the rapid production of a substantial book, *La Réforme Gouvernmentale*. This was for Blum a strangely empirical work. There was very little sweep of political philosophy about it. It amounted to a series of sensible, sometimes rather mundane proposals for improving the machinery of government. It was somewhat Anglo-Saxon, rather Benthamite in spirit. Its main weakness was that it was too attracted by the introduction of business methods into government. But it balanced this by a firm denunciation of the specialist as minister. If a man was only capable of filling an office for which he had specially prepared himself, then he was not really fit even for that. On the whole it was as though Blum were consciously disciplining his writing and thought after the intellectual leaps and extravagances of his previous books.

More importantly he was becoming accepted as a figure of moderate note within the Socialist Party. He was still at least half in the shadow of the dead hero, for in most years his major public engagement was the delivery of the annual *éloge* to Jaurès. But just as Blum was moving into Socialist prominence, so the Socialist Party was moving away from the positions of Jaurès and himself. Following the 1917 prohibition on continued participation in government, the 1918 conference carried by a vote of nearly three to two a resolution moved by Jean Longuet, Marx's grandson, which had the effect of transferring party power to the old minority. Ludovic-Oscar Frossard and Marcel Cachin, future leaders of the French Communist Party, became respectively general secretary of the party, and editor-in-chief of *Humanité*.

In 1919 there was a temporary ebbing of the ideological conflict. A commission was set up to draft a party programme. It was a widely based body of 52 members, and, surprisingly on both personal and political grounds at that stage, Blum was elected to the chair. He carried 37 of the members with him and successfully propelled the resultant document through the party conference. That autumn he resigned from the *Conseil d'État* and stood for election to the Chamber. The Socialists as a whole did badly, falling from the 102 seats which they had secured in 1914 to 67. But Blum's own result was not in doubt. He was put on the list for the multiple member seat of the north-east third of Paris, and was comfortably elected for that predominantly working-class sector. He celebrated his entry to the Chamber by making a noteless four-hour maiden speech on the organization of railways, which so impressed his colleagues that he was almost immediately elected secretary of the socialist group. And he compensated for his retirement from the *Conseil d'État* by becoming a somewhat middle-aged recruit to the Paris bar and earning a substantial income, mostly from commercial cases, for the next decade and a half. By the beginning of 1920 his life, while markedly and designedly different from its pre-1914 pattern, was bowling satisfactorily along upon a number of axles. But the smoothness was illusory. 1920 ended by being one of the most testing years of Blum's life.

In the spring of 1919, the Russians had set up the Third International or Comintern. Its attraction for most of the socialist parties of the West was magnetic. It symbolized both revolution and success. It stood out in happy contrast with the shop-soiled, over-respectable Second International which had achieved so little in its 25 years of pre-1914 existence. The Italian, Swiss and Hungarian parties quickly switched from the old to the new. Within the French party there were great pressures, fortified by the repudiation of the old majority, to go the same way. For the new majority the only restraining force was Gallic national pride.

Blum at first, although never bemused by the Russian Revolution, took a somewhat ambivalent view. He was a great believer in 'unity'. He was also capable of a cloudy optimism, which on one occasion during this period led his oratory to recall at once some of the poems of Robert Browning and some of the speeches of Ramsay MacDonald:

When we feel ourselves sometimes hemmed in by divisions, dissensions or intrigues, there is only one thing to do, to rise higher, to climb a little and look at our goal. And then we shall see we are in perfect harmony. We are like travellers in the mountains, who cannot see for the cloud and mist. Climb, climb higher, and when you climb higher you will find the air pure, the light undimmed, and the sun shining.

Accordingly he did not take a decisive part in the first stage of the controversy, at the Strasbourg conference of February, 1920. Withdrawal from the Second International was there carried by a majority of more than ten to one, without Blum voting against. But a decision to join the Comintern was postponed. There was carried instead a motion of Longuet's, which suggested that the best solution would be for the Third International itself, the French party, and, if possible, every other socialist party to be subsumed into a new and so far unnumbered international, but that, as a fall-back, Cachin and Frossard should go to Moscow to investigate the conditions of adherence to the Comintern. These travellers found themselves a good deal more investigated than investigating. They brought back a list of nine hard conditions, which were later expanded to 21. These amounted not to affiliation but to total subordination to Moscow. The name was to be changed to French Communist Party; any recalcitrant elements (including, it subsequently emerged, some like Longuet himself who had long been leaders of the left), were to be purged from positions of responsibility; and policy was to be rigidly laid down by the executive committee of the new international, which meant Zinoviev acting as Lenin's agent.

The 'offer' was to be decided upon at a special conference, which met at Tours over Christmas, 1920. Blum was clear that he could not accept the terms. He objected to the laying down of a strategy for French socialism upon the basis of the very different Russian experience. He objected to the acceptance of dictatorship and terrorism, not as temporary weapons of last resort, but as normal methods of government. And he objected to the creation of a hierarchical party, subject to almost military discipline, in place of one of argument and tolerance. His position was by no means that of a modern reformist. He insisted that he was as much in favour of the revolution as anyone, but he wanted it to be his own sort of revolution, which meant that it should be a French sort and, if possible, a peaceful sort.

He believed that similar considerations would weigh with a great number of delegates. He was wrong. The pull of Moscow was too powerful. Tours was a tumultuous and bitter gathering. Sembat and others had great difficulty in getting a hearing. Blum was more fortunate, perhaps because he wisely began by announcing that his very weak voice made it impossible for him to overcome noise. But his speech was not otherwise weak. He attacked the Communist doctrine centrally and audaciously. It was 'contrary to the essential and invariable principles of Marxist socialism'. He left no doubt that he was not staying in a Third International Party where he would be 'a hostage or a slave'. But it was not he who was deserting. While others departed in a new direction it was the duty of some to stay and 'guard the old house'.

This was one of Blum's few memorable phrases. *La Vieille Maison* became an evocative rallying-cry for French socialism throughout the 'twenties and early 'thirties. But when the vote had been taken and even the Longuet position, too close to Cachin for Blum to vote for it, defeated by three to one, and when Blum's own allies amounted to fewer than 400 in a conference of 4,500, there was not much of the old house, beyond the nameplate, for Blum to guard. The funds, the offices, the newspaper, and 120,000 out of 150,000 members went with the victory.

Blum, and those who thought with him, had to start to build almost afresh. He was not nominally the leader. There were others senior and more famous. But most of these were quickly removed. Albert Thomas went to the League of Nations in 1921, and both Sembat and Guesde died in 1922. From the beginning Blum was the dominant parliamentary personality, and in 1924 he succeeded to the full Jaurès position.

Parliament was crucial to the Socialist rump. Unable to rival the Communists in local organization, unable to sustain the *Populaire* (to replace the lost *Humanité*) on a daily basis until 1927, they had substantially more deputies from the moment of the split; and after the 1924 elections, which were a success for the 'bourgeois' as well as the socialist left, they had 105 against only 10 Communists. Militants and voters did not march together.

Nevertheless, the 1924 triumph of the *Cartel des Gauches* and the continuing facts of the political equation over the next decade presented Blum with great problems. The balance of parliamentary power could only be tilted away from the right by a firm electoral alliance, at least on the second ballot, between the Radicals and the Socialists. But what was then to happen? Blum's answer was that the Socialists should in general support Radical cabinets—those of Herriot, Briand, Painlevé and later Daladier—from the outside. To participate fully, he feared, was to hand over the torch of social revolution to the Communists and to find himself going the way of Millerand or Viviani. But his chosen course also had great disadvantages. Participation might have secured an effective if limited common programme. Without it, the more left-wing, Radical leaders had to cast the nets of their governments farther to the right. Then they would offend the Socialists on some specific issue and the government would fall. A new and less satisfactory Prime Minister would emerge from the amorphous recesses of the Radical Party would compensate for Socialist defection by support from the centre-right and France would revert to the unstable equilibrium of a new government of opportunism.

This pattern repeated itself several times. Not unnaturally it led to pressure on Blum to play a more constructive rôle. On different occasions most of his principal colleagues felt the pull of office. These included Renaudel, Paul-Boncour and Vincent Auriol. Eventually Renaudel, assisted by the less reputable Marquet and Déat, led 30 deputies into a breakaway neo-socialist group. Blum was deeply distressed, but he persisted in preserving the purity of the Socialist Party. He would enter only a government which he could control. As this appeared highly unlikely in the 'twenties and early 'thirties, he acquired a reputation as a man with more conscience than impact. In the Chamber he was respected for his own qualities, but was at the same time regarded as something of an impractical pedant.

This intransigence towards the 'bourgeois' parties in no way assuaged the hostility of the Communists towards Blum. He was the 'social fascist' who had split the party, stolen their votes, and challenged their moral authority. At the elections of 1928 they took their cold-blooded revenge. With the return to single member constituencies Blum had become candidate for the 20*th arrondissement*, for the hills of Ménilmontant, for the abattoirs and warehouses of Belleville, for the cemetery of Père Lachaise, as well as for 100,000 or so of the most solidly working-class electors of Paris. The Communists put up against him Jacques Duclos, the pastrycook who was later to share their leadership with Thorez, and whose appeal as candidate was not diminished by the fact that he had to fight the campaign from jail. Blum had to fight his campaign against a cross-fire of vicious clamour and vilification from both left and right. On the first ballot he was two thousand votes ahead of Duclos. On the second, as had always been the strategy, the small but disciplined band of right-wing voters switched almost unanimously to Duclos and put him ahead by a few hundred. *Humanité* (still bearing on its masthead the proud message that it was founded by Jaurès) and the press of the right were equally enthusiastic about the outcome.

* *

Blum remained out of the Chamber for nearly a year. It was a bad time in his life, for his wife had already begun to suffer from the disease that killed her two years later. In 1929 a vacancy occurred in the Narbonne district of the cheap wine-growing department of the Aude. It was good left-of-centre territory (not far from Jaurès's Tarn), but about as far from the 20th *arrondissement*, geographically and in feeling, as anywhere in France. Blum had both to overcome the natural local resistance to a political refugee (always less acceptable in France than in England) and face another difficult campaign. Again the left and the right attempted a pincer movement. The violence of their opposition gave him a certain *hubris*. He flashed defiance in both directions. 'This hatred by the forces of reaction is my honour, my merit, my pride', he proclaimed. And when he encountered Cachin, the Communist leader, across the square in Narbonne he engaged him in a passage of verbal arms which is both memorable for its own sake and superbly illustrative of the difficulty of rendering French oratory into English:

Very well, Cachin, I face you openly, you, director of *Humanité*, where I am traduced daily, you, representative of the Communist Party, you, who have been my friend and the guest of my house, you come now to affirm publicly that you consider me a traitor to the working class. For years you have represented me as an agent of the bourgeoisie. Here, I demand justice.

On this occasion the combined onslaught was unsuccessful. Blum was elected and Narbonne remained his constituency to the end of the Third Republic.

The 1932 elections gave the Socialists 130 seats, although the neo-socialist defection was soon to cost them nearly a quarter of these. Still Blum resisted any participation in government. Indeed in the autumn of 1933 he suddenly swung his votes against Daladier even though this had the predictable result of securing a more right-wing replacement, Chautemps in this instance. Blum, already 61, showed every sign of living out his political life as permanent leader of the opposition, as sterile as he was incorruptible.

This was changed by the events of February, 1934, when, in the wake of the Stavisky scandal, Paris was swept by right-wing riots, the Chamber was besieged, and the Republic seemed in greater internal danger than at any time since General Boulanger had postured on his white horse in 1886. For Blum it was the Dreyfus battle over again.

It was a defensive battle, which in many ways he preferred, and he was at once cool and exhilarated. During the night of February 6-7, while the mob howled across the river in the Place de la Concorde, he was one of the few deputies to offer any leadership, and he offered it in terms which broke with his habit of abstention from office:

If the Government wages the struggle with enough energy, with enough faith in the will of the people, they can count on us . . . In the battle now engaged, we claim our place in the front line. The fascist reaction shall not pass.

The offer to serve under Daladier, again Prime Minister, was too late. Daladier's nerve had collapsed. He resigned on February 7, and was replaced by a cabinet of the right under Doumergue.

Five days later Blum gave an explanation of his change of line, and did so in characteristically Jaurèsian terms: 'When the Republic is threatened, the word republican changes its meaning. It regains its old significance, historic and heroic.' More important than Blum's explanation, however, were the circumstances in which he delivered it. He was speaking to a huge demonstration, assembled in the Place de la Nation on a day of general strike, called in defence of the Republic, and he was sharing the platform with Cachin. February 7 was the first time since 1917 that he offered to serve with a Radical Prime Minister. February 12 was the first time since 1920 that he appeared in collaboration with a Communist.

The beginnings of the Popular Front therefore sprang directly and immediately out of the February days. But the alliance took time to mature and did so uneasily. Blum remained deeply suspicious of the Communists. And they, for nearly six months after the Place de la Nation meeting, continued their attacks upon him. Then the Russian line changed. There began a five-year period in which the Soviet Union pursued a foreign policy of collective resistance to fascist aggression and instructed the Communist parties abroad to match this by seeking political allies in their respective countries. Blum was still not happy. Typically, he searched hard for a satisfactory intellectual explanation for the shift. He failed to find one, but on the whole he none the less welcomed the consequences of the mystery.

He also had to deal with the Radicals: Herriot, whom he liked but who was stubbornly anti-socialist, and Daladier and Chautemps, both of whom he distrusted. A programme which could be accepted by all three parties had to be moulded. Much of the moulding took place in Blum's new apartment, on the Quai Bourbon, in the Île Saint-Louis. He had moved there after the death of his first wife in 1931, and remained when he remarried in 1932. Thérèse Pereira, his second wife, Jewish, war-time nurse and peace-time antique dealer, was a friend and contemporary of Lise Blum but, unlike her, was a dedicated Socialist Party member, who gave Blum six years of political assistance as well as marital companionship Blum was the nodal figure in the tripartite negotiations, but he was not the centre of compromise. Once the line had changed the Communists were more willing to water the programme to suit the Radicals than were the Socialists. Eventually a brief and fairly hard prgramme for 'bread, peace and liberty' was agreed upon. The defence of the Republic, the freedom of the press, collective security and support for the Franco-Soviet pact, the nationalization of armament manufacture, and in a somewhat convoluted form of the Bank of France, were the main planks. Oddly, neither holidays with pay nor the 40-hour week, which were to be the two main achievements of the alliance, were in the programme.

By Bastille Day, 1935, the confluence was symbolized by Blum, Daladier and Cachin marching together at the head of the traditional procession. The Front was a working reality for the elections due in the spring of 1936. Meanwhile governments of the centre-right followed each other with the usual Third Republican rapidity. Flandin succeeded Doumergue, Laval succeeded Flandin, Sarraut succeeded Laval.

Two months before the elections, Blum was nearly killed. He and another Socialist deputy were driving away from the Palais Bourbon for lunch. In the Boulevard Saint-Germain they encountered a funeral demonstration for the royalist Jacques Bainville. The car was stopped and surrounded and the passengers dragged out. One of the distraught mourners tore off the tail light and hit Blum with it behind the ear, severing an artery. For weeks Blum was swathed in bandages. *Action Française* produced a splendid version of the incident. It described Blum as 'this roadhog, whom not even respect for death can restrain', who forced 'his magnificent motor car' across the funeral procession, shouting disdainfully: 'Who are these cads?' A cine-camera produced a rather different version of events. Apart from anything else, the car was an old Citroën.

Blum gained fame, sympathy and even votes from the incident. It helped along an already strong-flowing current. The elections, on the last Sunday in April and the first in May, gave the Socialists a gain of 40 seats, to make them, with 146, for the first time the biggest group in the Chamber. The Radicals lost almost equally and went down from 159 to 116. Proportionally the greatest beneficiaries were the Communists, who, warmed by electoral alliance, moved up from 10 to 72 deputies.

The Socialists were the leaders and co-ordinators of the victorious alliance. Blum clearly had to be Prime Minister. He accepted with a mixture of curiosity, humility and hope. 'How can I tell how I will do a job I have never attempted before?' was his inaugural comment, perhaps more accurate than inspiring.

He became Prime Minister on the evening of June 18, 1936. The constitution of 1875 provided for a month's delay after elections before either the meeting of the new Chamber or the formation of a new Government. It was a good recipe for periods of leaderless chaos, and proved peculiarly effective to this end in the circumstances of 1936. During May, the French Treasury almost ran out of funds. There was heavy pressure on the franc, and a great wave of 'sit-in' strikes paralysed much of French industry, particularly the motor, aircraft and other metal-using plants in the Paris region.

The system did, however, have the advantage that, as with Roosevelt in 1933, Blum took over after several weeks of preparation. He had had time to think and to face the problems of Cabinet formation. The most acute of these was the refusal of the Communists to participate. It was not what Blum had expected, but it was in a sense what he deserved. Thorez and Cachin behaved to him as he had behaved towards the Radicals in 1924 and 1932. They offered support from the outside, arousing all the fears which always stem from such detached adherence. Blum had therefore to share the offices only between his own party and the Radicals.

The division reflected the direction of his interest. He kept the main domestic ministries for his own party, even though, with the franc weak, there were obvious advantages in having a property-conscious Radical at the Ministry of Finance. But Blum was more concerned with the control of the Bank of France. Vincent Auriol went to Finance and Roger Salengro to the Interior. The Radicals were compensated by responsibility for the foreign policy and defence of France. Yvon Delbos, *vice* Herriot, who had declined, went to the Quai d'Orsay. Daladier, Pierre Cot, and a third, less well-known Radical filled the three service ministries.

Blum's first task was to get the factories working again. This he was resolved to do without confrontation with the strikers. His conscience about taking office was delicate in any event; he was certainly not willing to affront it further by starting his ministerial career as a strike-breaker. Furthermore, he appreciated that most of the strikers were in a muddled way on his side, not even instigated by the Communists, who were themselves caught unawares by the spontaneity of the outbreak. In this resolve he was successful. Two days after he took office he negotiated the Matignon Agreements between the employers and the unions.

These amounted to a shift of several notches in the terms of the French social contract. They included wage increases of between 12 per cent and 15 per cent, the 40-hour week, holidays with pay, and the right to full union recognition and general collective bargaining. In some respects the Agreements merely enabled the French workers, whose standard of living had lagged since 1914, to catch up with the rest of the advanced world; in others they sent them well ahead.

This executive negotiation was followed by a spate of legislative activity. The majority in the Chamber was substantial and temporarily secure. The Senate was sullen but stunned ('I think no, but I vote yes', was Caillaux's cynical confession after collective bargaining had gone through the second chamber by a vote of 279 to 8). The Matignon Agreements (apart from the wage increases) had themselves to be given statutory form. In addition the Government in its first 10 weeks dissolved the semi-fascist leagues, gave an amnesty to political prisoners, brought the Bank of France under rather loose public control, carried permissive legislation for the nationalization of defence industries (vigorously used by Cot as Air Minister, weakly by Daladier as Army Minister), raised the school leaving age to 14 (the fact that it needed raising to this modest level was an example of French social backwardness), set up a commodity board for wheat, and secured the voting of a substantial programme of public works. As a first seventy days, it bore comparison with the first hundred of Roosevelt.

When Parliament adjourned on August 14, Blum could feel domestically satisfied. But only domestically. On July 18 the Spanish Civil War had begun. In Britain and even America its effects were traumatic, but they were most concentrated upon France. The ideological contiguity of the *Frente Popular* and the *Front Populaire* matched the geographical contiguity of the two countries. The gradual defeat of the Spanish Republicans and the guilt and tension which this aroused on the French left drained the spirit out of the Popular Front, and most of all out of its leader. And the germs of destructive bitterness were carried from their Iberian breeding grounds across the Pyrenees to infect French society with deeper divisions than had been known since the Commune, and a longer-lasting malaise than had even then been experienced. 'Better Hitler than Blum' was a cry which needed the irrational extremism of the Spanish conflict to give it currency.

From the moment of General Franco's revolt, Blum was on a rack of indecision and misery. The Spanish Government asked him for arms. He instinctively agreed to supply them. On July 22 he went to London for his first official visit. Eden warned him of the consequences of embroilment in terms which were moderate but unmistakable. 'It's your business, but I beg you to be careful', was how Blum subsequently summed up the warning. This was bad enough, for Blum attached overwhelming importance to the British alliance. Deputy for Narbonne and man of the left though he was, he had no intention of sacrificing London for Madrid. But what was worse was that when he got back to Paris he found Vice-Premier Chautemps waiting for him on the tarmac with the news that the leakage of the arms plan (through the pro-Franco military attaché at the Spanish Embassy) was producing a major French political crisis, and that the Radical members of the cabinet, fortified by the growling of Herriot from his new position as President of the Chamber, would not stand it. Blum at first wanted to force the issue, whatever the consequences to his Government. But he was dissuaded, not least, ironically enough, by the tearful argument of the Spanish Republican representative in Paris, who recoiled in horror from the prospect of the break-up. Instead Blum spawned what grew into the monstrosity of the non-intervention policy. He was a most reluctant parent and he never fully recovered from the birth. By September 6 he found himself defending the policy he so disliked before a vast and restive audience of 'supporters' at Luna Park. '*Blum à l'action*' became the not wholly satisfactory riposte of the left to the right's cry of preference for Hitler. The honeymoon of the Government was over.

On September 26 Blum announced a 25 per cent devaluation of the franc. It was a sensible economic decision (the franc was to go much lower after Blum ceased to be Prime Minister), which removed only a small part of the working class gains of the summer, and ought to have been done in June: coming in September it looked too much like the first of the chickens coming home to roost. In November, Salengro, the Minister of the Interior, was subjected to an unusually foul campaign of press calumny, which aroused Blum to a noble and victorious defence in the Chamber, but none the less led to Salengro's suicide, and hence to a deep depression of Blum's spirits.

By January there was an urgent need to float a large and successful government loan. An attempt the previous summer had proved a failure. A repetition of this could not be afforded. The money was urgently necessary both for rearmament and for the programme of civilian public works. Accordingly, in February, Blum found it necessary to announce 'a pause' in the programme of the Popular Front. 'We must get our breath', he said. The Communists did not vote against him in the Chamber, but the combination of the pause and the deteriorating position in Spain made them, and a lot of Socialists (including, it might almost be said, Blum himself), increasingly dissatisfied with his leadership.

This self-dissatisfaction was increased by the Clichy riots on March 16. A clash between the extreme right and Socialists and Communists took place in north-east Paris. The police killed six by their pacifying methods, and wounded a good number of others, including André Blumel, Blum's *chef de cabinet*, who had been sent by his master to see what was happening. Blum himself was attending an Anglo-French gala at the Opéra. Late at night he went to Clichy and visited the hospital. It was an agitated rather than a wise move. The white of his tie and waistcoat was too sharp a contrast with the blood of the wounded. No one felt the incongruity, or the shock of the incident as a whole, more than he did himself. It strengthened his growing but defeated feeling that it was impossible for one man to be at once leader of the Socialist Party and Prime Minister of a country as deeply divided as France had become.

This greatly influenced his attitude to the crisis, partly financial but mainly constitutional, which erupted in June. The continuing flight of capital forced Blum to ask for special powers relating mainly to exchange control. It was not an extreme or, in general form, an unusual request. The Chamber granted it without difficulty. The Senate substituted for the Chamber's Bill a new and much weaker one of its own. Caillaux, recovering his courage to vote as he thought, took the lead. The Chamber then proposed a compromise, which Blum accepted. The Senate was less accommodating. It rejected the compromise by a vote of 168 to 96. There was thus a direct conflict not only between the Government and the Senate, but also between the directly and the indirectly elected chambers.

It was the stuff of which constitutional changes are made, particularly as the Government was being remarkably successful in retaining its popular support. It achieved three resounding by-election victories during the course of the dispute. But Blum refused the fence. With his usual clarity he outlined three possible courses: to capitulate; to fight; to let the leadership pass to the Radicals and hope by that means both to get the special powers and preserve some sort of Popular Front cohesion. The first course was unacceptable. The second, he decided, was too divisive for the nation. He therefore opted for the third and did it thoroughly by becoming Vice-Premier under Chautemps. Chautemps got the powers but kept only the shell of the Popular Front.

Blum's Ministry had lasted a year and two weeks. It is difficult to believe that he had not lost the will to office well before three o'clock on midsummer's morning, 1937, when he left the Hôtel Matignon to drive to the Elysée and hand in his resignation as Prime Minister. Possibly it began to die as soon as a combination of the British and the Radicals made him retreat over arms to Spain. Probably it perished finally during the night of blood and guilt at Clichy.

The 26 months between his demission and the outbreak of war were all anticlimax for Blum. He served under Chautemps as long as that Government lasted—until January, 1938. Then in March, his second wife having died in the meantime, he was summoned back from a dismal retreat in the country to attempt the formation of a wide-based Government of national union, embracing all those with a will to resist Nazism, to the full menace of which he was much more alive than in 1936. 'From Thorez to Reynaud' was the cry. It remained a cry. The Government he in fact formed was only the old coalition of Socialists and Radicals. It lasted no more than three weeks, once again falling in a vain attempt to obtain special powers from the Senate.

That was Blum's last period of office under the Third Republic. But his troubles were far from over. As he became more intransigent, so much of the Socialist Party became more defeatist. Paul Faure, the secretary-general of the party, his Socialist Vice-Premier in 1936, his most considerable colleague right through from the Tours conference, was a dedicated appeaser. To preserve some sort of party unity, Blum found it necessary to cast an unhappy vote for the Munich settlement.

Only the onset of complete misfortune began the revival of his spirits and his reputation. The outbreak of war did not dismay him. He gave much readier support to the Daladier Government after September 3, 1939, than he had done in the last 18 months of the peace. Equally the Nazi-Soviet Pact, grave blow to the western democracies though it was, freed him from what had become the incubus of the Communist alliance. In May, 1940, on the eve of the collapse of France, he came to the Labour Party Conference at Bournemouth and delivered a speech which could perhaps be faulted for excess of optimism, but not for lack of resolution. Nor, despite the fact that it was delivered in a language uncomprehended by most of his audience (Blum was an appalling linguist; despite his intelligence and education he could not converse, let alone orate, in either English or German) did it fail to seize and enthuse the audience. Yet he took no refuge in easy messages of goodwill. It was a hard argument for fighting 'one of the most monstrous products of mankind', and for doing so by methods which included the exclusion of the 70 Communist deputies—most of them owing their election to the Blum ticket—from the working of the French Parliament:

That action was not imposed by the Government on the popular will; it was imposed on the Government by the people's will; it was imposed by the will of a people who would not tolerate any longer that there should be in our free National Assembly seventy deputies who publicly, openly, officially, received their orders from a foreign, and what may perhaps be, an enemy state . . . If you had seventy Nazis here in Britain working under orders from Berlin, would you tolerate it?

It was a long road to have travelled in the four years since the triumphant election of the Popular Front, but it was a road which was consistent with the heritage of Jaurès and with Blum's own attitude in the first world war, at Tours and at Narbonne.

Soon after his return to Paris from Bournemouth, Blum, together with most other French politicians, set off on another road, that which took them, as the seat of Government moved, south-west to Bordeaux, and then, according to a mixture of chance and choice, to England, to North Africa, to Vichy or to some less voluntary destination. Blum's defiance of defeat made some new friends (Paul Reynaud and Georges Mandel, in particular) and kept some old ones (Herriot, Vincent Auriol, Marx Dormoy), but it also lost him some (Faure, Chautemps and, ironically enough, Frossard, the 1920 emissary to Moscow, his old adversary of the

Tours conference, who became one of the pillars of the Pétain Government), as well as deepening old enmities. 'His life is really in danger', Mandel told General Spears. 'To many who yearn for a capitulation and hope to make friends with Hitler, he stands for that section of the population which will fight on at any cost.'

The danger caused Blum no fear, but, what was perhaps worse, a dismay at the impotence which stemmed from the antipathy he aroused: 'I wondered whether the upopularity which was growing up round my name had not already made my actions sterile—even harmful to the ideas I wished to sustain, to the companions who joined with me in defending them.' From Bordeaux he was prepared to sail to North Africa, on the assumption that the Government went, too, and carried on the fight from there. Rather pathetically he shuttled to and fro across the south-west of France, not sure whether he was supposed to embark from near Perpignan or from the estuary of the Gironde. Finally he discovered that the boat had sailed without him.

Then, in the early dawn of a June Sunday (three years nearly to the day since he had driven through another summer dawn to hand in the resignation of his first Government) he sat in his car outside Toulouse railway station and read in a late edition of the famous *Dépêche* (almost as much Jaurès's paper as *Humanité* had been) that the capitulation was complete, that 'the irreparable was consummated'.

For a time he stayed with friends near Toulouse. An untroubled garden gave him an island of calm in that sad but beautiful summer. His bodily equilibrium, he wrote, was restored, but the desolation of his spirit persisted. After a few weeks he went to Vichy and tried to rally the remnants of the Socialist Party against Laval. He failed. Only 28 of the great band of Socialist deputies elected in 1936 voted with him against the destruction of the Republic. He retired once more to the garden outside Toulouse. He was arrested there on September 15.

He was taken first to the Château de Chazeron, in the Auvergne, and then transferred after two months to Bourassol, which was a little nearer to Riom, the seat of the new Supreme Court. Blum's conditions of life in these two châteaux were physically perfectly tolerable. He was a prisoner and was closely guarded (although not much more so than as Prime Minister, he wrote in one letter), but he had spacious and reasonably furnished rooms, with full opportunity for reading, correspondence and other writing.

His fellow prisoners included Daladier and General Gamelin. He could talk to them, but they do not appear to have played much part in his life.

With Reynaud, and Mandel, who were similarly arrested and would have been more intellectually congenial, he rarely coincided. His closest Socialist collaborators—Vincent Auriol, Marx Dormoy, Jules Moch, who had all been amongst the twenty-eight who were with him at Vichy in July, were temporarily incarcerated elsewhere, but were given limited freedom in early 1941. Auriol was assigned to his house, but Dormoy, Mayor of Montluçon, was perversely ordered to Montélimar, where, six months later, he was assassinated in a hotel. This was a heavy blow for Blum, much of whose life had come to be bound up in correspondence with these three, and perhaps most of all with Dormoy. No sooner had he settled down to captivity at Chazeron than he was writing to him with a remarkable combination of warmth, intellectual vivacity and calm detachment:

Mon cher Marx,
Renée [Blum's daughter-in-law] *me dit que vous désirez savoir ce que je pense de Talleyrand. C'est bien simple* . . . [there followed 300 crisp words of analysis, information and aphorism].
Je vous embrasse
L.B.

It was the same note which he struck in the 60,000-word memoir of the months of collapse which he also wrote in this early period of imprisonment. It was compellingly lucid, assured in its standpoint, yet cool and comprehending in its acceptance of vicissitudes and its judgements of both friends and enemies. The faint note of self-pity, which had sometimes been present in Blum's speeches in the plenitude of his success, was wholly absent from his writings in the trough of his adversity.

Blum was formally charged on October 8, 1940. As Prime Minister and later deputy Prime Minister, it was alleged, he had betrayed his duty in such a way as to lead France into war and defeat. But the counts, as they developed, related solely to his domestic policy: it was the 40-hour week, paid holidays and the nationalization of armament firms which were held responsible for the plight of France and for which he was required to answer.

The course of the proceedings was at once dilatory, farcical and disgraceful. During the winter of 1940-41 there were sporadic private interrogations, with Blum reserving his defence for open court. Then for months nothing happened at all. The whole summer of 1941 passed in inactivity. In October, Pétain indulged in one of the most curious acts ever to be perpetrated by a head of State. On the same day that Blum was first given a full statement of the case against him, Pétain broadcast to the French people to announce that he had found Blum guilty, together with Daladier and Gamelin, and ordered their indefinite detention in the Fort du Portalet in the Pyrenees. But at the same time he asked the Riom court to hasten its consideration of the cases on which he had already given his verdict.

On November 22 Blum was accordingly moved to Portalet, an altogether bleaker establishment than those to which he had been used. But as, in the conditions of wartime France, it was a 14-hour journey from Bourassol, he manifestly could not be tried at Riom while he was there. So, five weeks later, he had to be brought back to Bourassol. After a further delay of two months, the trial eventually opened on February 20, 1942, 17 months after Blum's arrest.

With judgment and punishment already given, the only objects could be to make propaganda for the régime and to attempt a cloak of retrospective legality. There was a total failure on both counts. Blum was supported not at all by Gamelin, who put up no defence, and only weakly and without spirit by Daladier. He was defended by Le Troquer, later to be president of the National Assembly, and by two other advocates. But their assistance, courageous though it was, was hardly necessary. Throughout several days of statement and interrogation Blum dominated the court. Intellectually and morally he stood a head taller than anybody else.

The fluency of his memory, the precision of his logic, and the *netteté* of his language were formidable weapons. But more striking still is the extent to which, from the records of those 30-year-old proceedings, there stands out the impression of a man, who, far on in his seventh decade and in the winter of his misfortune, was immune to lethargy or despair. He answered all the detailed points with energy and ingenuity, but much more impressively he challenged the probity of the court and the core of the indictment. The wretched president constantly tried to restrict the political sweep of his argument: it was the effect of his measures upon war output, not upon the state of France, which was at issue. It was of course a ludicrous ruling in one of the most political of all trials, and one which could not possibly be sustained. Blum transcended the attempted limitations, not merely to set the charges in the context of the political needs of 1936, but in that of the whole republican tradition. It was the Republic which was on trial, he claimed. And it was the republican spirit, freed of defeats and compromises, which was being vindicated as Blum demolished each charge and then moved towards his final rejection, contemptuous and inspired, not only of the case but of the whole ethos of the Vichy Government.

At this stage, Pétain simply stopped the trial. Admiral Darlan had sent him a submission that the 'allegations of the accused' (a remarkable phrase) were dividing public opinion and harming international relations. Hitler had complained. It was the greatest possible triumph for Blum. It occured two days after his 70th birthday, and he was immediately racked by an appalling attack of rheumatism and sciatica. It was a month before he could sit at a table and write. At least this resolved the question of whether or not he should be sent back to the grim fortress of Portalet. He remained at Bourassol for almost another year.

During this period he was much occupied with the politics of the Free French in London, and sent, by clandestine means, a series of important letters to his Socialist friends there, to General de Gaulle himself, and through de Gaulle, to Churchill and Roosevelt. His position was then determinedly Gaullist. Only a soldier could lead the Free French, he had faith in the General, and he believed that he was the indispensable man, not only to assist the liberation, but subsequently to lead France in the transition to a new democratic régime. He firmly communicated these views to a number of anti-Gaullist Socialists who were organized in the *Groupe Jean Jaurès*, as well as to the British and American leaders. The only point on which Blum differed substantially from de Gaulle was over the accord which the General made with the French Communist Party at the end of 1942, and which in Blum's view exaggerated their force, gave them too special a position within the Resistance, and showed some political naiveté on the part of de Gaulle.

* *

On March 30, 1943, Blum made another change of prison. He was handed over to the Germans and transferred from Bourassol to Buchenwald. His physical conditions remained tolerable. He was not put in the concentration camp itself, but allowed to reside in a house on the periphery. It was the rule that political prisoners of Blum's stature could take with them a wife (or other member of the family) and one servant. Yet, even with these ameliorations, it was not only the name of Buchenwald which made the transfer menacing. Day to day, from then until the end of the war, Blum had no security of life. His fate was a matter of whim. Georges Mandel, who shared the house with him, was taken back to France and shot in 1944. Blum had to learn to live beneath this hanging sword. The whole arrangement, semi-comfort, total insecurity, and life within range of the continuing sound and smell of death, was an extraordinary mixture of deference and torment.

Blum had no wife to take with him, but he had Jeanne Reichenbach (née Levilliers), who was the companion of his old age. She was 30 years his junior, the daughter of a family friend, and had attached herself to Blum when the misfortunes of war began to fall upon him. She was with him near Toulouse at the time of his arrest, and had then travelled around France staying in the village nearest to each of his prisons. She had been married first to Henri Torrès, who traversed the political spectrum from Communism to post-war Gaullism; and then, after a divorce, to Reichenbach, the owner of the chain store Pris Unic. Reichenbach, who had been a close friend of Blum's, left for New York in 1940, and died there in 1942. Jeanne Reichenbach chose to remain in France. She succeeded in following Blum to Buchenwald and married him there in 1943. She survived him, and is indeed still alive. Like the second Mme Blum, but unlike the first, her political views were almost as strong as those of her husband.

Blum was liberated by the American armies on May 4, 1945. He returned to Paris by way of Italy, arriving at Orly airfield 10 days later. There were family and friends and a crowd of supporters to greet him. In one sense he quickly took up his old life. His first article in *Le Populaire* appeared within 48 hours—just as his last was to be read only the day before his death. He retained his desire to influence others, to pronounce upon questions both of the day and of the decade, and to do so above all by means of the written word. He moved quickly back into politics, and into Socialist politics. Yet there was a detachment which had not previously existed.

The scars of 1940, which he had concealed during the war years, suddenly became more obvious. He never again stood for elected office. Jules Moch asked him if he would accept nomination for Narbonne in the new Assembly, and was amazed by the vehemence of his refusal. Not merely would he not seek to represent them, but he never wished again to see the town or the *département*—and never did so. When he was at Toulouse in 1940 they had not wished to see him. After 1945 he did not wish to see them. 'Our comrades were not very courageous', he added grimly. Equally, he did not wish to live in Paris. He spent nearly all his time at a small but attractive house, village on one side, garden on the other, at Jouy-en-Josas, between Versailles and Villacoublay.

The Socialist Party had been purged of the 115 deputies and senators who had rejected his leadership at Vichy and voted for Laval. Yet he did not find the younger replacements wholly congenial. At the 1945 party conference he succeeded in persuading the majority to reject amalgamation with the Communists. But at the 1946 conference the left-wing minority, improbably led, as it now seems, by Guy Mollet, had their revenge, swung the party towards a more rigid Marxist position, and repeated the left-wing takeover of 1918. Blum's friend Daniel Mayer was replaced as secretary-general by Mollet.

Despite this defeat, Blum put before the party and the world his view of social democracy in a post-war context. Essentially it was Jaurès brought up to date. Marxism needed to be transcended but not rejected. Economic liberalism was dying if not dead, but the rights of individuals to develop their own capacities and to find, not merely their own usefulness, but their own happiness, was as essential to socialism as the freedom from economic thraldom: 'There is no free proletariat in an enslaved people; there are no free men if all men are not free . . .' The end was not economic, the aims of socialism could be bounded no more by class than they could by nationalism. 'Humane socialism', a term which he rather disliked, but which became associated with his name, was democratic, tolerant and internationalist.

Part of the difficulty of this period stemmed from the fact that Blum had transcended the party of which he was the brightest ornament but which he no longer effectively led. Many of its activists loved and revered him. Others regarded him with an uncomfortable mixture of pride and jealousy. He was faithful to *La Vieille Maison* even if not altogether comfortable under its new roof. But his triumphs were non-party. In early 1946 he had a brief but remarkably successful period as ambassador to Washington. Speaking no English, never having previously visited America, and knowing little economics, he arguably obtained a better agreement of assistance for France than the combined efforts of Keynes and Halifax had been able to obtain for Britain. He played a leading part in the setting up of UNESCO and its establishment in Paris. And then at the end of 1946, when de Gaulle had withdrawn to his long sojourn at Colombey, and when neither of the two biggest parties, the Communists and the *Mouvement Républicain Populaire* could either govern on their own or coalesce, Blum, although outside parliament, accepted an invitation from a group of party leaders to form a purely Socialist government, of strictly limited duration, to usher in the Fourth Republic, and had his investiture voted for by 575 out of 590 deputies.

For the third time he was Prime Minister of France, and during a brief month, rather successfully so. He secured a temporary halt to inflation, even a reduction in prices, and did the ground work for the Treaty of Dunkirk between Britain and France, the first of that network of accords which were to help raise Western Europe out of its slough of penury and fear. Ten months later, when the new Republic was challenged alike by Communist strikes and Gaullist menace, he was asked to try again, this time to form a 'Third Force' government. The attempt was notable, if for nothing else, for a picture of this famous private citizen, unelected, sitting alone on the ministers' bench in the National Assembly, and waiting calmly to hear that he had failed, even though by only 10 votes, to secure the necessary majority.

This was effectively the end of his public career. The next year he served for a few weeks as deputy Prime Minister in the coalition government of André Marie. He supported the Marshall Plan. He was an enthusiast for the Council of Europe. He received an honorary degree at Oxford, which gave him peculiar pleasure. For the first half of 1949 he was ill. His heart had begun to fail. Then he recovered, but only briefly. He died in March, 1950, a few days before his seventy-eighth birthday. He was given a great funeral beginning outside the offices of the *Populaire* and ending in the Place de la Concorde. The French Socialist Party was not a growing force, but there were plenty of old members remaining, who wished to come and say goodbye to *le Patron*. The cortège, headed by a hundred miners from the Pas-de-Calais, proceeded from the crowded Paris of journalism and commerce, to the spacious Paris of official grandeur. It was a procession of nostalgia and fidelity. It was a fitting route and a fitting obsequy.

In the Concorde there were major orations which recalled the Blum of the pre-war as well as the post-war years, the Blum of international socialism as well as the Blum of France. But his pervading influence was perhaps best summed up by Daniel Mayer, who eschewed the flourishes of Gallic oratory and said simply: 'There is hardly anything which can happen in our lives about which we will not spontaneously ask ourselves, "what would he have thought?".'

He was buried at Jouy. His grave carries the succinct inscription: '*Léon Blum, Homme d'État Francais*, 1872-1950'. So indeed he was, and the span of his life, perhaps the most undulating and fascinating in the whole of French history, is as significant to his character as are his own qualities as sparkling intellectual, hesitant statesman, and resolute resister.

ERNEST BEVIN

Ernest Bevin

Towards the end of a morning in the middle years of the 1945 Government Bevin arrived late at a meeting of the Defence Committee of the Cabinet, and waddled round the table to his seat. Attlee was just beginning his summing up. This terse exercise was not allowed to continue to its rapid conclusion. As soon as he caught the drift, Bevin interrupted. 'That won't do, Prime Minister', he said. 'That won't do at all. It don't fit in with my policy.' Attlee allowed Bevin his way, as he would have allowed no other member of the Government. The discussion began again and reached the opposite conclusion.

This story, unless more apocryphal than I believe it to be, shows that Bevin was capable of a greater exercise of single-handed, somewhat brutal Cabinet power than any man I ever saw in action around the table in Downing Street. And the feat was the greater because no one now believes that he was dealing with a weak Prime Minister.

It is not unusual for a Minister, particularly one as senior as Bevin was, to get a Cabinet or a Cabinet Committee to reverse its original intention. I have seen it done by serpentine skill; by the sheer weight of persuasive argument; by coming back after an adjournment with the claim that the development of the facts was more powerful than the theory of the earlier decision. And it can be done too—although then the result is more often a compromise—by sustained petulance and bad temper. But all these methods were quite different from that used by Bevin on this occasion. He simply stopped the engine in its tracks, lifted it up, and put it back facing in the other direction. He got what he wanted. He was concerned neither to give himself the pleasure of delivering a great Cabinet oration, nor to save the faces of those whose time he had wasted by being late. The bad manners were incidental. The exercise of power on the side of good sense (as he saw it) was central.

His life gave him unusual opportunity for such exercise. In one sense, of course, this is so obviously the case with any man who spends ten years as a major Minister that the point is hardly worth making. But it was true in a rather special sense with Bevin. Most politicians, even the most successful, spend a lot of their time as little fish in big ponds. Mr Heath, as an Assistant Government Whip, or Mr Wilson as parliamentary secretary to the Ministry of Works, could not, at those stages, have had much opportunity for throwing their weight about.

But Bevin was always big in relation to *his* pond. He had to be a general union and not a craft union man, for he served no apprenticeships. At twenty he achieved a relatively independent job, a mineral water delivery man with two horses and dray, an opportunity to plan his own route, make his own sales and draw commission. At thirty he became a full-time official within six months of joining a union. At forty-five, within one year of joining the General Council of the TUC, he became its most dominant member and remained so for the next 14 years. On the threshold of sixty, he became a minister (soon to be one of eight in the War Cabinet) before he was a Member of Parliament. Five years later he became Foreign Secretary, starting with the qualification that there was no other position in the Foreign Office, unless it was that of a rather truculent liftman on the verge of retirement, which it would have been possible to imagine his filling. He could not possibly have been a senior or a junior official, a political under-secretary, or even a Minister of State. It was Secretary of State or nothing. There are few other Foreign Secretaries of either party of whom this could be said.

Bevin as Foreign Secretary clearly left a lasting impression, both on the course of British foreign policy and on those who served under him. In this century there are only four occupants of the office with whom it is possible to compare him. The first is Lansdowne, the second Grey, the third Curzon, and the fourth Lord Avon. And for sheer weight of impression he beats them all.

Lansdowne must be included, not because he was a strong or colourful figure, but because he was the architect of the Anglo-French Entente of 1903 and therefore set the course of British foreign and defence policy for the next 37 years. But Bevin's work to launch the Marshall Plan, to create NATO, to commit the United States to Europe, and to commit Britain to the United States, while its results have not yet lasted as long, was at least equally decisive, and probably more consciously so.

Curzon left no remotely comparable imprint on the path of foreign policy. Indeed he was in many ways a weak Foreign Secretary, who failed to defend his department against the depredations of Lloyd George, and was therefore, despite the grandeur of his appearance, often little more than an agent for carrying out a fluctuating and uncertain policy. But he was Bevin's rival in ability to impress his personality on those who worked for him, and to be remembered with the vividness which only a richly anecdotal figure can achieve.

Grey and Lord Avon must be considered by virtue of their Foreign Office longevity: the one occupied the post for eleven continuous years, the other for a twice-broken aggregate of nearly ten. It is impossible to serve as head of a great department for these lengths of time without leaving a substantial deposit of influence and recollection behind. But not on the Bevin scale. Grey I believe to be an overrated figure, an insular Englishman of high but priggish character and limited imagination, who confined his contacts with foreigners to the minimum and led Britain into war with a policy which was at once stubborn and imprecise.

Lord Avon is still very difficult to appraise, but I think it fair to say that in his pre-war period he made a gallant failure of his attempt to shift the course of British foreign policy; that in the conduct of war-time foreign policy he was inevitably much overshadowed by Churchill (although not nearly as much as Cordell Hull was by Roosevelt); and that between 1951 and 1955 he broadly pursued lines laid down by Bevin rather than struck out in new directions of his own. Suez, of course, was his work as Prime Minister not as Foreign Secretary.

Bevin's imprint on the Foreign Office must therefore be regarded as remarkable by any standards. There is room for dispute about the rightness of his policies, as about the amiability of his character. But there is little danger of his being forgotten.

How did his career build up to this apogee? He was born in 1881, in the most remote part of Somerset. At the age of eight, his mother dead and his father always unknown, he was taken into the mid-Devon countryside to live with a married sister. This regional provenance is unusual. The West Country has not been much of a breeding-ground for politicians. There is no other figure clearly of the first rank for at least the last hundred years for whom it provided both the birthplace and the background of upbringing. It was moreover a peculiarly paradoxical provenance for Bevin. He was the symbol of the 'industrial' side of the Labour movement. More almost than any other minister he brought industry into the Cabinet room. But his childhood memories were all of a purely rural life. And when he left village life at the age of thirteen it was to Bristol—the least moulded by the industrial revolution of all the great provincial cities—that he went, and there he kept his home for 26 years.

His ideological development is not easy to categorize. Most people of his generation came into Labour politics under one of three dominant influences: the Marxism of Hyndman's Social Democratic Federation, the ethical socialism of the Independent Labour Party, or the intellectual gradualism of the Fabians. None of the three had a clear and obvious effect upon Bevin. He was against intellectuals, and for most of his middle life regarded middle-class socialists as patronising. This could sometimes take an almost childish turn, as when he wrote to H. N. Brailsford in 1926:

With regard to our refusal to talk to you and people in your category in the movement, believe me we have very good reasons. The 'superior class' attitude is always there in relation to the trade union leader who comes from the rank and file. We do not like your patronage and naturally withdraw from it..... I do not feel at home outside my own circle of trade union work.

This was written in an exceptionally sour and defensive post-General Strike mood. Even so it represented enough of his continuing feeling as completely to exclude the Fabian influence. Nor did he ever think much of ILP sermonizing, although he probably disliked the preachers more than the sermons. In some ways the SDF was more temperamentally congenial to him, and the first political body to which he belonged, the Bristol Socialist Society, was affiliated to it. But neither Marxist doctrine, nor revolutionary prospects made much appeal to him, and he was soon devoting his main political energies to the 'Right-to-Work' Committee. He preferred applying himself to a specific problem.

Bevin's intellectual route into Labour politics is not therefore easy to chart. Partly this is because in one sense he never came wholly into Labour politics until 1945. He always had strong political views, at times quite far to the Left, often well outside the compass not merely of industrial politics but of the ordinary range of contemporary political discussion as a whole. Once he had created his big union, by the middle 'twenties, he had a good deal of energy to spare for wider activities.

At first he devoted this mainly to influencing the industrial policy of the TUC. During the General Strike he made himself the organisation man, and tried to get a semblance of order into the chaotic conditions at TUC headquarters. At the same time he used his influence in favour of making the toughest bargain that was realistically possible. He was equally hostile to the soft accommodations of J. H. Thomas and the emotional intransigence of A. J. Cook. He always liked to believe that he—and perhaps he alone—was dealing with the facts of the situation. But these 'facts' were not quite so objective as he liked to pretend. They could change shape and colour according to the light which he chose to shine on them. But they were rarely pure figments of his imagination. Whether it was a question of detailed negotiation or of the general direction of trade union policy he had an instinctive sense of relative bargaining strengths and of their likely development into the future.

This told him more quickly than most that 1926 was the end of an era. Massive and frequent industrial action, which with a war interruption, had been the pattern since 1911, was no longer a matter for serious consideration. The battered unions had to be held together and their financial strength re-built. This meant less conflict and more negotiation. It led on to the Mond-Turner talks between both sides of industry, and more slowly but more importantly to the successful development of the general Bevin/Citrine strategy of trade union involvement in almost every aspect of the business of Government. If the unions were to use the strike threat only sparingly, they had to show that there were a great number of other ways in which they could represent their members. Bevin and Citrine achieved this during the 'thirties. Trade union leaders began to go to Downing Street when there was an international crisis and not merely when there was an industrial one. And Bevin solidified the position at many lower and possibly more relevant levels during his war years as Minister of Labour.

The reaction from 1926 also made Bevin more interested in politics. He distrusted nearly all the leaders of the 1929 Government, but he was nevertheless much more involved with its life and death than he had been with the Government of 1924. Then his main contribution was to greet the advent in January of the first Labour administration in history with a national dock strike in February and a London tram strike in March. '... Governments may come and Governments may go', he wrote indifferently in reply to a storm of criticism, 'but the workers' fight for betterment of conditions must go on all the time....'

By 1929 his vision was broader. He brushed aside MacDonald's offer of a peerage, but he treated more attractive invitations less roughly. He became a member both of the Macmillan Committee on Finance and Industry and of MacDonald's own Economic Advisory Council. The first proved more worth while than the second. Both, however, had the surprising effect of bringing Bevin for the first time into alliance with two of the normally despised 'intellectuals', one outside the Labour Party and the other inside. The outside one was Maynard Keynes. He like Bevin was a member of both bodies, but it was the Macmillan Committee which brought them together. There were only two other left-of-centre members, and one of these was useless and the other a crank. If the conventional wisdom was to be effectively challenged, Bevin and Keynes had together to do it. This they did, in a remarkably equal partnership, providing in almost perfect harmony a complementary balance of attack against august and complacent witnesses. They split on only one point of importance in the recommendations, with Bevin taking the more adventurous side. Both agreed that the return to gold in 1925 had been disastrous, but Keynes as in some other aspects of his beliefs thought that 'bygones were bygones', and did not advocate a reversal of what had been done. Bevin did, and wanted urgent consideration given to a devaluation. Despite this difference they achieved, and maintained, a high degree of mutual comprehension and respect. An echo of it reached me in Cambridge nearly thirty years later. Professor Kaldor, not an unreserved admirer of Bevin's foreign policy, was holding forth about the iniquity of the policy and of the man who had upheld it. Professor (now Lord) Kahn, perhaps the best qualified of all the would-be keepers of the bones of the saint, listened for sometime with a good deal of agreement, but then decided the attack had gone too far. 'Nicky', he said magisterially, 'you should remember that Maynard knew him on the Macmillan Committee and thought well of him.' That ended the attack. No torrent of defence on my part could have produced one-tenth of the effect.

Bevin's other intellectual ally was G. D. H. Cole. He too was a member of the ineffective Economic Advisory Council. After the fall of the Government they even wrote a pamphlet together, entitled simply *The Crisis*, and published under their joint names by the *New Statesman*. This alliance also led to Bevin becoming chairman of the Society for Socialist Information and Propaganda, one of a series of similar ventures inspired by Cole, but Bevin's only excursion into organisations on the fringe of the Labour movement. It turned out badly. The SSIP developed into the Socialist League, the main rallying point of the Labour left of the midthirties, and in the course of this evolution pushed Bevin out of the chairmanship. Cole was displeased by this, and against most of his natural inclinations left the executive with Bevin. But this loyalty could not repair the damage. Bevin repulsed an offer to compensate him with office in the New Fabian Research Bureau. 'I think it better I should stick to my last', he wrote. But he also stuck to some sort of relations with Cole for a few years. Principally this took the form of an occasional exchange of letters, couched on Bevin's part in surprisingly polite terms, but attempting to bridg an increasingly wide gulf of incomprehension. And by 1937 Cole was writing that: 'Bevin and Dalton . . . appear to have gone quite mad'.

The 1931 defections of MacDonald, Snowden and Thomas not only confirmed Bevin's worst forebodings but also aroused his strongest pugnacious interests. At a 'council of war' in Henderson's room on the day of the formation of the National Government, Bevin was described (by Hugh Dalton) as saying 'This is like the general strike. I am prepared to put everything in'. Primarily this meant financial assistance. But Bevin also allowed himself to be reluctantly nominated as Labour candidate for Gateshead. The result was hardly a triumph. A 1929 Labour majority of 16,000 was turned into a 12,000 defeat for Bevin. But big swings were common in 1931, and Bevin had performed his act of solidarity.

From 1932 to 1939 he played a major role in rebuilding the Labour Party in the form in which he wished to see it: very closely linked with the trade unions and therefore exclusive in its approach to political alliance, whether on the left or the right; committed to a short, hard, practical programme, which gave a future Labour Government the prospect of being more left-wing than its predecessors if measured by the test of likely achievement, but more right-wing if measured by the imposition of limitations on its aspirations; and firmly in favour of resistance to Nazism and Fascism, even if too wobbly on rearmament for Bevin's own taste.

Bevin did not achieve these results on his own. Attlee, Dalton, Morrison and Citrine all contributed substantially, some perhaps even more so than Bevin. But Bevin's role was none the less unique. He was the man who battered the Labour Party Conference into shape from the floor. He was the prototype of the union leader without whose intervention few major debates were complete. And he behaved in a more arrogant (or, according to taste, self-assured) fashion than anyone does today.

He chose his time to speak so as to achieve the maximum impact on the debate. He would then rise to his feet, make a brief signal to the chairman, and start to walk slowly, somewhat menacingly, towards the rostrum. It never occurred to him that he would not be called whenever he chose. When he had arrived at the rostrum there would be an appreciable interval while he looked round appraisingly at his audience. He had no need to start in a hurry for, within limits, he took little notice of time restrictions. Then he would begin. The content of his speeches was usually fairly well worked out in advance, although the phraseology mostly came as he went along. And a very odd phraseology it was. The syntax was erratic, to say the least, but he transcended grammar more often than he defied it. A sentence would frequently be put together out of two syntactically incompatible parts. Either would have been all right on its own. But the meaning was usually clear, although more so when heard than when read. There was no elegance, and rarely any grandeur of words as opposed to ideas.

Nor was there much intimate colloquialism of language. His oratory had little of the simple raciness of a J. H. Thomas or a Governor Al Smith. He may have been the authentic voice of ordinary people, but he certainly did not speak as they spoke. He was far too fond of a sort of committee jargon for that. Francis Williams, who published a short but highly perceptive life within a year of Bevin's death, wrote of 'a peculiarly trade union English (born, out of wedlock, somewhere between Smith Square and Whitehall) to which he was much addicted'.

Yet, for all these deficiencies, his oratory was a most powerful weapon. It gave his ideas, as they clambered with difficulty through the viscosity of his words, an additional force by virtue of having survived the ordeal. He often defied rather than coaxed his audience. But he rarely failed to engage with them. There was the crunch of metal against metal, rather than any flailing of the air. It was by no means only by the exercise of the block vote that he influenced the course of debate.

But despite his greater post-1926 interest in political action, despite his emotional involvement in the break-up of 1931, despite his part in re-shaping the Labour Party in the mid-thirties, despite his position as a great Conference figure, his involvement in Labour politics was not comparable with that of Attlee or Morrison, Greenwood or Dalton. Had he to choose, at any time up to the outbreak of war, between the slaughter of the Labour Party and that of the Transport and General Workers' Union, there can be no doubt that it would have been the Labour Party, reluctantly but unhesitatingly, which he would have sent to the abattoir. Between 1940 and 1945 there would have been more doubt, but I think the Labour Party would still have been sacrificed. Between 1945 and his death in 1951, probably but not certainly, his judgement would have gone the other way.

This detachment from politicians' politics is illustrated by the form in which he set up the new *Daily Herald* in 1929. Lansbury's *Daily Herald* had passed into joint Labour Party/TUC ownership in 1922 and continued for the next seven years as a small circulation socialist newspaper. Bevin and a number of others wanted to give it a mass circulation. For this he judged that a commercial partner with plenty of capital was necessary. His first step was to get rid of the Labour Party shareholding and vest the full financial control in the TUC. Then he made an arrangement with Odhams Press. There were to be five Odhams directors, including the chairman, and four TUC directors, including Bevin as vice-chairman. Only the TUC directors were to vote on policy matters. Under this aegis the paper bounded forward for ten years and more. The Labour Movement had a major daily mouthpiece, but one which, by Bevin's deliberate design, offered no place on its board to any representation of the Parliamentary Labour Party. At first he could justify this by his suspicion of MacDonald, but long after MacDonald had gone he made no move to change the composition of the board. The Labour Party got its newspaper support by courtesy of the TUC.

As late as 1936, following that year's Labour Party Conference at Edinburgh, his suspicion of 'politicians' boiled up again. He thought a lot of weasel words had been spoken on collective security and rearmament. Dalton had interpreted an ambiguous resolution in a way of which Bevin approved, but Morrison (of whom Bevin never approved) had been dreadful and Attlee, for whom his later affection and respect had not then matured, had been as ambiguous as the resolution. Bevin went round muttering that the TUC might be more influential if it were not so closely tied to the Labour Party. The Government might take more notice of its views. In any event that Conference fortified his opinion that politicians were not fit to be entrusted with the political direction of 'my paper'.

Later still, in 1943, when Bevin had been Minister of Labour for three years and was clearly at least the second man in the party, he responded truculently and extremely to a dispute between the Labour Ministers and the bulk of the Parliamentary party over the Beveridge Report by effectively severing all relations between himself and the party for a year or more. He attended neither the annual conference nor any meeting of the Parliamentary party. He operated as a member of the War Cabinet in his own right, indifferent for the time to any party affiliation.

From 1931 to 1945 Bevin's attitude to the Labour Party, paradoxically, was much more akin to that of Cripps, whom he spent much of his time denouncing and for whose expulsion from the party he cheerfully cast his block vote in 1939, than to that of the central core of Labour leadership, to which on the whole he gave his support. Attlee, Morrison, Dalton, were all in the Labour Party unconditionally. They often strove to change its policy, but whether they succeeded or not, in the last resort they accepted the position. The Labour Party was their life. Bevin and Cripps were both in conditionally. In Cripps's case this was much more obvious than with Bevin. This was because Cripps at this period was a man of the minority, whereas Bevin got so used to having the majority on his side that he almost came to regard it as identified with himself by a system of pre-ordained harmony. When Cripps could not get his way he acted so as to get expelled from the party, or, in Bevin's words 'drove himself out'. Bevin disapproved of Cripps's behaviour. He set great store by the loyal acceptance of the properly reached decisions of bodies to which he belonged. He could afford to. But if he had found himself consistently in opposition to the outlook and policy of the Labour Party, I think he would have endeavoured to take the Transport and General Workers out and probably the whole TUC too.

He never accepted opposition easily or tolerantly. He personalised it, quickly imported a deep note of bitterness into most disputes and used phrases like 'the stab in the back' more freely than reasoned argument. He could occasionally show a certain rough magnanimity in victory—who cannot?—but he hated defeat, or the threat of defeat, and fought against it without much respect, not merely for civility and convention but for more basic rules of human conduct as well. If his power base was threatened he would react with all the tenacity and viciousness of a primeval beast struggling for survival. There was only one rule he accepted. He would never break his word once he had given it. He may have loved the class from which he sprang—his loyalty to his own vision of that class was certainly complete and there has never been a British politician more free from snobbery—but his capacity for hating individual members of it was considerable. 'Not while I'm alive, he ain't', he replied with sardonic grimness when someone charitably suggested that Aneurin Bevan was his own worst enemy.

Bevin left a number of casualties behind him on his road to power. The three most frequently cited are Ben Tillett, the great hero of the early days of the Dockers' Union, whom he refused to allow to be President of the newly amalgamated Transport and General Workers' Union, and thus condemned to a long old age of ineffective reminiscence; Robert Williams, the President of the Transport Workers' Federation, for whom no place was found in the new union, and who subsequently committed suicide; and George Lansbury, Leader of the Labour Party from 1931 to 1935.

Bevin destroyed Lansbury at the 1935 Labour Conference. It was one of the most formidable feats of oratorical bulldozing in British political history. Lansbury's highly emotional pacifist speech was received with great warmth, although not with full agreement by the majority of delegates. It ended with a standing ovation and the singing of 'For he's a jolly good fellow'. Only Bevin and his own delegates failed to rise. But he rose immediately after the ovation and went to the rostrum, not merely to refute Lansbury but to excoriate him. He drove straight for the weak point in the relations of the Conference with Lansbury—sentimental attachment without intellectual conviction. Again he lifted the engine up in its tracks and put it down facing the other way. 'I hope this Conference will not be influenced by either sentiment or personal attachment', he said. 'It is placing the Executive in an absolutely wrong position to be trailing your conscience round from body to body asking to be told what to do with it.' And so he continued for ten minutes or so. At the beginning he aroused shouts of shocked disagreement, at the end another ovation, less excited but a good deal more solidly based than Lansbury's. More significant, however, was the fact that when Lansbury rose to demand a special right of reply the Conference would not hear him. Never had so much emotional soil been shifted in so short a time. Afterwards Bevin showed some of the complacency but not, on this occasion, a great deal of the magnanimity of victory. 'Lansbury had been going about for years dressed in saint's clothes and waiting for martyrdom', he said. 'I merely set fire to the faggots.'

Was he unduly harsh with his victims? Not, I think, with Tillett, whose accession to the presidency would have upset the balance of the new union and might have endangered its stability. The same may well have been true of Williams. With Lansbury he used more brute force than was necessary. But nearly everyone else would have failed to do the job at all.

The number of casualties Bevin left was not excessive. Those he felt he had to deal with were nastily mangled, but almost always for 'organisational' (an ugly and imprecise word which he would have liked) rather than for personal reasons. He dealt with those who threatened his policy or his base, but he never manoeuvred in order to elevate himself into a higher position. On the contrary he was one of the few men who has had the premiership within his foreseeable grasp, and turned it down. In 1947 he exploded an intrigue of Cripps and Dalton to make him Prime Minister in Attlee's place.

This was not done from modesty, but from a combination of loyalty to Attlee and self-confidence in his own position. His power was such that he did not need place. In this respect he was comparable with Joseph Chamberlain, who had a ruthless thrust, but never cared much for the premiership, and left an uncomfortable number of broken men behind him. But in Chamberlain's case they were mostly mysteriously broken. There was nothing of this with Bevin. What was done was openly done.

The greater count against Bevin's character was not ruthlessness with enemies but an inability to work on terms of friendly equality with political allies. His persistent, pervading dislike of Morrison, with whom he had little real political disagreement after 1936, was unfortunate, although one prejudice is perhaps understandable. But much more extraordinary were his relations with Citrine, the General Secretary of the Trades Union Congress. They worked together for 15 years, dominating the TUC, moulding it to their common purpose. They agreed on domestic affairs, they agreed on foreign affairs. In a sense they were made for each other. Citrine's meticulous lucidity combined perfectly with Bevin's force and imagination. In double harness, Citrine opening and Bevin winding up, they carried every controversial policy through the TUC. Neither could have accomplished nearly as much without the other.

Yet their personal relations were always frigid. They never throughout the whole 15 years had a friendly meal or drink together. And in 1941 (admittedly when Bevin as Minister of Labour was having some disagreement with the TUC) they engaged in an almost incredible exchange of letters. Citrine was trying to improve relations. 'Dear Bevin', he somewhat stiffly began, '. . . I have never regarded you as a superman but definitely as the most outstanding personality in the Labour Movement. You may find it hard to swallow that, but it is true just the same.'

Bevin's reply, still more remarkably in view of their past relationship, began 'Dear Sir Walter'. 'I am glad you do not regard me as a superman, so no one will expect too much', he wrote, 'but I am not concerned with how people regard me personally. . . . Finally I do not desire to quarrel with anyone and certainly a vendetta is foreign to my nature. I respect other peoples' positions and opinions but I expect mine to be respected also: and that is all.' It was certainly all so far as an attempt at a conciliatory correspondence was concerned.

Bevin shared no partnership, except with his wife, until his last years. In the late 'thirties he agreed, above all, with Dalton, but he did not give him his friendship, greatly though that rather unselfconfident Etonian would have valued it. In the War Coalition, he skirmished constantly with Beaverbrook, which was of no great account, except when Bevin contemplated prosecuting him, as Minister of Aircraft Production, for ignoring an Essential Work Order. He had tolerably good relations with Lord Avon and Sir John Anderson, but again these stopped well short of friendship. With Churchill there was considerable mutual respect. When the Prime Minister was in trouble Bevin defended him most vigorously in the country. His loyalty to the Coalition was complete. And Churchill fully reciprocated this support. For the first 18 months of the Government, when Bevin was much criticised, partly because of his lack of skill in the House of Commons, partly because of doubts about the success of his manpower policy, Churchill's confidence never wavered. Still more significantly, he always treated Bevin with great circumspection in the War Cabinet or in Cabinet Committees. He never allowed the vagaries of his mood or temper to play against him. He knew a dangerous animal when he saw one. But respect was not the same as friendship. Bevin was never a crony of Churchill's—probably because he did not wish to be one. Their dealings were mutually satisfactory but essentially those of business.

The one exception to Bevin's 'no partnership' practice was his relationship with Attlee. This grew slowly but with great strength. In the 'thirties he thought of Attlee as a second-rate leader. But that was what he wanted. He had had enough of those who thought they were first-rate with MacDonald. During the war, when for the first time he got to know Attlee well, his attitude changed. He could still make the occasional patronizing remark. 'We must look after little Clem', he told a colleague in 1946. But this was superficial. By then he believed that Attlee was not merely the best leader the Labour Party had got, but the best it was ever likely to get. He made it clear that he would serve under no one else.

In return he received complete Prime Ministerial support as Foreign Secretary. Bad relations between 10 Downing Street and the Foreign Office have damaged many a British Government. In the administration of 1945 the reverse was if anything the danger. Bevin's position was strengthened by Attlee's rock-like support. But his policy might at times have benefited from passing through the sieve of slightly more sceptical Prime Ministerial questioning.

This relationship was not purely one of business. Vastly different though they were, in personality, origin, methods of thought and expression, there was genuine affection as well as respect between them. They both needed each other, although it is arguable that Bevin, as a working-class sheet anchor was more important to Attlee than *vice versa*. He gave the Government a balance and stability which disappeared when he went. Even so, Attlee never allowed this dependence to affect his prerogative of appointment and dismissal. In 1945, as is well-known, he switched Bevin from the Treasury to the Foreign Office over a lunch-time. 'I thought a heavy tank was what was required, rather than a light sniper', he subsequently explained. And in 1951, when Bevin's health had manifestly failed, Attlee removed him from the Foreign Office, not with equal speed but with equal determination. Bevin was not pleased. It is doubtful if he forgave Attlee, for he had only five remaining weeks of life in which to do so. This was the only occasion when he had to be sacrificed in the way that he had sacrificed others in the past. And Attlee, almost the only man to whom he ever gave trust and affection on a basis of equality, had to be the man to do it. It was not without irony or pathos.

Bevin's anger at the manner of his removal from the Foreign Office was understandable but irrational. He was old and ill. So was the Government. If he had only a few weeks still to live, it had only a few months. He could hardly at that stage have made any difference to the outcome, and any remaining time as Foreign Secretary, even had he lived a little longer and dealt more skilfully than his successor with the Persian oil crisis of the summer of 1951, could have added little to his achievement and reputation. In a British context these should rest at least as much on his pre-war and wartime work as upon his final period. But in a world context his fame necessarily rests upon his $5\frac{3}{4}$ years at the Foreign Office, and it is by this that he must be judged.

How does his foreign policy now look, seen with the perspective given by the passing of over twenty years? On the central front it stands up remarkably well. On the flanks there is more crumbling. In his early days as Foreign Secretary he appreciated three salient and essential facts. First he realised that as a legacy of the war he had to play his hand from a weak economic base. Britain's role as the founder architect of victory gave her a nominally unassailable membership of the triumvirate of world power. But our power base, unlike that of the other two members, had been eroded by the events of the preceding five years. Bevin might bemoan this. 'If only I had 50 million tons of coal to export, what a difference it would make to my foreign policy', was one of his favourite and typically personalized sayings. But although he bemoaned it, he did not deceive himself, at least about the immediate position.

He also appreciated quickly and reasonably calmly that the intentions of the Soviet Union, towards both Britain under a Labour Government and the West in general, were far from benevolent. He had begun with higher hopes, and it was he who at the 1945 Labour Conference, two weeks after VE day and eight weeks before he became Foreign Secretary, coined the phrase, specifically in the Russian context, that 'left would be able to speak to left'. But he escaped from these illusions more quickly than most. He had to. From Potsdam onwards he came hard up against the solid wall of Russian hostility. He had to open the eyes of a Government and a party which had more than shared his hopes of a few weeks previously and which did not have his opportunities to see at first hand the difference between the theory of socialist brotherhood and the practice of Soviet foreign policy.

With Attlee's solid if taciturn support he had little difficulty with the Government, although a good deal more with the party, both inside and outside the House of Commons. He waged a continuous and fluctuating battle with the Labour left. At times it looked as though a good third of the Parliamentary Labour Party were against him. At others, aided generally by some act of exceptional Russian provocation, he temporarily reduced his opponents to a rump of little more than twenty. He never began to convince them. But they never began to shift him.

In this as in other phases of his career Bevin was undoubtedly intransigent with his opponents at home. But he rarely allowed this to spill over into undue obduracy in dealing with the Russians. In early 1946 he was the first Western statesman to denounce them with ferocity at the United Nations. But in negotiations with them he kept his impatience under a tight rein. 'What you have got to do in foreign affairs', he announced in Bevinese on one occasion, 'is not to create a situation.'

Bevin's first clashes with the Russians could not be blamed on too close an attachment to the Americans. In the early post-war days Soviet-American relations were better than Soviet-British relations. The spirit of Yalta did not die with Franklin Roosevelt. At and after Potsdam there was a real danger of America and Russia doing deals over Britain's head and at Britain's expense. Even if these fears were not realized, the desire of the Americans to go home in 1945, just as they had in 1919, was likely to leave a weakened Britain vainly trying to organize war-destroyed countries against Russian pressure in Europe. Bevin saw his major task as that of achieving a continuing American commitment, political, military and economic, to Europe. In this he was brilliantly successful, and his role was pivotal.

First, in the early months of 1947, he got the beginning of a military commitment by a firm announcement that responsibility for the defence of Greece and Turkey could no longer be carried by Britain. There were risks in this course, but President Truman accepted the baby which Bevin with excellent timing had placed in his lap.

Then in June of that year, his response to General Marshall's Harvard speech played a crucial part in turning it, in Bevin's own words, into 'one of the greatest speeches in world history'. Without Bevin's determination to make it so, it might have remained merely an interesting academic address instead of becoming the foundation of Europe's recovery. At first the speech created no great stir in the United States, and if the original official Foreign Office suggestion that the Embassy in Washington should approach the State Department to enquire quizzically exactly what the

Secretary had in his mind, its possibilities might have got lost in a maze of careful reservations.

Bevin stopped this, and decided to act as though the tide were already at its flood. He sent the Americans the warmest possible message assuring them that he knew exactly what they had in mind, he aroused the French and within a couple of days had created a momentum which led on to the implementation of the Marshall Plan and the setting up of the 16-nation Organisation for European Economic Co-operation. It was Bevin's finest hour as well as Marshall's.

It also illustrated something of his methods of work and his relations with the Foreign Office. Bevin was almost certainly more popular with most of his officials than any Foreign Secretary within living official memory. This was partly because of his innate capacity to inspire loyalty —and to give it, when he was not dealing with rivals. But not only were his officials not possible rivals to him. He was not a rival to them. His training and mental processes were so different that there could be no question of his attempting to do their work for them. He could not draft; he was not concerned with the meticulous details of presentation, or with the accurate recollection of precedents. What he liked to do, in his own phrase, was to get officials to 'put clothes on his ideas'. But he provided many of the ideas, and as in his reaction to the original proposal for tentative enquiries in Washington about the Marshall speech, he did not hesitate to stamp upon any advice of which he did not approve.

The Foreign Office also liked him because he won battles in the Cabinet, because he was a world figure, because his behaviour provided them with plenty of anecdotes for their friends, and because they had never met anyone quite like him before. Some critics of Bevin would argue that it was the officials' battles rather than his own that he won in the Cabinet. They see his popularity being based on his having become a tame lion, a mascot for the Foreign Office which looked splendid and ferocious to the outside world, but was no danger to them.

I find this unconvincing. When men become tame they become tame all through. An old lion led on a cord by the permanent under-secretary of the Foreign Office would quickly have lost his power with the Cabinet, the Labour Party and the other principal Foreign Ministers of the world. This is not to deny that a considerable community of outlook as well as affection grew up between Bevin and his principal officials. He found himself defending individuals and institutions of which he would not previously have thought much. Occasionally his defence took a fairly ludicrous form. 'I am not one of those who decry Eton and Harrow', he told the Labour Party Conference in 1946. 'I was very glad of them in the Battle of Britain.' (Apart from anything else, this remark was based on a rather inaccurate view of the social background of most officers in the Royal Air Force.) Even so, Bevin was never remotely the victim of an aristocratic embrace. It would have taken an outsize bear rather than a duchess to get their arms around him. His 'Eton and Harrow' defence was made at just about the same time that he turned his back on a man who came up to him outside a London hotel to express his deep personal admiration, combined with his dislike of the rest of the Labour Government. Bevin's reaction on both occasions sprang from the same cause—a hostility to anyone, except occasionally himself, criticizing those with whom he was working.

In his achievements at the Foreign Office he received enthusiastic official co-operation. But he made the basic policy. The triumphs were his own, just as were the mistakes, in which the co-operation was equally enthusiastic.

What were the mistakes? Palestine is clearly a strong candidate. Here he was both stubborn and provocative. It does not now seem to me possible to say with certainty that he was either right or wrong. He believed that British influence in the Arab world was of great importance both to the security of the Commonwealth and to our own standard of living. But by the time he was responsible the Balfour Declaration was a thirty-year-old fact. He always claimed to be a great man for dealing with 'facts'. This fact he tried to ignore. And he showed a lack of imagination in his failure to appreciate the force of the Jewish determination to establish a state in Palestine. Furthermore, and to put it at its lowest, he allowed his handling of the Palestine question, a difficult but peripheral issue, gravely to endanger his central policy objective of good relations with the United States. This at the very least showed a lack of proportion.

His language exacerbated the effect of his policy. 'I hope it will not be misunderstood in America', he told the 1946 Labour Conference, 'if I say with the purest of motives that their policy (towards Jewish immigration into Palestine) was because they did not want too many of them in New York.' It was misunderstood—if that is the right word—and for a time he became markedly unpopular in the United States. Longshoremen refused to unload his luggage when he arrived for a UN meeting, and he was loudly booed at a baseball game in Brooklyn. Much more important, his relations with President Truman were temporarily damaged. He recovered from this, but he had run unnecessary risks.

The second main ground on which he is open to criticism is that he showed no more (and no less) prescience than nearly all other politicians of his day about Britain's future role in the world. He saw our immediate weakness and danger. But he regarded these as more of a temporary phenomenon than the result of a long-term change, and he saw a large part of his duty as that of performing a covering-up operation until we could recover our old strength. He played weak cards with great force, but he believed that if he could hold on long enough we would in time be dealt much better ones. He was wrong, and as a result of his error he began the mishandling of our relations with Europe which was to be developed to a much greater pitch of refinement by his successors after 1951.

He signed the Dunkirk Treaty and the Brussels Pact, but he cold-shouldered the Schuman Plan for the Coal and Steel Community because he did not then believe that we were as other European nations were. In 1928 he had advocated a European 'economic entity', but by 1948 he thought we could help Europe without joining it. He believed, as did Lord Avon after him, that our relationship with other European countries should be more akin to that of America with them to that of themselves with each other. His roles in the creation of NATO and in the spurning of the Schuman Plan were symbolic. In order to maintain this position he required an unsustainable level of British defence expenditure. In the last year of his Foreign Secretaryship we were spending 7.7 per cent of our national income on defence, compared with an American figure of 5.9 per cent, a French figure of 5.0 per cent and a negligible German figure. He helped Europe from outside to such an extent that within 15 years its economic strength had recovered far more completely than our own.

Nevertheless, his foreign policy achievements were massive. He led Britain into the postwar world. And in prewar days he provided a quality of trade union leadership rarely seen before or since, in this or any other country. His personality was unique. Its like may never be seen again. More recent educational opportunities preclude such a combination of an untutored mind, a far-ranging intelligence and absolute self-confidence. Those who knew him well and worked with him will never forget him. Nor should his country.

STAFFORD CRIPPS

Stafford Cripps

I had five predecessors as Labour Chancellors of the Exchequer. Three of them I knew well, two as intimate friends. Snowden I never met. Cripps occupied an intermediate position. I frequently saw him, listened to him, admired him, followed him. Occasionally I spoke to him. Once I visited him at his house. But there was never any approach to closeness. I was in the House of Commons for only two and a half years before his health drove him to Switzerland and retirement, and he was 31 years older than I. But the generation gap seemed infinitely wider than with his precursor and senior, Hugh Dalton.

Yet Cripps exercised a considerable fascination over me at the time, and left a reputation at the Treasury which, 17 years later, was still immanent and intriguing. Despite the 1949 devaluation, he was almost the only post-war Chancellor to depart with his colours flying high. Neither his party nor his policies had been defeated: merely his body. It is also probably the case that he shared with Lord Butler the distinction of being the Chancellor whose habits and idiosyncrasies officials remembered with most interest, and recalled most often. This is not necessarily a sign of being a great minister. In the Foreign Office it applied outstandingly to Curzon, who was not so. But it is a sign of having left a certain residue behind one.

In addition, there is a curious ambiguity about the shape of Cripps's career. It had no natural progression. Although he came of a political family, he took no part in politics until he was over 40. Then he came into the Labour Party with a golden spoon in his mouth. He was imposed upon a constituency in order that he might take his place on the front bench as Solicitor-General. After a brief post-1931 period in a triumvirate of leadership he plunged further and further to the left. The content of his statements, still delivered in a precise legal voice, became increasingly shrill. The clerk of the Labour establishment became a self-appointed tribune of the minority. In 1939 he was expelled from the Labour Party, and remained an isolated but at times extremely powerful voice until

1945. As ambassador to Moscow he somewhat fortuitously became the symbol in Britain of successful Russian resistance to Hitler. There was a short period, in 1942, when it almost seemed as though he might replace Churchill. Then his star faded, and he served out the rest of the war as an effective but hardly famous departmental minister.

By the beginning of the Attlee Government he was back in communion with official Labour, and rose inexorably over the next two years to be the dominating economic minister. As an austere but commanding Chancellor of the Exchequer he became the very embodiment of responsible government and self-disciplined patriotism. The connexion between this dedicated servant of the state—almost a twentieth-century Peel—and the unanchored agitator of the 'thirties became difficult to recall. It was almost as though the Russians, during his embassy, had performed some motiveless feat of substitution.

Cripp's authority again became great, but longer-lasting than in 1942. Supporting his economic leadership was the role which he had played in negotiating Indian independence, his contribution to which was a recurring sub-theme over the last 10 years of his political life. Seven years Attlee's junior, it seemed not impossible, in 1948 and 1949, that he might be his successor. Probably this would not have occurred in any event. Whether as iconoclast or as consul, Cripps was hardly a rounded enough personality to make a leader under a party system. But the issue was never put to the proof. He retired five years before Attlee, and predeceased him by 14. He remains a figure who, for a short time, exercised an authority as great as it is possible to achieve without occupying the premiership itself, and who came to it by a route which was one of the least obviously charted in the history of British politics.

Cripps was born in London in the spring of 1889. His father, Alfred Cripps, was an intellectually elegant lawyer ('the little jewel of an advocate', was how his own father-in-law described him) who came from a long line of Gloucestershire squires. His mother was one of the numerous Potter daughters, a scion of a rich nineteenth-century industrial family and a sister of Beatrice Webb. She died when Stafford was four. Alfred Cripps's father, himself an ecclesiastical lawyer of some note, had moved his branch of the family to a substantial estate at Parmoor, above Henley-on-Thames. This was where Stafford grew up. Alfred Cripps became a Conservative member of Parliament in 1900, and again, after an interval, in 1910. He was made a member of the Judicial Committee of the Privy Council and a peer by Asquith in 1914. In 1924, having moved to a pacifist internationalist position during the First World War, he accepted the Lord Presidency of the Council in MacDonald's first Labour Government. He thus achieved the remarkable feat of being a Conservative MP who was elevated to the peerage by a Liberal Prime Minister and became a Labour Cabinet Minister. He was a man of grave views and warm family feeling. He wrote frequently and over a long period to Stafford, addressing him most often as 'My very dear Staff', and ending 'Your affect. father, Parmoor', or occasionally 'P'. He supported him in most of his political enterprises, but became a little worried in the late 'thirties.

Like his father, Stafford Cripps went to school at Winchester, where he was not a scholar, but did outstandingly well. He accepted the Wykamical spirit with enthusiasm. Thereafter his career began to diverge a little from the conventional pattern of hereditary lawyer servants of the state. He was a scientist, and his papers for a chemistry scholarship at New College attracted sufficient notice that he not only won the scholarship but, instead of taking it up, was diverted to work specially under Sir William Ramsay at University College, London. After a few years of laboratory work, however, he began to read for the Bar, and was called in 1913. By then he was already married, to Miss Swithinbank, who as Dame Isobel Cripps is still alive and active. The granddaughter of Mr Eno, of fruit salts fame, she was relatively rich, and he met her in the Conservative Committee Rooms at one of his father's High Wycombe elections.

Cripps had barely established himself at the Bar before August, 1914. Unlike his brothers, he did not join the Army. This was not due to any pacifist feeling: he was rejected by a medical board. He did however spend six months in France driving a Red Cross lorry. Then he entered the service of Lloyd George's new Ministry of Munitions and was sent as assistant superintendent to a large high explosive factory near Chester. After a few months his health collapsed. It was the beginning of the intestinal trouble which was to be with him intermittently for the rest of his life. He was rescued from the brink of death by a somewhat unorthodox nature cure. He remained a semi-invalid for the rest of the war.

In 1919, at the age of 30, he was well enough to resume practice at the Bar. Almost from the moment of this new beginning he was an outstanding professional success. He never became a jury advocate. He disliked the tumultuous arena where the law jostled with human conduct and human emotions. He specialized in complicated commercial actions, where the issues turned upon legal precedent, technical knowledge and business practice. As a cross-examiner his *forte* lay not in exposing an unconvincing interpretation of a course of events but in probing the judgment of expert witnesses. He was very much a lawyer's lawyer. He was lucid and meticulous. His practice was of high quality and brought him very substantial rewards. He took silk in 1927, becoming at 37 the youngest K.C. of his day, and passed through this change of gear without even a temporary loss of momentum.

During this period he removed himself back to the Cotswold country which had been the earlier centre of the Cripps family and where several of its branches were still embedded. He established a farm and moderate sized country house at Filkins, near Lechlade. He took no interest in the sports of the countryside, but he enjoyed landscape and estate management. Outside his professional work his main activity was in a particular aspect of church affairs. The tradition of his family was strongly Anglican. It was also internationalist. He combined the two by working closely with Dr Burge, his old Winchester headmaster who had recently been translated as bishop from Southwark to Oxford, in the World Alliance for Promoting International Friendship through the Churches. He became treasurer of the British Council of this Alliance, and spoke extensively for it throughout the country. He also became a member of the House of Laity of the Church Assembly. It was hardly a revolutionary introduction to public affairs.

To party politics he paid almost no attention. Although both his father and his uncle by marriage (Sidney Webb) were leading members of the 1924 Labour Government, he regarded that venture with little more than benevolent detachment. So far from rushing into socialist politics in order to shock his church and state father, he remained a good five years behind him in any leftward move.

When it eventually took place, Herbert Morrison was the recruiting sergeant. As a leading member of the London County Council he had encountered Cripps in a long transport costs case before the Railways Rates Tribunal. They had each formed a high view of the other. Encouraged by Morrison, and inspired by the writings of Tawney, Cripps joined the Labour Party immediately after the 1929 election. Within six months, again largely by Morrison's agency, he was adopted as parliamentary candidate for West Woolwich, a seat which in the relatively optimistic days of 1929 seemed a tolerable Labour prospect.

He never fought it. In the autumn of 1930 the Solicitor-General resigned because of ill health. Cripps was appointed in his place. A strenuous effort was then made to find him an immediate place in the House of Commons. East Bristol was vacant, but the local Labour Party was unenthusiastic. They were a working-class constituency and many of them wanted a working-class member. They had some natural scepticism about Cripps's fulfilment of this qualification. They were also doubtful of the depth of his roots in the Labour Party. Transport House did not share these doubts. The national agent descended upon Bristol, with all the authority which he then possessed. 'I urge you, nay, I implore you to accept him', he is reported to have said.

They did, although with considerable grumbling and misgiving. Ironically, Cripps's leading local opponent became his staunchest constituency supporter in the later days of stress. Although he never went a great deal to Bristol, Cripps had no subsequent difficulty in establishing a strong constituency position. In 1939 much of the East Bristol Labour Party chose to be expelled with him rather than to disavow his views.

At the by-election in January, 1931, Cripps secured an adequate majority. He plunged quickly into the technical House of Commons work which is required of the junior law officer. He spoke on a minor Bill within two days of his introduction; a few months later he gave a somewhat over-legalistic reply on a delicate trades union issue, which led to a row with the TUC, and his effective repudiation by the Prime Minister; but he balanced this by a notably accomplished performance on some complicated clauses of the Finance Bill.

By the end of the session he was exhausted and unwell. When the crisis broke at the end of August and the National Government was formed, he was caught in sadly quintessential circumstances, rather as a flash of lightning in a dark night can illuminate some truth about a landscape which daylight does not wholly show. He was at Dr Döngler's Clinic, Baden-Baden. MacDonald telegraphed asking him to continue in office. Cripps sent back an ambiguous reply, which led to some newspaper speculation that he might be willing to do so, and immediately returned to London. Once there, so 'technical' was his position within the Government, he consulted only the Lord Chancellor (Sankey) and the Attorney General (Jowitt). It is difficult to believe that either fired his party spirit, but he none the less wrote to MacDonald almost immediately, from the less characteristic address of the Royal Automobile Club, declining his offer. His tone was friendly: 'May I be allowed—without being considered impertinent—to say that I admire immensely the courage and conviction which have led you and other Labour Ministers associated with you to take the action you have taken.' It was also firm: '... I will content myself with saying that I disagree with the policy of the Labour Party taking any part in a National Government having the programme of the present Government.'

Although so emollient in tone, this letter marked a climacteric in Cripps's life. Hitherto a moderate and orthodox politician, somewhat corralled in interests and activities by his legal position, he began almost from the moment of its composition a straight-line bolt, not only towards the freedom of general politics, but also towards the horizon of extremism. It was a bolt which lasted for most of the decade. At first, however, its singularity was not noticeable. There were a lot of others stampeding with him. Even Attlee made some very odd statements about this time. But after a year or so he and the others mostly paused, looked around, and began to recover their equanimity and previous positions. This did not apply to Cripps. He continued in a cloud of dust, unswerving, towards the increasing isolation of his horizon.

The result of the 1931 election gave him a premature prominence for which his extremely limited political experience was a quite inadequate preparation. East Bristol, for which he had become member purely by the chance that its previous MP's death had coincided with his appointment as Solicitor-General, turned out to be one of the safest Labour seats in the country. In the conditions of 1931, it was the solitary one in the whole South of England, west of the East End of London, which could be held. Cripps did so by the narrow margin of 400 votes. He had inherited an isolated Labour island in a Tory sea. It made him one of a small, embattled band of 46 Labour members. It made him, with George Lansbury and Attlee, one of the only three with ministerial experience. It therefore made him the third member of a triumvirate of truncated leadership. So strong was the post-holocaust feeling that they are all clustered together, sharing the room of the Leader of the Opposition. They all spoke in the House with excessive but necessary frequency.

Cripps had a good enough relationship with Attlee, although I doubt if either was ever close to or much influenced by the other. With Lansbury, 30 years his senior, he forged close bonds of affection and partnership. They had little in common except an ardent Christianity, which in both cases, somewhat surprisingly, expressed itself through the forms of the established church. (Nevertheless, there was no period of Cripps's life when religious beliefs figured less prominently in his public utterances than during the three or four years of his intimacy with Lansbury.) Lansbury combined an inspiring personality, a warm-hearted and uncompromising utopianism and a certain shrewd commonsense which enabled him to be an effective First Commissioner of Works. The influence of these qualities, filtered through the clear but sometimes naive and over-rigid mind of his lieutenant, produced, in the circumstances of post-1931 dismay, a rather harsh and mechanistic semi-revolutionary doctrine which led Cripps into a whole series of mutually debilitating quarrels with the majority of the Labour Party.

First Cripps became obsessed with the prospect of extra-constitutional obstruction to a future Labour Government, and with the need for a 'committee of public safety' approach to counteract this. The House of Lords should be swept away. The House of Commons would need to make extensive use of emergency powers and general enabling legislation. There was no doubt that there would be opposition to overcome 'from Buckingham Palace and other places as well'. There might be an uprising of the capitalists which would have to be quelled by force. 'The one thing which is not inevitable now is gradualness', he proclaimed.

It was an unwise theme for a politician to devote himself to, as Cripps did for two years or more. Independently of the truth or otherwise of the analysis, it sought to concentrate people's minds not upon the benefits which a Labour Government might bring but upon the appalling upheaval which would have to be gone through before there could be a chance of any results at all. It caused deep embarrassment to Arthur Henderson, the old leader, and considerable resentment in Bevin and Citrine, the dominant trade union chiefs. It led to a confrontation at the 1934 Labour Party Conference when the official statement said clearly that there was no reason 'why a people who, first in the world, achieved through parliamentary institutions their political and religious freedom should not, by the same reasons, achieve their economic emancipation', and voted down, by large majorities, a series of amendments proposed by Cripps and his associates.

The next year Cripps chose a different ground of dissent. The major issue then was support for the attempt, through the League of Nations, to frustrate Mussolini's aggression against Abyssinia. The main confrontation was between Bevin's responsible but brutal realism and Lansbury's pacifism. Cripps was not a pacifist but evolved a somewhat convoluted line of his own. Nothing could be accomplished until all capitalist governments had been replaced, and in the meantime it was dangerous for a workers' party even to try. Support for the League was merely support for a capitalist combination. His speech arguing this thesis marked the nadir of his 1930s foolishness:

I have been accused of changing my views on this topic. I have changed them because events have satisfied me that now the League of Nations . . . has become nothing but the tool of the satiated imperialist powers . . . I wish to God the workers were in control in this country so that they could make their power effective as the Russian workers can do today in their own country. . . . If we feel a desperate need to do something at all costs we must fall back on the attempt to use working-class sanctions.

Once again he was defeated by an overwhelming majority. A more representative working class figure, the leader of the National Union of Railwaymen, poured deep scorn on his talk of 'working-class sanctions'.

Cripps's next initiative was to launch the 'United Front' campaign. It was a direct response to the outbreak of the Civil War in Spain, and was influenced by the shape of the governments there and in the France of Léon Blum. But this initiative was still within the ambit of his semi-revolutionary outlook. Its main aim was to unite in alliance the Labour and Communist Parties (although the ILP and a radical fringe from the Liberal Party were to be brought in as well). It was to be anti-National Government, indifferent to military defence, and in favour of the working-class solidarity approach which he had developed in 1935. It in no way envisaged the subordination of class struggle politics to collective security against the dictators. Indeed, on one occasion in this phase, the *Manchester Guardian* reported him as saying that it would be no bad thing for the English working-class if Germany defeated Britain. He had not said this, but he had said something uncomfortably like it.

The vehicles for this campaign were, first, the Socialist League, over which Cripps had presided since 1933; second, *Tribune*, which he founded and largely financed at the beginning of 1937; and third, the Left Book Club, influential but more independent of his leadership. The official Labour leadership, for whom alliance with the Communist Party was the sticking point, and who in any event were disposed by this stage to react violently against anything which emanated from Cripps, responded by proscribing the Socialist League. Those who continued to associate with it would be excluded from the Party. Cripps was not at this stage in a mood for ultimate defiance. His supporters—Harold Laski, Aneurin Bevan, George Strauss and Ellen Wilkinson were the most prominent—did not desire excommunication. In any event, he recognised that if the Labour Party would not provide the nucleus, a 'unity campaign' made little sense. He wound up both the League and the unity campaign, while protesting and again being massively defeated at yet another Labour Conference. *Tribune*, however, survived, and went forward to a long and adventurous life.

After this third defeat Cripps withdrew somewhat from politics. He had been leading a life of immense strain, and was again unwell. His pattern involved long days in court, often on his feet for three or four hours, evenings with frequent interventions in the House of Commons, and weekend visits about the country with a quartet of speeches on the Saturday and Sunday. He spoke mostly from prepared texts, but except in the courts, they were not very carefully considered. His legal work continued to be both successful and recondite, totally detached in the main from his other activities. He would appear with matchless skill in the day for some great financial institution—one of his most famous cases was on behalf of the Westminster Bank—and in the evening would denounce that whole world and its assumptions.

There was at least one exception to his non-political legal work. He appeared free for the miners at the long inquiry which followed the Gresford colliery disaster of 1934, and in a sustained and devastating cross-examination of the colliery manager did a great deal both for mining safety and for his reputation with the Miners' Federation.

He still had his Cotswold country house, but spent all too little time there. Nor did he take extensive holidays. He went once or twice to the United States, lunching alone with Roosevelt in the White House on one occasion and getting on remarkably well with him (much better than did Keynes at about the same time), but these were essentially political visits. He did little travelling in Europe. Then, in the summer of 1938, the pattern changed. Under the pressure of ill health he went to Jamaica for nearly 10 weeks of holiday; and the next year, when his ill health had receded, he took another long and indeed almost lavish holiday, chartering a small yacht from Cannes and sailing round the Tyrrhenian Sea almost to the outbreak of war. These holidays, straddling his fiftieth birthday, marked, I think, a change towards a broader and less shrill view of the world and its problems.

Between them he conducted the fourth of his pre-war campaigns. In January, 1939, he launched his Popular Front manifesto. Although to most of his supporters it appeared a natural development from the United Front campaign, there were certain crucial differences. The linchpin was no longer an alliance with the Communist Party. Much more important was the appeal to the Liberal Party, to anti-appeasement Conservatives, and to politically uncommitted voters. There was no more talk of working-class exclusivity, either at home or abroad. It was to be an alliance to get rid of Chamberlain, to support collective security, to strengthen the defences of the country, and to stand up to the dictators. To achieve these immediate and urgent aims the Labour Party must be prepared to sacrifice its socialist although not its reformist programme. It was at once an extension of and a contradiction to the United Front approach.

It met with the same opposition. The Labour Party National Executive rejected his manifesto by 17 votes to three. When he refused to withdraw it from circulation they decided to exclude him from membership of the party. Bevan and Strauss went with him. He continued with the campaign until May, when the party conference, at Whitsun that year, after according him a chilly hearing, which he used to present an ill-judged legalistic argument, upheld the expulsion.

When the war came Cripps was regarded by the majority of his fellow politicians as an irresponsible disrupter. This was particularly so among the trade union leadership and those Labour front benchers, such as Dalton and Greenwood, who had never known him well and were glad to set their own robust loyalty against his alleged tergiversations. Others, such as Attlee and Morrison, who had at one time or another been closely associated with him, tempered their disapproval with retrospective affection. They shook their heads sadly rather than angrily. Those few who agreed with him were bound by the strongest bonds of personal loyalty and affection.

Ernest Bevin was the harshest and most resolute of Cripps's opponents. These two men, who were later to be the twin and reasonably harmonious pillars of the Attlee administration, had entirely different conceptions of loyalty. Bevin's was that of loyalty to organisations. He was interested in ideas, but he believed, rightly for himself, that if he fostered his organisations he could mould them to his own views. Cripps believed in moral purpose and in treating organisations as vehicles on the road along which the pursuit of his ideas led him. If they ceased to serve, they should be abandoned. His attitude to the Labour Party as a whole was not vastly different from that to his own creature the Socialist League, which, when he thought it tactically necessary, he quietly strangled. In his own way he could be as ruthless as Bevin.

Cripps used his large earnings to finance his campaigns. He had the money and he believed the causes were right. He could see no objection. Others could. There was resentment and jealousy. A much respected trade union MP wrote: 'By accident of birth and a privileged capacity to earn a fabulous income, a privately controlled political machine is being created that gravely menaces the authority of the Party'. Bevin had the same point in mind when in one of his less agreeable and more inaccurate conference interventions, he told Cripps that lawyers had not done too badly out of Fascism.

Outside the Labour Party the view of Cripps had changed somewhat in the last year or so of peace. Until then Churchill, for instance, would probably have been inclined to apply to him the soubriquet of 'a squalid nuisance' which he subsequently bestowed on Aneurin Bevan. Certainly, in 1937, when Cripps endeavoured to enlist his support against the refusal of the trustees of the Albert Hall to give him a booking for a United Front meeting, Churchill responded with a sharp brush-off: 'I cannot feel that right of free speech is directly involved in the inability of a particular person to procure a particular hall. You are working in close association with the Communists at the present time. . . . Most people will think that (they) have a pretty good run over here, certainly much better than they are given by the German Nazis, by whom, if I remember rightly, you declared it would be a good thing if we were conquered.'

By 1939 both Cripps and Churchill had moved somewhat towards the centre. Churchill wanted some left-wing allies, and Cripps had become firmly in favour of resistance to the dictators. The Popular Front campaign had opened a window to liberal opinion. Archibald Sinclair, Lady Violet Bonham-Carter and Keynes all supported it enthusiastically. When he was expelled from the Labour Party he did not fall back, as he would have done a few years before, upon a base of the extreme left. He acted with a full but not misplaced sense of his own importance as an independent statesman. He began a private personal campaign for an 'All-In Government'. He visited, at his own request and in quick succession, Churchill, Halifax, Kingsley Wood and Oliver Stanley. He even tried to enlist the support from retirement of Lord Baldwin. He was generally well-received. Churchill's attitude was very different from that of his 1937 letter. He recorded that Cripps was 'deeply distressed about the national danger'.

Cripps's new position was both symbolized and aided by an alteration in his appearance which had coincided with his ill-health of 1937-8. In the early and middle 'thirties he had been black-haired and rather chubby. He wore round spectacles with rims. It was possible to think of him as a precocious schoolboy who had turned into a clever but immature lawyer. At the age of about 48 he thinned down and assumed a more ascetic and formidable visage. He also became converted to a system of 'conscious bodily control' which, whatever it did for his health in the long run, gave him a peculiarly erect and detached but dedicated carriage. And the spectacles became smaller and rimless. The Cripps of his Chancellorship had assumed bodily shape. It was the Cripps who later prompted Churchill to make his growling witticism, 'there, but for the grace of God, goes God'. It was the Cripps to whom, when he indicated dissent from the Government front bench a Tory member could say 'the right honourable member must not shake his halo at me'. Jokes apart, the new appearance gave him an increasingly authoritative and statesmanlike air.

After September 1939, Cripps wound up his legal practice. He wanted a public role, but found it difficult to achieve one. He gave the Government a little help with the drafting of price control and other emergency regulations. There was a suggestion that he might become chairman of a price regulation committee, but it was vetoed by trade interests. He had talks, both with the Soviet Ambassador and with ministers about improving relations with Russia, and elicited the suggestion from Churchill that he might go there as British Ambassador. He was keener on going on a semi-official mission, but failed to arouse the enthusiasm of Halifax. Eventually he decided to set off on a private tour. On November 30th, 1939, accompanied as assistant and private secretary by Geoffrey Wilson (now Chairman of the Race Relations Board, formerly permanent secretary of the Ministry of Overseas Development), he set out for India, China, Japan, and the United States, with the possibility of an intermediate visit to Russia.

It was an extraordinary journey by any standards, covering 45,000 miles and lasting five months, but particularly so in the depths of the first uncertain wartime winter. India lasted three weeks, and involved intensive internal travelling and talks with all leaders of opinion. It was not Cripps's first meeting with Nehru (who had been often to Filkins), but it was the beginning of their close working relationship. From Calcutta he went to Rangoon and over the Burma Road to Chungking which was in 1940 the capital of Nationalist China. Chiang Kai-shek and his wife were then heroes of the progressive world. Cripps got on well with them, and was strangely offered a semi-permanent job as planner of Chinese industries. His main desire, however, was to use China as a somewhat roundabout staging post to Moscow. Through the Soviet Ambassador in Chungking he arranged this, and set off on an 8,000 mile round trip, mainly by the limited range aircraft of the day but partly by motor-car. The journey was made more difficult by bad weather. They were away from Chungking for nearly three weeks. It was a vast expenditure of effort for a limited objective. When he got to Moscow he did not see Stalin. He had a two-hour interview with a cautious Molotov. But he felt he had achieved something. He was the only western politician who had seen a major Soviet official since the Russo-German Pact.

Continuing eastwards via Japan and the United States he got back to London at the end of April, in time for the British defeat in Norway and the repercussions which followed from it. He had acquired a greater knowledge of the hidden parts of the wartime world than any other British politician. In the famous debate which led to the fall of the Chamberlain Government he played only a limited role. His speech was not of great note. More significant was his publication of his own list for an alternative government in the *Daily Mail* a few days beforehand. He had arranged this with Lord Rothermere, having been turned down by *The Times*. It was typical both of his self-confidence and of his willingness to use any vehicle which came to hand.

In the first week of the Coalition Government he was asked to go as a trade envoy to Moscow. At first he was hesitant about accepting the offer. He would probably have preferred to be a minister, but Churchill was forming a coalition of parties rather than of individuals. His hesitation was brief, and within five weeks of his return to England he was on his way back to Russia. Before he got there he was appointed ambassador. The Russians had insisted that they would only receive him in this role. For nearly a year his ambassadorship was unrewarding. He saw Stalin once in July, but the meeting was bleak. He could make little contact with the Soviet Government, his wife could not join him until October, he did not enjoy diplomatic society, he did not have deep literary or intellectual interests outside the job of the day. He decided to teach himself not Russian but French. He spent much of the summer in the company of a dog.

In the autumn he was able to make slightly closer contact, but his position remained difficult even though, during the first half of 1941, there came increasing evidence of a German build-up against the Soviet frontier. Cripps disliked the delays and secrecy and cruelty of the Russian system. But he remained convinced of the need to widen every possible chink in the walls of suspicion. When the invasion came, at the end of June, he was back in London on a short visit of consultation. But this did not make him look irrelevant. He had predicted the attack, even though he, like everyone else, had been unable to gauge its exact time. On the Sunday when the cataclysmic news came through he lunched at Chequers with Churchill. He was one of the few who could be consulted before the Prime Minister made his decisive broadcast that evening: 'Any man or state who fights on against Nazidom will have our aid. . . . It follows that we shall give whatever help we can to Russia and the Russian people.' The next day Churchill paid a notable tribute to Cripps in the House of Commons and had him made a Privy Councillor.

Cripps returned almost immediately to a more welcoming Moscow than the city which he had left. Thereafter he had adequate contact, not only with Molotov, but with Stalin. On July 12th he signed the Anglo-Russian treaty of alliance with the Soviet leader. It was the culmination of his work there. The Germans, not he, had brought it about, but it was nonetheless a satisfaction to be there for the fulfilment. He advocated the Russian cause to London, including support for Stalin's demand for an immediate second front. He took a hard line, however, in negotiating on matters of supply with the Russians, demanding disclosures of their resources which they were typically loath to give. When the Beaverbrook mission arrived at the end of September its leader took a much more compliant attitude than Cripps had done. Beaverbrook also enjoyed undermining Cripps's position with Stalin: 'I then asked him about Cripps', Beaverbrook recorded after a Kremlin banquet. 'Stalin gave what I thought was a negative shrug and said: "Oh, he's all right" without enthusiasm. I said: "He's a bore?" and Stalin said "Like Maisky?" I said, "No, like Mme Maisky". Stalin enjoyed the joke immensely.'

This piece of mischief was not without success. In mid-October Cripps, against his will, was evacuated to Kuibyshev and left in the impotent isolation of this 500-mile distant town for the next two months. It was not an act of positive discrimination, for the rest of the diplomatic corps went too. But neither was it an act of outstanding friendship to the specially chosen ambassador of Russia's principal ally. It made Cripps increasingly anxious to return to London and British politics. In January, 1942, Churchill agreed that he should do so.

His re-entry was not without its problems for everyone concerned. He came back trailing clouds of glory. He appeared as the symbol of the successful Russian resistance before Moscow, as the man who, from his experience, must know how to wage total war. And he came at a time when the fortunes of the Churchill Government were not high, and were just about to take a further downward plunge. In the retrospect of history the beginning of 1942 looks a favourable time for Britain. The Japanese attack on Pearl Harbour had ended American hesitations and made ultimate victory almost inevitable. But in the narrower perspective of the day it was a period of doubt and criticism. Churchill came back from a long Christmas visit to the White House to find both parliamentary and public opinion more critical of his administration than at any time since its formation. In February the fall of Singapore and the escape up the Channel of the Scharnhorst and the Gneisenau accentuated this hostile wave.

Between these two groups of events Churchill sought to persuade Cripps to become Minister of Supply. It was not an attractive offer. It did not carry membership of the War Cabinet, and it involved some subordination to the new Minister of Production, who was to be Beaverbrook. Cripps declined, politely but firmly. He addressed a large public meeting in Bristol and delivered a major broadcast. He stressed the totality of Russian effort, compared with the relatively easy-going British performance: 'There seems to be a lack of urgency in the atmosphere of the country. It is almost as if we were spectators rather than participants.' The phrases, as was always the case with Cripps, were not especially exciting but he struck a public response. He was hailed as one of the few men in the country, in or out of government, who commanded popular confidence. Two weeks after the rejected offer of the Ministry of Supply Churchill offered him the leadership of the House of Commons as a member of the War Cabinet with the office of Lord Privy Seal. Attlee, compensated with the title of Deputy Prime Minister, moved over to the Dominions Office to make way. Beaverbrook left the Government. Churchill retrospectively wrote of 'the need to accommodate Sir Stafford Cripps'. Cripps had certainly won that round.

He did not win the next. Perhaps he was never intended to. The Leadership of the House was ill-suited to his style and talents. He had no party. He had at the best only a handful of MP followers. He had no experience of and little interest in the manipulation of parliamentary majorities. He was not agile. His speaking style, while it could occasionally inspire the public, could never cajole an assembly of nominal equals. He had a brief honeymoon in the House, and then began to appear as a querulous lecturer.

Outside the House he had prestige but little power. He had no specific role, whether as a leader of a group or as the organizer of a sphere of government. He could not be complementary to Churchill. He was a shadowy alternative, at once the Prime Minister's ineffectual rival and his effective prisoner. For a few weeks he found a role as a conveyor to India of new proposals for the government of the sub-continent. For the first time ultimate independence was offered, but it was hedged around by the British need to ensure that the country was effectively defended against the Japanese. This, indeed, was the motive which led Churchill and others to agree to the offer. It was fatal to its acceptance. Nehru, even Jinnah, were tempted. But Gandhi, who cared little about the threat of the new invaders, moved in and snatched the prospect of achievement away from Cripps. After three weeks he had to return in failure, but not in ignominy.

During the summer and early autumn of 1942 Cripps then engaged in a private and surprisingly good-tempered dispute with Churchill about the central conduct of the war. In some ways, except for the difference in the power and personalities of the disputants, it was reminiscent of the Lloyd George-Asquith argument of 1916. Cripps wanted a small War Cabinet, independent of the Chiefs of Staff, to make strategic decisions. Churchill wished to keep the existing organisation, by which the Chiefs of Staff advised him and he made the decisions, nominally endorsed by others—Attlee, Anderson, Eden—who were engrossed in strategically non-central work. The issue came to turn on the success or otherwise of the North African offensive, due in November. If it worked, Churchill could sustain his power. If it did not, he might again have 'to accommodate Sir Stafford Cripps'.

Churchill recognised this by writing: 'Although it was evident that if we won the impending battles in North Africa my position would be overwhelmingly strengthened and his proportionately reduced, his patriotism ruled his conduct'. Cripps held his hand until the decisive battle had taken place. Montgomery won at El Alamein, and Cripps lost in London. Cripps accepted the national victory and his own defeat with a good grace and retired for the rest of the war to the important but peripheral office of Minister of Aircraft Production. He was no longer a member of the War Cabinet. He was no longer a principal figure, no longer a threat or a rival. The second major phase of his disjointed career was over.

* *

Through most of the war Cripps valued his independent position. So long as the end of the tunnel was not near he had no desire to rejoin the Labour Party. While he was a pivotal figure in the War Cabinet he was no doubt right. He was more powerful on his own than if he was a member of Attlee's section of the coalition team. When he became Minister of Aircraft Production this mattered much less. And in any event peace-time politics were beginning to loom.

Towards the end of 1944 overtures were made. There was then an enthusiastic response from both sides. Attlee wrote an unusually warm pre-Christmas letter, which Cripps received with particular pleasure: 'It is a very real joy to me that we shall be again together in the Party in the New Year.' Cripps however still treated his own position so meticulously that he sent his resignation as a minister to Churchill. Churchill brushed this aside with humour and friendliness:

My dear Stafford, I have always considered you a Socialist and as belonging to the Socialist representation in the Government. Your decision ... raises no question affecting the balance in the Government, except of course that you will henceforth count as a Socialist instead of something even worse.

At the 1945 election Cripps played a full part in the Labour campaign. As soon as the victory was known, Attlee made him President of the Board of Trade, the last name on the list of five senior appointments which he announced before returning to the Potsdam Conference. Cripps had shown prescience by foreseeing more clearly than most the peacetime problems of the British economy: the dominating need for exports and the shortage of resources from which to meet this and the other competing needs. This, combined with his Ministry of Aircraft Production experience, directed his mind towards problems of productivity and management. He took a somewhat technocratic line, and on one occasion ran into a good deal of Bristol trouble by announcing that there were few workers in Britain who were capable of running large-scale enterprises. He regarded it as a necessary plea for professionalism, but others saw it as class prejudice.

Increasingly he intermingled his religion with his day-to-day problems, and sought the aid of one for the solution of the others in an unusually direct way: 'Do not let us be afraid of bringing the force of our moral, ethical and religious ideals to bear upon our everyday life', he told a Chamber of Commerce. 'As soon as we realize that straight dealing with one another, sympathetic understanding of mutual difficulties and high moral standards are an essential part of that co-operation which alone can lead to the increased industrial production which is vital to the nation, we shall appreciate that our religious and ethical standards have a very direct bearing upon the solution of our economic difficulties.'

In the spring of 1946 Cripps's mind was removed for three months from working parties and production targets for industry. The Indian sub-plot again came to the centre of his stage. A Cabinet triumvirate was sent out to negotiate the terms of independence. Apart from Cripps it was composed of the elderly Secretary of State, Pethick-Lawrence, and A. V. Alexander, the pugnaciously British First Lord of the Admiralty. A combination of knowledge of India and intellectual vigour inevitably made Cripps the central figure. He produced the draft constitutions (the one which survived he wrote one morning before breakfast) and, until he collapsed into hospital, did much of the negotiating. He had two main schemes, one for a single Indian state, the other for a Hindustan—as it was then called—and a Pakistan, preferably linked in some form of loose federation. Unlike 1942, provided he could carry his two Cabinet colleagues with him, his hands were not tied. He was free to seek the highest common level of agreement. Although on this occasion, again unlike 1942, he established a working but wearing relationship with Gandhi, the most powerful man in India, this was not easy. The preferred solution of a united India proved impossible. The second best had to be fallen back upon, with all the strife and movement of populations there involved. The Indian Independence Act passed through Parliament a few months later. Cripps more than anyone else was its begetter.

On the whole 1946 was a good year for the Labour Government. 1947 was a bad year. It began with a bitter winter and an extended fuel crisis. As these seasonal problems receded it became increasingly apparent that the American loan was disappearing fast, and that so far from relief being imminent, the drain would be accentuated by the commitment to make sterling convertible on July 15th. Cripps's speeches struck a more sombre and consequently more realistic note than those of most of his colleagues, notably Dalton, the Chancellor of the Exchequer, and Morrison, the Lord President of the Council, who was in ministerial charge of the new Economic Planning Staff. He was also less partisan. As the press reputations of the other economic ministers declined, so his rose.

As in 1942, he sought to change the machinery of government. He wanted, not unreasonably, the concentration of economic authority at least into a single committee. He also wanted a change of Prime Minister. He decided that Attlee was not forceful enough for the gathering crisis. He wanted Ernest Bevin in his place, a strange turn of the wheel from the quarrels of the 'thirties, illustrative above all of the impermanence of political hostility. Attlee, he thought, could go to the Foreign Office, or perhaps take over the Treasury from Dalton, if the move were made triangular. For himself he wanted power rather than place, the effective economic overlordship under Bevin.

During the late summer he determinedly discussed various permutations with his principal colleagues. Dalton, who always liked an intrigue and was in any event near to the end of his tether at the Exchequer, was friendly. Morrison was strongly in favour of any move which would depose Attlee, subject to the important and unacceptable proviso that it should end with himself in the top place. Bevin, although reported as growling discontentedly to Dalton in mid-July, was more loyal. There is a widely believed story that when Cripps went to see him at the Foreign Office and suggested he should take over from Attlee, he responded challengingly rather than encouragingly: 'I'll come over with you now, and you can tell little Clem that's what you think'. They never paid such a joint visit.

But Cripps cannot be faulted for lack of courage. He told Attlee exactly what he thought in early September. Attlee took it calmly and politely, discussing his own lack of aptitude for the Treasury, but raising no question of *lèse-majesté*. He was probably fairly confident that Cripps would be no more successful in forming a united front in 1947 than he had been in 1937. He showed more response to his proposals for a change in the machinery of government. He decided to depose Morrison from his economic role and amalgamate the two principal economic committees under himself as a nominal chairman and Cripps as effective vice-chairman with the title of Minister for Economic Affairs. Such are the methods by which even the most self-effacing Prime Ministers comfortably dispose of threats to their own position. But yet again it had been necessary 'to accommodate Sir Stafford Cripps'.

There was one substantial loose end left. What were to be the relations between Cripps and the battered but still powerful Treasury? It was an issue which was to re-present itself 17 years later. On this earlier occasion, however, it was quickly—but accidentally—solved. Six weeks after Cripps's appointment an exhausted Dalton, 20 minutes before presenting an autumn Budget, committed a characteristic but venial indiscretion. Attlee's standards were strict. Within 48 hours Dalton resigned, and Cripps filled his place. He retained his powers and title as Minister for Economic Affairs. The planning staff, under Edwin Plowden, came home to the bosom of the Treasury. The new Chancellor was in undisputed economic command.

Cripps was 58 when he became Chancellor. He held the office for two years and ten months. It was a period for him of fluctuating health and fluctuating success, but of unvarying toil concentrated upon a single issue, the dollar shortage. In a world of largely inconvertible currencies what counted was the balance with the single dominating economy, which alone had the surplus supplies which Britain needed, and with the single dominating money. The sterling area was intact, although often a drain on Britain's own resources, and the trading balance with the still ravaged soft currency countries of Western Europe presented no great problems. Dollars, spent either by Britain or by the rest of the sterling area, were the key to success or failure. Marshall Aid was on the horizon and gave substantial hope. But Cripps who played a notable part in organizing the European response to it, saw clearly that this in itself could only give only temporary respite, and that, unlike the American loan, it must be used to underpin the future and not merely to ameliorate the present.

All his principal policies—disinflationary budgets, tighter money, firm restraint on wages and dividends, the elevation of the need for higher productivity into a moral imperative, restricted imports, priority for exports over the needs of the home—market, were directed towards enabling Britain to pay her way in dollars. How right was this concentration, and how successful were the results? The concentration was almost unavoidable, as much so, *mutatis mutandis* as in the post-1967 situation. And, having decided where the objective lay, Cripps had outstanding gifts, both of moral conviction and of lucid exposition, for focusing the mind of the nation upon it. His weakness came from too mechanistic and quantitative a view of the functioning of an economy. He saw it in terms of a physical equation or a sealed-off model, giving too stark a choice between good and evil, exports and consumption, too direct and certain a relationship between a change of x per cent in the level of wages or y per cent in the volume of imports and the future state of the dollar balance. Unlike his less logical successor Lord Butler, he was not skilled at nudging the economy round a curve, appreciating that progress can often be crabwise.

Success first came in 1948, when our overseas accounts were almost in balance, for the first time since the beginning of the war. Then in 1949, as is the way in the early stages of a recovery, the prize receded. The trouble lay more in the sterling area than in the United Kingdom, although British prices were clearly out of line with those of North America. Cripps, as in 1946, but not 1947, had to spend August at the Birchner Benner Clinic in Zurich. While he was there the other principal economic ministers decided that devaluation was inevitable, and carried the Prime Minister with them. The Chancellor was informed by letter. He accepted the advice, embarrassing though it was for his personal position, but made the curiously impractical suggestion that implementation should be preceded by a general election. Attlee dismissed this out of hand.

Viewed in perspective the 1949 devaluation was not a defeat for Cripps or his policy. Independently of the run on the pound which had built up that summer, it was neither desirable nor practicable to maintain the $4.03 rate. It bore no relationship to the competitive facts of the post-war world. Moreover, it was in reality not so much a devaluation of the pound as a revaluation of the dollar. Two-thirds of the world followed us down, including Western Europe and the whole of the sterling area. But it was personally difficult for Cripps. When the run had begun he had given, as Finance Ministers must, some very firm denials of intention. These were the more embarrassing because of his reputation for unblemished probity. Churchill, as a somewhat frustrated leader of the opposition, made the most of them:

The question is much discussed in the country of the Chancellor's political honesty. Ordinary people find it difficult to understand how a minister, with all his knowledge and reputation for integrity, should have felt it right to turn completely round, abandon his former convictions and do what he repeatedly said he would never do ... I am surprised, I must say, that the Chancellor's own self-respect did not make him feel that, however honest and necessary was his change of view, his was not the hand that should carry forward the opposite policy. Certainly he stands woefully weakened in reputation ... although his personal honour and private character are in no way to be impugned, it will be impossible in the future for any one to believe or accept with confidence any statements which he may make as Chancellor of the Exchequer.

Churchill regarded this as the legitimate small change of party politics. Cripps regarded it as a destructive and unfair attack from his wartime leader. He was the more shocked because, when he had told Churchill of the decision he had received private congratulations upon his firm and courageous handling of the economy. He took to the very end of his life to forgive. He immediately declined to receive an honorary degree at Bristol University from the hand of its Chancellor, his traducer. Churchill's object had been to leave a few stains on the shining armour, so valuable to the Labour Government, of his adversary. To a limited extent he succeeded, but he sacrificed Cripps's respect in the process.

Cripps did not resign. He continued through the general election of 1950 and for another seven months thereafter. During the period he again moved into a successful phase. The economy, until inevitably disrupted by the effects of the Korean war, responded well to devaluation. The fullest of full employment, as throughout Cripps's whole period as Chancellor, was maintained. Inflation, remarkably in the aftermath of a 30 per cent devaluation, was contained. And the foreign balance improved. The foundations of the full recovery of the early 'fifties had been securely laid. Then, in September, 1950, he succumbed to the intolerable strains of ill health. He resigned both his office and his seat in Parliament, and retired, semi-permanently, to the Birchner-Benner Clinic. He was succeeded at the Treasury by Hugh Gaitskell and in Bristol by Mr Wedgwood Benn.

Throughout his period as Chancellor Cripps worked long hours. He would habitually wake at 4.30 or 5.00, and do four solid hours of paperwork before breakfast. My thought, as one of his successors, about this habit has always been, what on earth did he do? It is not necessary, particularly for a man of quick mind and weak body, to steal this additional four hours from sleep or leisure for the administration of the Treasury. The answer is that he devoted them to writing, with fluency, lucidity and a certain flatness, long drafts of speeches and Cabinet papers, as well as numerous private letters. They poured out from his restless pen with the strength of a river bounteously flowing across a hard but regular countryside.

Was the exercise pointful? On the whole, no. Much of what he did could have been done by others, less near to the edge of their endurance. Much of it need never have been done at all, as on one occasion when he devoted a long early morning to the meticulous preparation of an address to the prisoners of Wandsworth about the need for Christian values in the management of the economy. It was not as though he imported a peculiarly personal quality to his papers and speech drafts. He was barren of memorable phrases. His force lay in the conviction with which they were delivered rather than in the choice of words. He was graphically compared with Stevenson's Weir of Hermiston, going 'up the broad, bare staircase of his duty, uncheered and undepressed'. It was more a form of self-punishment than a purposeful use of his time.

Accompanying this misapplication of effort went a singularly bad judgment of people. It was his major weakness. The corrupt and the self-seeking, it need hardly be said, had no attraction for him, although he was sometimes slow to recognise their corruption or their self-interest. It was more that he was often taken in by the foolish and the unbalanced. He took almost everyone at their own valuation of themselves. With individuals, as with medical remedies, he had little critical faculty. Yet he had a most remarkable mind. He once described it as being made up of a series of well-fitted drawers, each of which contained part of his accumulated information and could be pulled out at will: 'If I had to do any of my major cases again', he told Edwin Plowden, 'an hour with the papers would be enough to remind me of the issues'. After a pause he said: 'No, I do not think I would need the hour, I could do any of them straightaway'. 'It is no credit to me', he added. 'My mind is just made that way.'

For all its lucidity his mind had a certain narrowness. It embraced no great store of literary culture. His houses, even the large one of the 'thirties, contained remarkably few books. When he had leisure he preferred carpentry to reading. But he enjoyed talk. He was a much warmer personality than was generally thought. Those who worked closely with him stress his charm as a companion, his humour, his tolerance, even his gaiety. It was, they say, a great pleasure to be in his company. His famous asceticism was medically imposed rather than self-generated. He never sought to impose on those around him the restrictions of food, wine and tobacco which he believed to have become necessary for himself.

After his resignation Cripps went to Switzerland for nearly a year. His general health improved, but a spinal infection had developed. In the autumn of 1951, as the Labour Government died, he came back to the Cotswolds for a weak autumn of convalescence. In January he went back to Zurich. By April, just before his sixty-third birthday, he was dead.

It had been a brief career, spanning less than 20 years of political activity, circumscribed by a late start and an early death. Although uneven it had been one of wide range and great achievement. Could Cripps have been a notable Prime Minister? He was free of many of the traditional disabilities of lawyer politicians. He argued from moral purpose not from a brief. He had an almost Gladstonian fervour and conviction of personal rightness, undisturbed by any change of his own views. But he set too much store by logical as opposed to emotional persuasiveness. He always strove to win an argument, and believed that when he had done so, or at least reduced his opponent to silence, he had both captured his mind and solved the problem at issue. He was at once clever and naive, penetrating and unsubtle. Although personally insular, his sympathy embraced the world, without understanding most of the people in it. He had the desire and the capacity to break old moulds and set new patterns. He had most of the qualities of leadership, including the less definable ones. His deficiencies were more mundane: a certain lack of common sense and of ability to see problems in perspective. They did not prevent his being one of the outstanding architects of post-war Britain. They may have made him at his best as a supporting general, not as commander-in-chief.

JOSEPH R. McCARTHY

Joseph R. McCarthy

The last man before Richard M. Nixon to rock the American political system was Joseph R. McCarthy. For five years, two decades ago, the junior Senator from Wisconsin, as he remained throughout his Washington career, became for the outside world one of the three or four best-known living Americans, and easily the most-hated. In his own country his lowering features and rather flat, dispassionate voice, became still more familiar than those of Truman, Eisenhower or Stevenson. He was the first demagogue of the television age, a poor speaker but the provider of compulsive viewing. In the United States also he aroused hatred, and contempt as well on the one side, mingled with a bewildered fascination about the irrational success of his methods; and on the other sympathy, identification, approval, but mostly something a little short of whole-hearted adherence.

At his high-water point, which was after he had levelled the most fantastic charges against public servants from General George Marshall downwards, 50 per cent of Americans expressed a generally favourable view of him, with another 21 per cent refusing to commit themselves the other way. He weakened two Presidents, but he was never himself a prospect for the White House. He was not even a good vote-gatherer in his own state. His demagogy did not set the nation alight. It was too wheedling, and his self-righteousness too shallow. He at least half knew that he was a fraud. He was amoral rather than immoral. In the words of Richard Rovere, 'though a demon himself, he was not a man possessed by demons'.

His anti-communism was more of a racket than a crusade. As a result he sapped other people's leadership rather than promoted his own. He weakened and sullied America, but he never seriously threatened to set it in a new and perverted direction. He did much damage, some of which took long to repair, but then he collapsed more quickly and completely than most of his victims. He died in 1957, after two or three years of obscurity, and probably as a result of a drinking bout instigated by bad news from his stockbroker. It was a death suitable for neither a hero nor a fanatic. It occasioned relatively little notice. Yet, had it occurred 50 months before, in March, 1953, it would have competed with that of Stalin in its world reverberations.

Two decades later McCarthy is half remembered and half forgotten. Few outside America who are not professional students of the politics of his time and country could go beyond one central fact and give a coherent account of the shape of his career. Some might even confuse him with another Senator of the same name, but of very different views and character, who has since come and gone from the world scene. Yet Joseph R. McCarthy did something which Eugene J. McCarthy as well as many greater men never did, and being a vain and self-obsessed man it would no doubt have given him pleasure. He made a noun out of his name and put it into the language. Like Captain Boycott and Major Quisling he is guaranteed a niche in history. But, unlike them, he fills it with more than an accidental label, for, almost at the zenith of American power, he illustrated the weaknesses and tested the strengths of that country's politics and society.

McCarthy, the Grand Chute township records show, was born on November 14th, 1908, a few miles from the north shore of Lake Winnebago in east-central Wisconsin. (The records are necessary because he habitually lied about the year, for a purpose, and sometimes about the day of the month, without one.) His father was born a citizen, half Irish and half German. His mother was wholly Irish and an immigrant. He was the fifth of seven children. The family farmed 142 acres of indifferent land. But his provenance was more notably uncultivated than poor. There had previously been a log cabin, but by the time of his birth it had become an eight-roomed clapboard house. The routine was one of grinding work. His parents were just literate. The family was shut-in, and so was the community. Almost the only outside influence came from the local Catholic church, eight miles away. Yet the locality was not particularly remote. It was only a hundred miles from Milwaukee, the Germanic half-million beer city on the shores of Lake Michigan, and less than two hundred from the great metropolis of Chicago. It was little further from the animation of the Loop than the urbane community in which Adlai Stevenson was brought up. Yet the psychological gap was immense. Grand Chute kept itself to itself, and distrusted Milwaukee, let alone Chicago or New York. Stevenson's Bloomington, set in its rich central Illinois land, had neither an envy nor a fear of the great cities.

McCarthy, apparently an awkward, withdrawn, industrious boy, never subsequently made much either of his childhood or his large family. He drifted quickly away from both. Wisconsin remained his base, and he never became remotely an Easterner, except for the purely political pull of Washington, but his natural habitat as a young man was the small, travelling salesman towns around but away from his birthplace. He left school at 14, worked for his father for a few months, and then from 15 to 19 branched out on his own as a chicken-rearer. Through ill-luck he failed, and then removed to the 5,000 inhabitant town of Manawa. Here he became a successful manager of a branch of the Cashway grocery chain. After a year he decided to put himself, sitting with fifteen-year olds, through a crash high school course. He went on to Marquette, a small Jesuit university in Milwaukee, working his way. He first tried engineering and then the law. He boxed, debated and played poker. He graduated in 1934, and set himself up in private legal practice in Waupaca, a similar town to Manawa. He had no connections and he was not a good lawyer. He made more money from poker.

In 1936 he tried yet another small town, Shawano, working for or in partnership with an older and more successful Republican lawyer, Mike G. Eberlain. In that same year he ran on the Democratic ticket for the District Attorneyship of Shawano County. There was nothing exceptional about a junior partner of a Republican running as a Democrat. It was known as 'working both sides of the street'. He lost, but did better than had been expected. At this stage McCarthy was a good grass-roots campaigner. He was a Roosevelt supporter, but without much ideological baggage. He was more interested in picking up votes through assiduous canvassing and a shrewd exploitation of local issues than in major political positions. But he was broadly internationalist and in favour of the New Deal.

Wisconsin, however, was not basically a Democratic state. Its presidential vote had been Republican in every election from 1892 to 1932, except when Wilson slipped through the split in that party in 1912, and 1924, when Robert M. La Follette, who had been a Republican Senator since 1904, ran on his own Progressive ticket and secured the electoral votes of his own state, but of no other. The progressivism of the La Follettes was semi-socialist and isolationist. Wisconsin then supported Roosevelt in each of his first three elections, although not in 1944. In 1925 Robert M. La Follette, Jr. succeeded his father in the Senate, nominally as a Republican again, although he set up his own party organisation in 1934. His younger brother was Governor for three terms in the 'thirties. In 1935 La Follette was joined in the Senate by Alexander Wiley, a more regular Republican. Despite these splits, the Democrats of Wisconsin, until recently, failed either to secure a firm hold, except in parts of Milwaukee, or to throw up a major figure.

The influence of these confused strands upon McCarthy is obscure. He never subsequently talked much about this part of his life, and even had he done so, he could not have been believed. What is clear, however, is that by 1939, at the age of 30, he had become a Republican. 'It was an advantage', he subsequently said, 'to be a Republican with a Democratic name.' And as such he ran in that first autumn of the European War for the office of Circuit Judge in Wisconsin District 10, which covered three counties, including Shawano and the one in which he had been born. It was an office which his partner, Eberlein, had long wanted. McCarthy listened sympathetically to his aspirations and then put his own name in first. Eberlein was bitter but silent. He immediately dissolved the partnership, but he allowed himself to be assuaged with McCarthy's powerful support for the same office when, seven years later, the latter moved on and no longer needed it.

McCarthy then had to win the election. His main opponent was the highly respected incumbent, who had been elected and re-elected for the past 24 years with massive majorities. McCarthy's recipe was an intensive personal canvassing campaign, accompanied by a flooding of the district with direct mail appeals, purporting to be signed in his own hand, and a frontal if inaccurate attack on what looked like the core of Judge Werner's strength. He was much too old for the job, he said. Werner was in fact 66. McCarthy decided to make him 73, or in one flight of extravagance 89. But the more moderate lie, even though it contradicted an easily verifiable truth, was the more effective. Werner had been born in 1873. By sometimes referring to him as 73 years old, and sometimes as having been born in '66, he left enough confusion for Werner never effectively to catch up with his misrepresentation. (He also falsified his own age by a year, in order to pretend that, if elected, he would be the youngest circuit judge in Wisconsin history.) For good measure he added that as Werner had received $170,000 to $200,000 from the taxpayer this ought to be enough for any one man. The fact that this only mildly inaccurate total stemmed from a salary which had never been more than $5,700 was not very carefully worked out by a lot of voters. $200,000 sounded a very deep dip at the public trough. McCarthy rounded off his campaign with the slogan that 'Justice is Truth in Action'. He won by a good majority.

In office McCarthy was quick, hardworking, relaxed and friendly with the press and most of those who appeared before him, and very doubtfully judicious. But he only once got into serious trouble with the appellate court, and that he brazened out. To a lot of people he appeared to be giving a human face to the flummery of the law. His work was civil rather than criminal, so he was not inflicting punishment. He built up as much goodwill as possible, being constantly willing to fill in for or exchange with judges in other circuit districts, and thus get more widely known throughout the state. His eyes were already firmly on higher elective office.

Six months after the United States entered the war he enlisted in the Marine Corps, and received an immediate commission. He served for 18 months or so in the Pacific. His main job was as an intelligence officer with an aircraft wing, interrogating pilots who had been on missions and collating the results. He also flew on some missions himself, acting, so he said, as a tail gunner, although the number is imprecise as he subsequently gave varying and ascending figures. In June, 1943, he broke his leg in several places, but this, despite subsequent claims, was an injury rather than a wound, for it occurred during an equator-crossing celebration in a troopship. Later he silenced a questioner who asked him why he wore built-up shoes by saying: 'It's because I carry 10 pounds of shrapnel in this leg.' That, however, was a small and once-only McCarthy fantasy. What was much more consistent was his subsequent portrayal of himself as a quintessential tail-gunner. 'McCarthy—Known in the Pacific as "Tail-Gunner Joe" ' was the heading of one of his campaign brochures. 'Congress Needs a Tail Gunner' became one of his central slogans. If so, it was unlucky not to get a better-trained one, for researches into his military record gave no evidence that he was ever so qualified, or could have been allowed to do more than sit occasionally in the seat.

Despite this storing up of bombast—and the sending of some of it back to Wisconsin newspapers at the time—he does not appear to have been an unpopular officer. He was efficient. He had considerable personal charm, of a somewhat sleazy sort. He had the prestige of being a judge who had not claimed exemption. He was clearly set on political advancement, but was prepared to take risks to achieve it, and this made him a figure of rough interest amidst the tedium of war. None of those with whom he served subsequently made serious efforts to denounce his fantasies. The more pedestrian truth had to be unearthed with difficulty by hostile journalists.

In 1943 he added to his military exploits by making a profit of $42,000 on the stock market, but omitting to declare it until the tax authorities later caught up with him. In 1944 he came home on extended leave to contest the Senate primary against Wiley. He was not near, but he came second out of a field of four. It was a trial run for two years later. At the end of that year he again asked for political leave and was refused it, but was allowed to resign his commission and came home permanently in early 1945.

Captain Judge McCarthy was back full-time in Wisconsin politics. Returned to the bench, he secured his re-election for a further term. He was very much a veterans' candidate, with few stops left unpulled. He was 'sick, sick at heart' (this was to become a favourite expression) over what 'his boys' would come home to. His nightly prayer in the Pacific had been: 'O God, for one more day, spare these, my boys.'

In 1946 Robert M. La Follette, Jr. had to seek re-election for his fourth term as his father's successor in the Senate. If he lacked the fire of his father, he was nonetheless a Senator of very high quality. He was a champion of civil liberties, and also a man who had taken the lead in reforming and modernising the processes of the Congress. He had recently been voted on a poll of newspaper correspondents and political scientists as 'the best' of the 96 members of the most powerful and independent legislative chamber in the world. He was not a sufficiently commanding figure or a formidable enough orator to stand with the greatest of nineteenth century Senators—Clay, Calhoun, Webster or William Hart Benton. But he was well into the next rank of quality. During the war years he had perhaps grown a little remote from Wisconsin, but he was its most distinguished representative, with the exception of his father, an exception which added only lustre to his name, since the admission of the state to the Union in 1845. For the fake tail-gunner to attempt to topple him was like Horatio Bottomley (had time stood still) trying to unseat John Bright. But this was precisely what McCarthy did. He fought a campaign of energy, calumny, indestructible bounce, and massive direct mail advertising. He won the primary by the narrowest but most unexpected of margins. He then proceeded, less unexpectedly, to win the election, against a respectable and academic Democratic candidate, by nearly two to one. La Follette was the first, the most complete, and one of the most notable of his victims. A few years later he shot himself.

McCarthy arrived in Washington in January, 1947, almost his first visit to the capital city, as a US Senator at the age of 38. (Typically he had been illegally elected. He had violated a clear provision of the Wisconsin constitution which prevented a judge from running for legislative office without first resigning his judgeship. A complaint went to the State Supreme Court, but they took a long time and then did nothing. The offence was unlikely to be repeated, they ludicrously ruled. McCarthy remained unmoved by such a 'technical' matter.)

For the next three years he thrashed around as a self-seeking Senator, anxious to make a name, but without intellectual resources, moral ballast, or much sense of direction. At first he tried to make himself more respectable, appearing quietly under Wiley's wing, dressing more conservatively, and seeking acceptance both in the Senate and in Washington society. He then quickly and rightly decided that this path was not for him. As an accepted figure, whether on Capitol Hill or in drawing rooms three or four miles to the west, he would always be in the outer ranks. As a deployer of logical argument he would be regarded as an uncouth third-rater. He must continue and develop his own style, which was a combination of going for his adversary's groin, spattering an issue with uncoordinated misrepresentation and sentiment, and hoping to attract attention by the uninhibited flamboyance of his statements.

During this phase he developed his technique but did not settle on his target. He was not sure whose groin he wanted to go for, and rather fitfully lunged at a number of unrelated ones, from public housing to, most surprisingly, the Army. It had, he said, attempted a framed-up trial of German S.S. guards who were alleged to have massacred some American troops in Belgium in 1944. He was anti-Communist, and freely labelled anyone he did not like as 'a pinko'. But he was no more so than a lot of Republican politicians at a period when, under the Democrats, Stalin's shadow lay heavily across Europe and Mao was taking over in China—and less so than quite a few. He was in no way a notable or early cold warrior.

For his technique he had several advantages. He half wanted to be liked, but he was quite indifferent to being respected. He simply did not understand the significance of logic or truth. He could not be effectively caught out, because this is at least half a subjective state, and he never felt it. He simply moved on. He was argumentatively indestructible. What cast him down was the failure to attract notice, not the failure to convince. And even when he had no memorable issues, he was good at the phrase which stuck, the scene which had to be reported.

He was in constant need of money. He sought no elegance of living. A couple of rooms and a few crumpled suits sufficed. But he drank a lot, he gambled a lot, both on race tracks and in late-night poker and crap games, and he wanted more than his salary for his political enterprises inside and outside Wisconsin. He drifted through a combination of need and inclination into Washington's less savoury circles. He was a natural target for a variety of commercial lobbyists and small-time fortune hunters. His pertinacity made him quite a good instrument to hire. He fought a hard fight on the sugar allocation for the cordial interests (which earned him no praise in Wisconsin; his log-rolling here might indeed have been regarded as inimical to Milwaukee beer), and became known for a time as 'the Pepsi-Cola kid'. His attack on public housing was largely activated by a connection with private construction and real estate concerns. But the scale of his corruption was small. It centred around his being paid $10,000, excessive admittedly in relation to its literary value, for a 7,000 word pamphlet ironically entitled *A Dollar's Worth of Housing for Every Dollar Spent*.

It was a tawdry three-year record, and one which earned him the reverse accolade from that which had been bestowed upon his predecessor: the pundits voted him 'the worst' Senator in Washington. But that exaggerates his abjectness. Their standards were quite different from those which the voters of Wisconsin had applied when they preferred him to La Follette. He had done a few things for his constituents, he had been home a good deal, and there was no evidence that his machine there, headed by two men with the splendid names of Urban P. Van Susteran and Loyal Eddy, was in or near revolt. Even in the Senate itself, which has always wisely mitigated the tightness of its inner ring with an acceptance of the whims of the electing states, he was tolerated rather than excoriated. It was slack water, with another election just beginning to loom on the very distant horizon (Wiley, had to test the water first) rather than imminent trouble which surrounded McCarthy in early 1950.

The accepted story that he was desperately seeking an election issue and found one with a blinding flash of revelation at a restaurant dinner in that January therefore seems to me implausible. What is certainly true, however, is that he then dined with three respectable figures (two from Georgetown University) and told them he was seeking an issue. One—to his subsequent bitter regret—suggested the subversive nature of Communism, but in a world-wide rather than a Washington context, and that McCarthy responded enthusiastically. 'That's it', he said, 'the Government is full of Communists'.

He then asked the Republican Campaign Committee to give him some speaking engagements for the Lincoln's Birthday weekend in early

February. He was given a rather undistinguished list, a Women's County Republican Club at Wheeling, West Virginia, and meetings of similar grade at Salt Lake City and Reno. He spoke without texts and there has always been some uncertainty as to what exactly he said. The best authenticated report is that at Wheeling he said:

While I cannot take the time to name all of the men in the State Department who have been named as members of the Communist Party and members of a spy ring, I have here in my hand a list of 205 that were known to the Secretary of State as being members of the Communist Party and who nevertheless are still working and shaping the policy of the State Department.

The speech was not an immediate nationwide sensation. It was reported the next day only in the *Wheeling Intelligencer* and the *Chicago Tribune*. No mention appeared in the *New York Times* until three days later. Nevertheless the Wheeling speech and its repercussions deflected the United States for the next five years. Even more decisively it changed the future of Senator McCarthy.

*   *

During the five years following his Wheeling speech, the apogee of his short career, McCarthy's life is the most tangled skein which I have ever attempted to unravel. It is a biographer's nightmare. The reasons are partly subjective to him, and partly objective. The subjective reasons arise from his passion for the confusing statement, the 'multiple untruth', and the throwing around of innumerable names, few of which meant much before the sudden projection of their possessors into notoriety and anguish, only a handful of which are now remembered, least of all outside the United States. Most of the cases he dropped as suddenly as he had taken them up. He acted only too thoroughly upon the frighteningly irresponsible advice which the moralistic Senator Taft (perhaps thoughtlessly) once gave him: 'If one case doesn't work, try another'.

The objective reasons arise partly from the methods of operation of the U.S. Senate, the main forum of his activities. It proliferates committees and sub-committees. Once launched they have a largely uncontrolled life of their own. Mostly they were used by McCarthy to investigate or intimidate others, but sometimes they were used to investigate him. At first he had to dominate sub-committees of which he was an ordinary member, and occasionally those of which he was not even a member but upon which, by a courtesy which he did not allow to influence his own conduct, he was permitted to sit in; then he got his chairmanship; then this same sub-committee, as a result of a transformation scene as spectacular as any in pantomime turned itself from a peculiarly poisonous pumpkin into a golden coach of truth and carried him off not to a ball but to rejection and obscurity.

There was also the fact that his reign of intimidation, formidable though it was, did not rise steadily to a crescendo. It flowed not as a great river of the plains but as a mountain torrent, running into several checks and even a few quiet pools before achieving its full spate of destruction. And the senatorial boulders which made the checks—Tydings, Lehmann, Benton, Margaret Chase Smith, Fulbright, Flanders—never seemed able to effect much co-ordination and changed bewilderingly. In several cases they were thrust out of the Senate for their pains.

The force of the flow grew massively if fluctuatingly as the years of the early 'fifties succeeded each other. Behind it there was a combination of fear, envy, the search for scapegoats, the desire to pay off old scores, and simple nastiness. But clearly the motives of all McCarthy supporters were not uniformly bad. They could not be when they affected so many people. And they went very wide, and sometimes in confusing political directions. Lodge, the Republican Senator from Massachusetts, once asked Dever, the Democratic Governor, about local opinion. 'Your people don't think much of him; I'm afraid mine do', was the answer. Nor was this to be explained because of the preponderance of Democratic Catholicism in the state. McCarthy's margin of Catholic over non-Catholic support was narrow. It was only in the overwhelming hostility of the Jews (although he was not anti-Semitic) that a clear religious difference showed. It was much more that his strength lay amongst blue collar workers and small (particularly unsuccessful) tradesmen rather than amongst professional and business people—the Texan oil millionaires apart. Geographically, he was weakest in the South, but that had always been internationally minded, despite its other flaws.

If there was a single, unifying force it was the protest of ordinary America as it uncomfortably adjusted itself—as it nonetheless did—to the buffetings and frustrations of a continuing but unaccustomed world leadership role. The old isolationist rôle was one thing. America running the world was another, but equally acceptable. What was difficult was America waging a fluctuating struggle with world Communism and having to accommodate itself to some of the views and hesitations of its allies in the process, and having also to be guided through these problems by the sophistries of an élite foreign policy establishment. A combination of the slump and Roosevelt had dethroned Wall Street, both as an oppressor and as a target. In its place, particularly when his own popular persuasiveness had gone, Roosevelt left the Foreign Policy Association, with its Yale/Harvard cohorts. Both his two successors were basically favourable to this legacy. But neither could defend it with his skill. Truman lacked guile, Eisenhower lacked courage. As a result a perverted but superficial form of populism arose. It was the wave which McCarthy chanced to mount at Wheeling, and upon which he floated for a quinquennium.

There were three main periods. There was 1950 to 1952, when Truman was still in the White House. The background was the conviction for perjury of Alger Hiss, a State Department 'flyer', in January, 1950, the recent 'loss' of China, and the shock and then the grind of the Korean War. In the Washington foreground there was the Truman administration, which looks so good in history, but the declining years of which were disfigured at the time by relatively minor but damaging scandals. At the head of the State Department was Dean Acheson, a Whig (in the British not the American sense) rather than a liberal, but in all other ways the quintessence of everything that McCarthy and his followers distrusted and disliked. He had taken over in 1949 from General Marshall, one of the three or four most distinguished soldier-statesmen in the history of the Republic, who in 1950 came back to office as Secretary of Defence. There was also, looming off stage, another famous soldier, although hardly a statesman, General MacArthur, who in 1951 Truman peremptorily relieved of his Far Eastern command for insubordination.

McCarthy, in this first period, was establishing his claim to be taken seriously. At the beginning it looked a hard fight. He did not help himself with his ludicrous playing with numbers. His 205 Communists at Wheeling, where what he 'held in his hand', if it was anything more than a random sheet of paper, was certainly no document which had not been in the public domain for several years, became 57 'card-carrying members' by the time he got to Salt Lake City. It was 81 when he was called to explain himself on the floor of the Senate 11 days later. Before the subcommittee of the Foreign Relations Committee (known as the Tydings Committee, after its Chairman, Millard Tydings, Democratic Senator from Maryland until 1950), which was set up to investigate his charges, it was variously 10, 116 and 121. Back on the floor of the Senate in June it was 121. 'I am tired of playing this silly numbers game', he splendidly announced on one occasion that summer.

His speech of self-justification before the Senate on February 20th was one of the most remarkable examples of rodomontade in the history of representative institutions. It lasted six hours, with many substantial interruptions, a few friendly, most strongly hostile, from both Republicans and Democrats. At this stage he was thought to be a bad joke rather than a danger to justice or an asset to witch-hunting. The speech sought to review the 81 cases on which he had temporarily settled. It contained such gems of logic as case number 72, which was notable, McCarthy said with a fine display of fairness, because it is 'the direct opposite of the cases I have been reading. . . . This individual (is) a high type of man . . . opposed to Communism'. Nothing approaching hard evidence was produced against anyone. Most of those named were not and never had been in the State Department.

After this performance many of the professional anti-Communists, including Congressman Nixon, then Chairman of the House Committee on Un-American Activities, and the hard-line China-lobby Senators, considered him a liability. He continued in similar style before the Tydings Committee. On March 10th he announced that he would present full evidence on at least one case on March 13th. On March 13th he appeared and said that he was ready but that a debate of pressing importance required his presence on the floor of the Senate. He was told that it had been postponed. He said that was good news for he had some constituents waiting in his office. He seized the bulging briefcase, which, always replete with meaningless documents, was soon to become as much his symbol as Donizetti's quack doctor's casket of potions in *L'Elisir d'Amore*, and attempted to leave the room. He was captured at the door, but produced little of significance.

At the end of July the Committee issued an interim report. It said that McCarthy had perpetrated 'a fraud and a hoax'. But the two Republican members did not sign. They were beginning to realise that McCarthy, although he failed to convince his fellow-Senators, was being listened to across the nation. His contradictions were too many and too complicated to follow, but his central message was falling on listening ears. Towards the end of 20 years of Democratic power, 'two decades of treason' as McCarthy was later hyperbolically to describe them, the Grand Old Party was sick for power. Perhaps this vulgar huckster had found the key. Perhaps he could help to achieve it, where Landon, Wilkie and Dewey, Taft, Vandenberg and Knowland had failed. They were not squeamish in its quest.

The Korean War at first stole his thunder. Then when it gave him a still more favourable climate in which to operate. He had a deceptively quiet late summer. He spent it working against Tydings in Maryland, and to a lesser extent in Illinois against Scott Lucas, who had been vociferous against him on the night of February 20th. Tydings was defeated; so was Lucas. There were other reasons, but he began to acquire a reputation for electoral omnipotence. And if there is one thing to which most Senators attach a still greater importance than to the standards of the club it is to their continued membership of it. The mood began to change.

In 1951 he had an even better year. His charges became still more wild, but this did not seem to matter. He inflicted major damage on two victims of moderate note, Owen Lattimore, professor at Johns Hopkins University and China expert, and Philip Jessup, United States representative at the UN. He climbed rapidly aboard the Douglas MacArthur train, despite the fact that he had skilfully smeared the General when he had been considering entering the Wisconsin presidential primary in 1948. He now described him as 'the greatest American that was ever born' and joined wholeheartedly in the attempt to use him as a weapon against Truman. There is little evidence that MacArthur ever took much notice of McCarthy, but the latter's contribution to this battle was nonetheless spectacular and unique. He took on General Marshall, whose style was the antithesis of MacArthur's, and went a long way towards neutralising him as a symbol of military duty and responsibility. On June 14th he half read on the Senate floor and half put unread into the Congressional Record a 60,000 word indictment of the former Chief of Staff and Secretary of State. Even he stopped short of the claim that Marshall was himself a Communist, but he did claim that, 'steeped in blood', he was a man 'whose every important act for years has contributed to the prosperity of the enemy'. He 'would sell his grandmother for any advantage'. How could he be believed 'under oath or otherwise'? The effrontery of this attack was almost unbelievable. It even earned a mild rebuke from Senator Taft. But, like all McCarthy's enterprises at that time, it half worked. Marshall was off his pedestal for up to half the American people.

At the level of personal resistance to these and other calumnies Truman and Acheson were rock-like, and in sharp and admirable contrast with the Republicans who followed them. They never wavered in their total defence of Marshall or in the contempt with which they spoke publicly of McCarthy. Acheson once had to share an elevator with him. 'Hello, Dean', he said with the off-duty false bonhomie of one man with a racket to another, a technique which often produced response from weak opponents. The murderously cold silence and apoplectic forehead of the Secretary penetrated even to McCarthy. But at another level the effect of McCarthy upon these nodal figures of the American Government should not be underestimated. He threw them on to the defensive. He made a misery of Acheson's last two years in the State Department. He weakened him abroad. He caused him to retire several officers. He gave him a morale-shattered Department over which to preside. How could it be otherwise when senior officials of high intelligence felt constrained to put in defences which were as humiliating as:

I was active in the YMCA from the age of 10. I went to YMCA summer camps and was President of the Hi-Y Club during my high-school years. From the age of 12 I was a Boy Scout. I became an Eagle Scout....

Still more seriously, McCarthyism imposed an intellectual rigidity upon policy thinking. Both Marshall and Acheson assured a Senate hearing that the recognition of Communist China would *never* take place and was not even *discussed* within the State Department. The Eisenhower Administration was to suffer still more, but McCarthy's imprint upon the Truman Government was nonetheless considerable. On Acheson in particular the scars stayed, albeit in a complicated form, for the remaining 20 years of his life.

The second period was that of McCarthy's greatest strength: over the 1952 election, during 1953, when for the first time he had his own sub-committee, and into 1954. At the Chicago Convention, which nominated Eisenhower with Nixon as his running-mate, he was given star-billing, and in the election itself he was encouraged by the Republican National Committee to play his full part in the presidential campaign as well as in that for his own re-election. Eisenhower, of course did not arouse his enthusiasm. He was much too close to the Eastern establishment. When he was asked what he thought of the ticket, McCarthy replied with studied insolence: 'I think Dick Nixon will make a fine Vice-President.' Nevertheless he campaigned with vigour and malice. (On television he talked about 'Alger—I mean Adlai—Stevenson'.) Any Republican would be a big improvement on the Democrats; he would flush out the Communists.

Eisenhower came to Wisconsin and went on a joint tour with McCarthy in his campaign train. He struck out the pro-Marshall passage which he had intended including in his major speech there. It was not clear who thought he needed the other's support more. In the event it was McCarthy. The local Republican candidates in Wisconsin won by majorities of between 400,000 and 500,000, Eisenhower by 357,000, McCarthy by 139,000. 'McCarthyism', as he proclaimed, might be 'Americanism with its sleeves rolled', but his home state apparently preferred them in a more conventional position. He could console himself with the defeat of

Benton in Connecticut, who had introduced a Senate resolution for his impeachment. On the other hand two of his strongest supporters (Kean of Missouri and Cain of Washington state) were also defeated. The destructive nature of his appeal is illustrated by these indications that he was better at defeating his enemies than at winning positive votes for himself or his friends.

Taft as Majority Leader thought he was fobbing off McCarthy by giving him the Government Operations Sub-Committee. He fondly but foolishly believed that McCarthy would spend his time studying audit accounts while the relatively responsible Jenner of Indiana looked after alleged Communists through the Internal Security Committee. After a post-election hesitation or feint, when he indicated that his previous witch-hunting would be unnecessary under the new Administration, McCarthy made it clear that he would do no such thing. He simply pre-empted Jenner, and used his own minor committee to summon, interrogate and abuse anyone connected (and a good many not connected) with any branch, however important or remote, of the U.S. Government. And for a time practically no-one effectively gainsaid him. The Administration and the majority of Senators were simple too frightened of his killer methods and the public support which appeared to be behind them. He made few real allies. He had too many rows, even with his near supporters, like Knowland and Taft, but when their anger had subsided they were only too willing to patch things up.

This was the time of his greatest presumption. He ignored all rules. In the name of security, he broke all security regulations. 'Wasn't that a classified document you were reading from?' a journalist asked him. 'It *was*, I declassified it.' He maintained a network of espionage of his own within the Army, and promised—and gave—his informants an immunity for their blatant indiscipline. He shared internal control of the State Department with the new Secretary of State. Scott McLeod, an ex-FBI man, became Personnel and Security Officer, effectively controlling nearly all appointments. And McLeod reported to McCarthy as freely as to Dulles. He hired, as agents of the Sub-Committee, Roy Cohn and David Schine, two very young men, whose age nonetheless exceeded their discretion, and allowed them to tour Europe, nominally looking at U.S. libraries overseas, on one of the most ludicrous and damaging missions ever mounted by America or any other country.

Eisenhower and Dulles were attempting to ride before the storm. Charles Bohlen, whose confirmation as Ambassador to Moscow (but not without allowing the five weeks to pass following the death of Stalin without the United States being fully represented there) was one of the very few setbacks suffered by McCarthy during the period, saw the President at the beginning of April and found this to be exactly his mood. Whenever a challenge was offered to McCarthy, it was quickly retracted. When the library investigation was in full spate, Eisenhower went to Dartmouth College and denounced 'book-burning'. A week or so later he explained that no reference to McCarthy was intended. When McCarthy pretended to have negotiated a deal with the Greeks not to trade with Communist China, and thus attempted not merely to supervise but to supersede the State Department, Harold Stassen as Mutual Security Director, delivered a strong counterblast; the next day Eisenhower effectively repudiated Stassen, and arranged a compromise luncheon between Dulles and McCarthy. When the Secretary of the Army proudly and properly announced that he would not allow a certain General Zwicker to be summoned before the sub-committee he had to turn round like a squirrel in a cage, and was soon attending another peace-making luncheon, graced this time by the presence of the Vice-President. It was an humiliating chapter, with the President and the Secretary of State aware of the damage which McCarthy was doing, yet assisting him, reluctantly but indisputably, with the prestige, the power and the patronage which he needed in order to do more.

In October, 1953, at the age of 44, McCarthy was married—for the first time. From his early days in Wisconsin he had cultivated a public reputation as a womaniser, interested in 'girls' in an almost professional way. Often when a conventionally attractive witness appeared before the sub-committee and her address was taken down as a matter of routine, he would roll his eyes before the television cameras and say 'Better get her telephone number as well'. But there had been little in the way of known emotional attachments. His bride was Jean Kerr, who had worked for him for a number of years. There was a great ceremony in the Washington Roman Catholic Cathedral, followed by a reception given by Mrs Miller the publisher of the *Times-Herald* and niece of Colonel McCormick of the *Chicago Tribune*.

During their West Indian honeymoon news came that the Army had suspended for security reasons several civilian employees at the highly sensitive Signal Center of Fort Monmouth in New Jersey. With a panoply of publicity he flew back to New York and began a new series of emergency hearings. It was the beginning of his major joust with the Army, but also the beginning of the end.

* *

In January, 1954, when the 83rd Congress re-convened for its second session, McCarthy like other chairmen had to secure from the Senate as a whole a renewal of funds to keep his committee in operation, to pay Cohn and Schine amongst other things. For this to have been refused would have been an exceptional step. But the circumstances were equally exceptional, both because of the damage which the committee was doing to the whole U.S. Government, and because of the irregular and autocratic methods by which he ran it. In the previous July its three Democratic members (McLellan, Symington and Jackson) had withdrawn in protest.

Even McCarthy had to trim a little. He promised procedural reform and more restraint. Unbelievably, he was believed. He got his money by 85 to 1, with 10 Senators absent or abstaining. Fulbright cast the single adverse vote. The three Democrats agreed to go back. The 50 per cent popular support (with 21 per cent of 'don't knows') was still casting its spell.

What were the methods (even if mitigated by a worthless promise) for the continuation of which 85 Senators cast this supine vote? By far the best description of what it was like to appear as a witness before McCarthy has been given by James A. Wechsler in his book *The Age of Suspicion*. The fact that Wechsler was summoned was in itself remarkable. He was not, and never had been, remotely a Government employee. He was the spirited and successful editor of the *New York Post*. He had been a Communist as a very young man, but had recoiled in 1938. Since then he had been a firm but discriminating anti-Communist, and was abundantly on the record as such. He had run his paper as a powerful voice of support for Truman's forward foreign policy. The nominal reason for his summons was that his books were on the shelves of some American libraries abroad. The real reason was that McCarthy disliked the *Post's* criticism of himself and was anxious to blacken the paper.

Wechsler at least half looked forward to the encounter. He was an intellectually self-confident man, who, after careful preparation, believed that he could win a bout with McCarthy. He believed in full disclosure, and was determined not to give McCarthy the handle of refusing to answer any question. His first session with the committee (in April, 1953) began 70 minutes late and lasted for 90 minutes. McCarthy received him coolly and apologised for the lateness. Cohn started the interrogation (there appear to have been only one or two other Senators present) and asked a few routine questions about his books and his Communist past. Then McCarthy took over and switched to the wholly irrelevant but real subject of his interest, the *Post*. How many Communists or former

Communists were on its staff? Four former ones Wechsler answered, determined to conceal nothing, and gave their anti-Communist credentials. McCarthy was uninterested. 'Your paper is next to and almost paralleling the *Daily Worker*', he pronounced almost blandly. Then Wechsler put in what he regarded as his irrefutable piece of evidence, the review by the Communist National Committee of the reasons for the disappointing showing of their front candidate in the 1952 elections: 'The major responsibility ... was the content of the policies of the Reuthers, Dubinskys, Wechslers, *et al.*, who paralyzed independent political action by projecting the myth that Stevenson was an obstacle to the advance of reaction.'

Wechsler waited for the devastating effect of this. He waited in vain. 'Did you take any part in promoting the passage of that resolution?', McCarthy responded. 'I thought I had expected anything', Wechsler recorded, 'but my imagination had been inadequate'. He spent the next 10 minutes or so on the defensive, trying heavily to explain that this was preposterous and impossible. 'Here indeed was a daring new concept in which the existence of innocence becomes the damning proof of guilt. This is the way it must feel to be committed to a madhouse through some medical mistake ...', he wrote subsequently. McCarthy then reverted to a series of questions about the staff and editorial policy of the *Post*, interlaced with attempts to get Wechsler to illustrate his continuing sympathy towards the far left by refusing to endorse the methods of professional Communist-hunters like Senator Jenner, and concluding with a protracted attempt to get Wechsler to answer the ridiculous 'when did you stop beating your wife' question of whether or not he had been 'intimidated' by the interrogation. He also asked him to prepare a list of all those he had known as Young Communists. This, under his full disclosure resolution, Wechsler subsequently felt bound to do, improper a decision though this would now seem to those who look at the period from outside.

McCarthy then summed up like a judge delivering his verdict after a weighty consideration of the evidence:

I have been following your record, not so closely perhaps as I would if you were a Communist, but I have been following you somewhat. I am convinced that you have done exactly what you would do if you were a member of the Communist Party. . . . I feel that you have not broken with Communist ideals. I feel that you are serving them, very, very actively. Whether you are doing it knowingly or not, that is in your own mind. I have no knowledge as to whether you have a card in the party. . . . I think you are doing tremendous damage to

America. ... I say this so that you need not say McCarthy intimated or insinuated. McCarthy did not intimate, he said that he thinks Wechsler is still very, very valuable to the Communist Party.

Wechsler began to reply. McCarthy, however, 'was on his feet, his face pre-occupied. He was a man who had much more justice to mete out before the day was done and who regarded the present defendant as belonging to the past'. Wechsler was left to expostulate before Senator Jackson, Cohn, Schine and a few others.

Sometime after he had recovered his equanimity he recorded his overall impression:

Throughout the interrogation the grand inquisitor was by turns truculent, contemptuous and bland. Yet I rarely had any feeling of authentic personal animosity. He acted like the gangster in a B-movie who faces the unpleasant necessity of rubbing out someone who has gotten in his way: he would really like the victim to feel that there is nothing personal about it and that he rather regrets the exorbitant demands of duty. At no time did I have the feeling that I was confronted by a fanatic. McCarthy is a poker player, not a zealot, a cold-blooded operator in a big game. There were a few off-the-record asides when he almost seemed to be saying: 'Look, don't get excited, old man, we've all got our rackets'. This detachment may be his greatest strength; at moments it endows him with a certain cold charm. ... I think he is one of the least passionate demagogues I have ever encountered.

This was McCarthy when he was running things exactly as he willed. This came to an end in the spring of 1954. The reasons sprang partly out of the activities of the tragi-comic team of Cohn and Schine, and partly out of his having gone so far as to leave too many people with no alternative but to stand and fight. In the late summer of 1953 Schine received his draft papers for the US Army. Schine, the son of a rich hotel proprietor, was the more amateur of the two. He was less valuable to McCarthy than was Cohn. But Cohn was devoted to Schine, and McCarthy was dependent upon and even loyal to Cohn. This variety of links forged the three into an unbroken chain of determination. And this determination became directed towards one of the most trivial and indefensible objectives which has ever deflected a major political operation: the resolve that Schine should not serve as an ordinary soldier. At times this took the form of Cohn, in McCarthy's name, putting intense pressure on generals to give him an immediate commission with non-combat duties. At another of Schine summoning the Secretary of the Army to his suite in the Waldorf Towers and expatiating on the advantage to the Secretary of employing him as his own special assistant; at a third of Schine (then briefly a private) simply absenting himself in the middle of an exercise to conduct 250 long-distance telephone calls.

Over the same period McCarthy was paralysing Fort Monmouth with a peculiarly vindictive and long drawn-out investigation. Fort Monmouth was a key installation for the development of the anti-missile warning system. McCarthy's system of national priorities was such that the doggedness (not always one of his characteristics) and even the bitterness of his attack was considerably influenced by his battle with the Army over Schine. It was also typical that he treated as of about equal importance the question of security at the installation and the promotion to major before his honourable discharge of an allegedly Communist dentist named Perres.

On a broader front he had used a major television appearance to proclaim that the 'Communists-in-Government' issue would be the main one between the Republicans and the Democrats at the 1954 mid-term elections. This was no longer as acceptable to the Republican leadership as it had been in 1952. They, after all, were now the Government. At last, both on behalf of himself and the Army, Eisenhower began to stiffen. In addition McCarthy's 1954 Lincoln week-end speeches had impugned the whole Democratic Party with an extravagance exceptional even by his own standards. 'Twenty years of treason' was supplemented by the claim that those who wore the Democratic badge 'wear it with the stain of a historic betrayal; wear it with the blood of the dying men who crawled up the hills of Korea while the politicians in the Democratic Party wrote invitations to the Communists to join them in the United Nations'. Not merely the liberals, but all Democrats up for election clearly had to hit back and not seek cover.

Against this background the Senate had to deal with a public complaint by the Army that McCarthy was using a committee improperly as an instrument by which to get special treatment for Schine; and McCarthy retaliated with the charge that the Army was holding Schine as a 'hostage' to force the abandonment of his investigations. It dealt with this by turning the Committee, but with McCarthy temporarily out of the chair and on to the witness stand, into a forum for confrontation. It was intended as a form of mediation. The Army/McCarthy hearings lasted 35 days over the late spring of 1954, and provided 187 hours of television time, often with an audience of 20 million or more.

The balance was quite different from that of previous McCarthy hearings. He was put on equal terms. He could no longer pursue his hit-and-run methods. He could be cross-examined for long periods at a time. And counsel for the Army did so ruthlessly and powerfully. To protect his own sources, McCarthy had to take refuge in the refusal to answer questions, a refusal for which he had so effectively damned others. Furthermore, the balance of the committee shifted. Three Republicans (Mundt of South Dakota, the chairman, Dirksen of Illinois and Dworshak of Idaho) remained broadly with him. But the three Democrats, joined by Potter of Michigan, were hostile and fighting. He accused McClellan of wanting to put him in jail. 'I'm asking no such thing', McClellan replied. 'No one's afraid of you out any more than in.' He accused Symington of cowardice and got the answer 'I want you to know from the bottom of my heart that I am not afraid of you or anything you've got to say any time, any place, anywhere.' Neither of these responses from middle of the road Senators qualify by their breathless prose for inclusion in an anthology of great libertarian pronouncements. It is a comment on the previous climate that, after they had been delivered before 20 million viewers, McCarthy's position could never again be the same.

He did not collapse at this stage. On the contrary he put up a sustained bravura performance. He more than held his firm adherents. He secured something very close to a draw with the Army which had beaten generals from Burgoyne to von Rundstedt. He got the Republicans to report that the Army Department had failed to sustain its charges against him, although he had maintained insufficient discipline over his staff. Dirksen went further and exonerated him completely. Potter, with a touch of bathos, said he had behaved badly. The Democrats were more wholeheartedly censorious. But McCarthy needed more than drawn battles. He had been exhibited to middle opinion as disruptive and snarlingly defensive, as a seditious enemy of one of the main institutions of order and power in a country whose might he was supposed to be so concerned in upholding.

On July 30th Ralph Flanders, an old Republican from Vermont, introduced a motion of censure on the floor of the Senate. This was a good deal more serious, even if less courageous, than the Benton motion three years before. On August 2nd there was a vote of 75 to 17 for yet another enquiry. Vice-President Nixon organised for the purpose a Select Committee which was deliberately rather dim. The only name amongst its members which now means much to the public (and even more to Mr Nixon) was Senator Samuel Ervin of North Carolina. It sat during the early autumn, somewhat under the shadow of the mid-term elections, and condemned him on two counts, but exonerated him on several others. Back on the floor, its consideration had to be postponed while McCarthy, in a foretaste of things to come, took to a hospital bed.

Then on December 2nd an amended version was voted upon. It was nominally 'condemnation' not 'censure'. It ended by saying that McCarthy had 'acted contrary to Senatorial ethics and tended to bring the Senate into dishonour and disrepute, to obstruct the constitutional processes of the Senate, and to impair its dignity; and is hereby condemned.' The vote was 67 to 27. The Democrats were almost unanimously in the majority. The Republicans split exactly equally, with the more influential ones in his favour.

After this McCarthy simply collapsed. There was no inherent reason why he should have done so. Nothing very dreadful had happened to him. He was not impeached, or expelled, or jailed. He lost his chairmanship, but as a result of the Republican defeat in November rather than his own turpitude. He kept his seat, his seniority, and his other committee assignments. He was not even in an unprecedently exposed position for a representative of Wisconsin. A previous Senator to be so condemned was, ironically enough, Robert M. La Follette, Sr., during World War I, and he went on to become a senatorial saint. In any event, what was a demagogue doing worrying about the judgement of his peers? As Richard Rovere has pointed out, Hitler would have been more likely to burn the place down than to subside under its judgement. Nor had he lost his hard core supporters. A million of them signed a petition against his condemnation, 13,000 of them assembled at a New York public meeting. But McCarthy was too ill to attend.

This was the pattern from then on. He was 46, but had only two and a half more years to live. He drank too much (as he had mostly done, but it began to affect him much more). He lurched around the Senate. He made a few speeches, some of them quite good. He declined to become a predictable conservative and took a rather pro-welfare state position on most domestic issues. He remained married, adopted a child, and talked about retirement to Arizona. He became more interested in money than power, but extremely erratic in his pursuit of it. He did not even attend the 1956 Republican Convention. There were many still willing to proclaim the old slogan of 'Nobody loves Joe but the Pee-pul', but there was no old Joe to respond to it. He was frequently in hospital, mostly for unconvincing diseases like a recurrence of his knee injury. He was often very agreeable, sometimes with old victims, and could not understand why they were not equally so. He died on May 2nd, 1957, at 6.02 pm, just at the right time for the seven o'clock news, as one journalist, remembering his professional understanding of deadlines, more nostalgically than spitefully recalled.

He was given a good funeral. His widow requested an obsequy on the floor of the Senate, the first for 17 years. Wiley, Mansfield and Wayne Morse, the last two resolute antagonists, spoke with discrimination but no rancour. Perhaps they thought they should give thanks for the limitations of America's latest destructive demagogue.

LORD HALIFAX

Lord Halifax

The career of Edward Wood, 3rd Viscount and 1st Earl of Halifax, illustrated the decline of Britain's power in the world. It also epitomised, in a late flowering way, the landed territorial politics of Victorian England. And, as a sub-theme it showed the relative ease with which an intensely devout but untormented High Churchman could reconcile God and Caesar.

There were three major phases in Halifax's political life. In his forties he was a notably liberal Viceroy of India, and prepared the way for the eclipse of British rule and the end of the great office, the grandest which a subject could occupy, in which he had only four successors. He was the last Viceroy to tread the road of Lansdowne and Curzon and return to a major role in British politics. A Baldwin man at heart, he became Neville Chamberlain's Foreign Secretary and, until almost the last, a complacent accomplice of appeasement. In 1940 he nearly succeeded to the premiership. Little more than a determined Churchill silence stood between Halifax and an office which was as unwanted as it would have been unsuitable.

Within a year he was found inadequately bellicose as a wartime Foreign Secretary, let alone as leader of the nation, and was shunted to the Embassy in Washington. There, against the likelihood and after an awkward beginning, he achieved an outstanding success. Fifteen years after riding imperial elephants in Delhi, he ate a much publicised hot dog at a Baltimore ball-game. He was more skilled in dealing with the Rotarians of Texas and the Elks of Illinois than he had been with Hitler and Mussolini. He played a large part in persuading the American democracy to sustain a Britain to whose weakness he had made his own special contribution. Despite an imposing and aristocratic manner, he was better at suppliance than at defiance.

Edward Wood was born at Powderham Castle, on the estuary below Exeter, in 1881. It was the house of his mother's father, the 11th Earl of

Devon. Despite this maternal provenance, it was an inappropriate birthplace, for his inheritance and background were essentially of Yorkshire, diluted by a Northumbrian grandmother, a daughter of the Lord Grey of the Reform Bill. The Woods had ambled along as a respectable Yorkshire county family for several hundred years, but it was only the nineteenth century which brought them both wealth and national eminence. The wealth came from the development of the South Yorkshire coalfield. Much of their land was between Doncaster and Barnsley. The eminence stemmed from Charles Wood, who was Chancellor of the Exchequer under Russell and Secretary of State for India under Palmerston, before becoming the first Halifax in 1866. The two principal family residences were bought during his lifetime, Garrowby in the wide and still agricultural landscape of the East Riding Wolds in 1803, and Hickleton, later to be heavily encroached upon by the coalfield, in 1829. Garrowby became Edward Wood's house after his marriage in 1909 and remained so until the end of his life. Hickleton, where he had spent much of his childhood, was kept up until the death of his nonagenarian father in 1934.

Edward Wood's father, the second viscount, engaged only in ecclesiastical politics. He became president of the 'Puseyite' English Church Union in 1869 and retained the office until 1919. Even after that he remained the natural head of the High Church faction within the Anglican communion. Most of his House of Lords speeches were about church affairs. In 1924 he conducted the Malines conversations on re-union with Mercier, the Belgian Cardinal Archbishop. His doctrinal position was always clear rather than subtle. He believed in the Catholic Church, its creeds, forms, and concept of the priesthood. But he believed equally strongly that the Church of England was the Catholic Church in this country. To follow Newman over to Rome simply did not occur to him. Re-union meant the acceptance by Rome of the validity of the High Anglican position in England.

These views were smoothly transmitted from father to son. Edward Wood followed his father both in the devoutness and the form of his belief. But he did not follow him in a great deal else, except for a dislike of change and a natural acceptance of his position in the world. He was both cleverer and better educated than his father, as well as nearly a foot taller; he was less irascible, more responsible, and less macabrely eccentric: he did not habitually terrorise his children by first reading the most chilling gothic ghost stories which he could find, and then acting them out on the way to bed. He was also a better squire and countryman, despite his father's somewhat self-conscious pride in his role as a great landlord and sportsman. But he lacked something of the second Halifax's spirit and originality. His personality was weightier, more conventional, more predictable. But the differences were not such as to prevent a very close relationship between father and son during the whole of the 53 years by which their lives overlapped.

Edward Wood was not born the eldest son. He had three older brothers, one of whom died at the age of seven, and the other two during their time at Eton or Oxford. This sequence of family tragedies had the odd effect of making his parents more concerned with his success than with his health. His father in particular was convinced that he would achieve every prize in life, from Oxford to Downing Street, and constantly urged him to harder work rather than to self-solicitude. At Eton he did fairly well, although without showing any great enthusiasm either for the place or for its intellectual offerings. At Christ Church he did much better, particularly for a 'nobleman commoner' who was much occupied with playing an appropriate role in Bullingdon and hunting-field life. In 1903 he took a First Class in the History Schools, and in the same year was elected to a Fellowship of All Souls.

He resided at All Souls for only two years, but the College attracted him for frequent visits throughout the rest of his life. After the two years he went on a grand tour of the Empire, including a vice-regal sojourn with Curzon in Calcutta. In 1906 he published a rather pedestrian life of John Keble. His intellectual quality did not embrace any considerable literary gift, nor make him a very systematic reader.

In 1909 he married Lady Dorothy Onslow to whom he had been introduced against the background, at once appropriate to the period and a little unconventional, of the station buffet at Berwick-on-Tweed. She was the daughter of the 4th Earl of Onslow, a former Governor-General of New Zealand. The marriage caused great rejoicing within his family. His parents had been anxious that he should make an early and suitable match. A short time before his mother had written complaining that he had let Lady Dorothy Legge go to his cousin. They were assuaged by another and at least equally suitable Lady Dorothy being produced within two years. Garrowby and a substantial London house in Eaton Square were made over to Edward Wood and his wife. In 1910 he was elected as Conservative Member of Parliament for Ripon. He was then 28.

He played little part in the pre-1914 House of Commons. It was a time of bitter and entrenched party warfare. The general Conservative mood was one of angry frustration at continued exclusion from office. Bonar

Law replaced Balfour and the front bench leaders sought to prove their virility by their virulence. On the back benches shouting was at a higher premium than argument. Wood found the atmosphere discouraging. Although an instinctive Conservative who had never, despite his Whig forbears, thought it necessary to reflect where his political allegiance lay, the habit of his mind was always to see both sides of a question, to seek compromise, to try to get his own way by showing sympathy with the views of others. He liked feudalism in the Yorkshire countryside and accommodation elsewhere. He disliked almost equally the flat intransigence of Law, the meretricious pyrotechnics of F. E. Smith, and the dogmatic histronics of the Cecil brothers. He hunted three days a week and cultivated his family.

At the outbreak of war he was mobilised with his yeomanry regiment, the Yorkshire Dragoons. There was some doubt as to whether he should go abroad, both on medical grounds (he had been born with only one hand and his heart, perhaps due to too much kneeling, his mother thought, was a little uncertain) and because of his responsibilities; but he decided firmly in favour and left for France in the summer of 1915. He stayed there over two years, suffering discomfort but not much danger. The cavalry was almost useless on the Western Front, and was left in perpetual reserve. In 1917 he came back to England and worked for the last year of the war in the Ministry of National Service.

He spoke occasionally in the House of Commons, during leaves or after his return to London, but on most of the political issues of the war years he was somewhat indeterminate. He preferred Asquith to Lloyd George, but he thought a change had probably become necessary. He was asked to support the Lansdowne 'peace' letter, but although he agreed with its substance, he thought the moment ill-judged. Only on Ireland, where the Ulster cause was always antipathetic to the Woods, did he match intelligence with boldness. For different reasons he found no more of a niche in the war-time House of Commons than in the pre-1914 one.

After the 1918 General Election this changed. Wood was one of the few who liked the Parliament of 'hard-faced men'. This was not because he was one of them. It was because the overwhelming Coalition majority broke the mould of pre-war party politics. As there was no sizeable Opposition it could not plausibly be regarded as the duty of Government back-benchers to spend their time in combat with it. There was less need to be partisan and more opportunity to be constructive. Wood established himself in a group of younger Conservatives who believed more in social cohesion than in profit. (They could afford to, one of the more struggling of the hard-faced men might have complained.) The other principal members of the group were Ormsby Gore (later Harlech), Lloyd-Greame (later Swinton), Wolmer (later Selborne), Lane Fox (later Bingley), Walter Guinness (later Moyne), Samuel Hoare, Walter Elliot, and Winterton. Wood spoke principally about Ireland, housing and agriculture. He continued to hunt three days a week and his ambitions for himself remained under much better control than those of his father for him. But he began for the first time to enjoy politics. He found minor fame as the principal author of a progressive Conservative pamphlet, entitled *The Great Opportunity*.

In 1921 within a week of his fortieth birthday, he achieved his first office. He became under-secretary for the Colonies, with Churchill as Secretary of State. It was a modest recovery from a false start, for a year before he had been offered, and had accepted, the Governor-Generalship of South Africa, and had then found the offer withdrawn because the South Africans did not consider him sufficiently senior. Nor did his undersecretaryship begin auspiciously. Churchill, with whom his life was to be awkwardly entangled for another quarter of a century, was not at all pleased by the appointment. He had wanted somebody else and his mind was in any event concentrated upon the sweep of history in the Middle East and not upon such trivia as the arrival of a new junior minister. Nor had the Prime Minister bothered to inform Wood directly of his appointment. He had left him to read it in the newspapers.

Wood approached the Colonial Office with doubt. Perhaps he was the victim of a hoax. He was not, but he then found himself the victim of several weeks' ostracism by his minister. He eventually broke through this and spoke faithfully to Churchill. He subsequently claimed that the latter's kindness and charm then made up for the initial chill. It is difficult to believe that this could really have been so. Even the most secure of new ministers is not likely to forget being ignored at the moment of his appointment. Wood reacted wisely by concentrating on those areas of the Empire which bored Churchill. The West Indies stood out. He paid a long visit and wrote a notable report. Soon after his return he participated enthusiastically in the break-up of the Coalition. The fact that this meant the end of office for the Prime Minister and a nasty break for Churchill did not unduly deter him. He preferred the Baldwin atmosphere which quickly suffused the new Government.

In this Government Wood was promoted to the Cabinet as President of the Board of Education. It was curious that this office should have been thought appropriate for him, not only by Bonar Law on this occasion, but also by Ramsay MacDonald 10 years later. 'The truth is', as the second Lord Birkenhead, Wood's accomplished biographer, clinically stated it, 'that Edward's imagination was not stirred by the subject of public education; that his heart was never in it, and this lack of interest can be measured by the fact that he makes no reference in his autobiography to either of his periods of office at the Board. He had little, if any, interest in educational problems, past or present. . . . Sometimes he would begin a conversation with his civil servants with a display of interest in some aspect of education, but it would quickly evaporate.'

After 14 months the Government evaporated and Wood no longer had to attempt event his mild degree of simulation. When the interlude of the first MacDonald Government had been disposed of and Baldwin came back at the end of 1924 he gave Wood the more congenial post of Minister of Agriculture. But although the department was more congenial he did not find the policy opportunities inspiring. 'In that administration', he wrote in his autobiography,

'I served as Minister of Agriculture, a post at the time of almost complete futility and frustration. . . . It was dispiriting to know that the soundest advice to give to any farmer was to get out of his head all fancy ideas of high production to lay his land down to grass, reduce his labour bill, and run his farm with the traditional "stick and dog".'

It was perhaps curious that his dismay at the lack of constructive opportunity in successive ministries (he attributed the dullness of Education to shortage of public funds) led him to no challenge of the assumptions of Baldwinian politics. But it certainly led him to a disenchantment with middle-rank departmental office, even under a Prime Minister who commanded his full loyalty and approval.

When in the autumn of 1925 there came the opportunity to escape— and to do so in a golden coach—he had some reservations but few regrets. The offer of the Viceroyalty was made to him by Birkenhead, who as Secretary of State for India was the appropriate channel. He was not otherwise appropriate. Birkenhead gloried in glittering prizes. He was offering, on the original suggestion of the King and after the decision of the Prime Minister, the one with the brightest gleam. But Wood did not believe in glitter. And his fingers had been somewhat burnt by the South African *dégringolade* five years before. He put up all the obvious objections—his father was old, his children were at school, there was his own inadequacy and attachment to Yorkshire. Birkenhead took all these reservations seriously. He would not have dreamt of making them himself and exhibited respect for the unfamiliar. But Baldwin, who would have thought and argued in exactly the same way, had no difficulty in seeing them in perspective. Wood required to be convinced, not of the road to glory, but of the path of duty. A Sunday at Chequers was more than enough to sweep away the doubts. Wood then accepted with exhilaration. At 44 he was young enough to run his term and return with a substantial future ahead of him. (But he was by no means unprecedentedly young for the job. Of his seven immediate predecessors, Lansdowne, Elgin and Curzon had been younger than he at the time of appointment. And, earlier, Clive had been only 33 and Wellesley only 37. India, throughout most of British rule, was regarded as a young man's task.)

He was escaping from a grim English political scene, in which he found it increasingly difficult to combine his Yorkshire feudalism with his progressive Conservatism, his departmental boredom with his personal loyalty. His appointment, together with the resignation of his office and his seat and his elevation to the peerage as Lord Irwin, was announced in October 1925. In March, 1926, two months before the General Strike, he made a ceremonial departure from Victoria Station, and two weeks later a still more ceremonial arrival at the Gateway of India in Bombay.

The India in which Irwin arrived was superficially and temporarily calm. But beneath the surface were tensions and contradictions which made his viceroyalty, not by plan, but by reaction to circumstances, the great watershed, the continental divide of the history of British rule. First, there was the anomaly of the nature of his office, always there, but only becoming apparent during his time. Viewed in retrospect the Raj was one of the most extraordinary political enterprises in the history of the world. It ruled directly over 270 million people, and indirectly, through the 600 Native States, over another 80 million. Over the former Irwin had the executive powers of a Governor General, over the latter, the vague suzerainty of a Viceroy. The dichotomy was indicative of the complexities, but did not begin to exhaust them. The Viceroy was a despot in a spider's web. His power and prestige were immense, but also limited, both by the home government, and by the facts and protocol of the country and the administrative machine over which he presided. He was responsible to the Secretary of State in London, and on appointment was often of junior political rank although usually of grander territorial provenance than his nominal superior. He was then separated from him by two or three weeks of slow communications. He lived in an unparalleled splendour, against which the everyday life of his Sovereign, let alone that of his Secretary of State, even when it was Birkenhead, was one of almost clerkly drabness. He became a more important figure, not only to those over whom he ruled, but probably to the home public as well. The history of the British in India is that of Governors General, not of Secretaries of State. To the Colonial Secretary, his governors were satraps. To the Indian Secretary, his single Governor-General was a planet to which he could easily become a moon. The resignation of the nominal subordinate would have been more serious than that of the nominal superior. In addition, the Viceroy, as head of the Government of India, assumed a power over British policy in a large part of the world which could not easily be challenged even by the Prime Minister or the Foreign Secretary. In Persia and Arabia, even in dealings with China, it was Delhi rather than Whitehall which counted.

Yet in Delhi, the capital since 1911, although without Lutyens's completed grandeur until 1929, the Viceroy was himself subject to many limitations. Assisted, or quite often impeded by the 160,000 'Europeans', one to every 2,000 Indians, he tried to exercise subordinate government through a system almost as complex as that of the United States. To the nine Governors' Provinces there was considerable devolution. In six of them the Governor was habitually an experienced and powerful member of the Indian Civil Service, in the other three, the Presidencies of Bengal, Bombay and Madras, he was often an English politician, a rival in home contacts with the Viceroy. In addition there was the hazy relationship with the Native Princes, conceived by some Viceroys, and not least by Irwin, as being rather like that of a high moral tone headmaster in a rich boys' school. Then, with the Viceroy at the centre, were the Commander-in-Chief, who, as Curzon found, could be a most formidable power in his own right, and the six other members of his Council, at least two of whom, the Home Secretary and the Finance Member, exercised responsibilities fully comparable with that of a major minister at home. There was also the Legislative Council, no longer with an official majority, but with the Viceroy able not only to veto its decisions but also to act, by means of Ordinances, wholly over its head. In the provinces, since the Montagu-Chelmsford reforms of 1919, there was *dyarchy*, the system by which the less sensitive departments were administered by ministers dependent on the votes of an elected legislature, but the more important ones were 'reserved' to the Governor.

This was the super-structure of government. Beneath it were the basic problems of India. Added to the perennial ones of poverty, illiteracy and 220 mostly mutually incomprehensible languages, all made the more complex by being intertwined with ancient civilisations and a pervading and long-established nexus of spiritual values, were the newer ones of communal strife and the demand for self-government. These added ingredients were in a sense a family responsibility of Irwin's. The reforms of his grandfather had opened the doors of Western education to a limited but important minority of Indians. The opportunity was much more taken by Hindus than by Moslems. The result was a substantial shift in the balance of power between the two communities. The Moslems, the old conquerors, the new soldiers of the Raj, contributed little to the new bourgeoisie of rich lawyers and businessmen. Their compensation, a dangerous one for India and themselves, was that of being preferred by the less perceptive majority of Englishmen in India. Greater communal violence than had been known for centuries was the outcome.

At the same time the new breed of sophisticated Hindus, assisted by a few militant Moslems, were more urgent for *Swaraj* than their forbears had been. The Inner Temple preserved the law in England but disrupted it in a subjugated India. The Congress Party which had accepted the Morley-Minto reforms with respectful gratitude, treated the more far-reaching but still limited Montagu-Chelmsford ones with a mixture of disdain and increasing appetite. Gandhi had returned from South Africa in the meantime, and had begun his campaign of Civil Disobedience in 1920. The movement had gathered momentum in the early 'twenties'. The other leading figures were Motilal Nehru, his son Jawaharlal, the two Patels, Vittnalbhai, the president of the Legislative Assembly, and his brother Vallabpbhavi, perhaps the ablest organiser, and Subesh Chandra Bose, the idol of Calcutta, who was later to carry his determination as far as defection to Germany. C. R. Das, another Bengali advocate, had died the year before Irwin arrived. They were lawyers to a man, as subtle and well-remunerated as Sir John Simon, but with rather firmer views.

Irwin's predecessor was another outstanding lawyer, Rufus Isaacs, first Marquess of Reading. He had been a strong but negative Viceroy. Handing over in Bombay, and with a combination of welcome and felineness, he told Irwin that he could look for 18 months of quiet, followed by a period of intensive squalls. Fortified by this prediction, Irwin set out in his white viceregal train, guarded for its thousand mile journey to the half-finished capital of Delhi by torch-carrying soldiers standing at 20 yard intervals. The Raj could exhibit its labour-intensive might more easily than it could solve his problems.

*   *

Irwin had few set views, and indeed little knowledge of India when he arrived. He was instinctively antipathetic to the swashbuckling obscurantism of the Secretary of State. (Birkenhead had been the only member of the Coalition Cabinet to oppose the Montagu-Chelmsford reforms.) And he was no great admirer of Reading's style. They both represented, as it appeared to a good Baldwin man, too much of the tinsel of the Coalition. Reading had governed with a worldly formality. He, and his wife, believed in rising to the great position to which they had been appointed. They much enjoyed the semi-regal aspects of the life. Irwin believed in less worldliness and more informality. He did not wish to rise to a new position. Whether in Doncaster or in Delhi he saw himself as a Yorkshire gentleman with sporting tastes and religious beliefs. He wanted his life in Vice-Regal House to be as close as possible to the way in which he lived in the Wolds of the East Riding.

To those who liked the ease of an assured position the change was welcome, although some of its forms had their own limitations. On the first Christmas Day there was a dinner party at Belvedere in Calcutta. 'How characteristic it was of the Irwins', his principal biographer has written, 'that this large gathering was just like a dinner party at Garrowby with Edward's presence merely encouraging the young, and Harry Stavordale leaping over chairs on all fours like a horse, and the Viceroy blowing his hunting horn'. 'Thoughts of the Reading Regime', the wife of the Governor of Bengal commented, 'helped, I think, to increase the general enjoyment.'

The religious rather than the sporting side of Irwin was more helpful to his relationship with Indians. In his first major speech, at Simla in July, 1926, which was designed primarily as an appeal against communal strife, he struck a note of simple gravity and high-minded sympathy which was to be characteristic of his viceroyalty and was to bring a considerable if fluctuating response. His relationships with the principal nationalists, notably with Gandhi and with President Patel—the exception was Jawarharlal Nehru—were sometimes remarkably close. But these bursts of sympathetic understanding were not sufficient to prevent the continuance and growth of communal violence or the movement of the Congress Party, in which moderation was nearly always outbid, to an increasingly intransigent position.

In the autumn of 1926 the early appointment of a Statutory Commission, to consider the whole constitutional future of India, was decided upon. This was due within 10 years of the Montagu-Chelmsford reforms. Birkenhead's blunt motive for the acceleration, not dissented from by Irwin at the time, was to ensure that the Commission should be at work before the danger of another Labour Government arose in 1929. The spirit in which the Secretary of State approached the future was well

1. *Above*, Keynes in the Second World War.
Below, Keynes with Bertrand Russell and Lytton Strachey at Garsington, *circa* 1917.

2. *Above*, Blum speaking at a Popular Front demonstration, 1936 (*Keystone Press*). *Below*, Blum on the witness stand, 1948 (*Keystone Press*).

3. *Above*, Bevin as trade unionist, 1920 (*The Times*).
Below, Bevin as world statesman, 1946 (*The Times*).

4. *Above*, Cripps at his country home with Aneurin Bevan and others in the thirties. *Below*, Cripps as a sparse and austere Chancellor.

5. *Above*, Joseph R. McCarthy with David Schine (*Associated Press*).
Below, Adlai Stevenson (*The Times*).

6. *Above*, Halifax as Viceroy (*Massers'*, *Malton*).
Below, Halifax greets Chamberlain, 1938.

7. *Above*, Hugh Gaitskell with his family, 1951 (*The Times*).
Below, Hugh Gaitskell with an audience, 1959 (*The Times*).

8. *Above*, Robert Kennedy in London, 1967 (*The Times*).
Below, Robert Kennedy campaigning in Philadelphia, 1968 (*Associated*).

illustrated in a letter which he subsequently wrote to the Viceroy: 'It does not do to take these people (the Congress leaders) too seriously: indeed I find it increasingly difficult to take any Indian politicians very seriously'. Birkenhead preserved himself from the infection of seriousness by never visiting India.

Irwin took them very seriously. But he was fully party to the decisions both to appoint the Commission under Sir John Simon and to confine its membership to six other members of the British Parliament, including Major Attlee (as he was then known) but, obviously, no Indians. Thereafter the Simon Commission hung like an incubus over the remainder of his viceroyalty. The exclusion of Indians from membership guaranteed the boycott of the Commission by Hindus and Moslems alike. From the moment of its first arrival in Bombay in February, 1928, its presence was a continuing provocation. And its pale and cautious recommendations, published in 1930, although known to Irwin a year earlier, provided no feasible axis of advance. Constantly protesting his respect for the Commission, constantly trying to pretend that he was acting within its ambit, Irwin in fact had to sterilize it if his purposes were not to be reduced to a nullity. But 'Indian Empire' opinion in London was willing to do no such thing. From Reading to Birkenhead, from Churchill to Rothermere, it was prepared to put its faith in Sir John Simon, a hazardous enterprise at any time, and began to regard Irwin as a dangerous heretic.

As a result, Irwin came positively to welcome the change of Government in May, 1929. He infinitely preferred working with Wedgwood Benn, the new Secretary of State, to attempting to do so with Birkenhead. He had faith in the cloudy vision of Ramsey MacDonald. The new circumstances might enable him to break out from the *impasse* into which Simon was leading, and enable him to do something more with the last two years of his viceroyalty than pass Public Safety Bills as Ordinances. He came home on leave in July of that year. There was germinating in his mind the idea of a 'Round Table' Conference to be held in London, representing all major shades of Indian and British opinion, prefaced and made possible by a firm declaration that Dominion Status was the clear if ultimate goal.

On his return to Delhi in October he was able to turn this idea into a definite announcement. It was greeted with a chorus of complaint from England. Much more important to Irwin, who was good at withstanding criticism, was the response in India. At first the prospect looked good. Gandhi, Jinnah, Motilal Nehru, all approached enthusiasm. Even Jawaharlal Nehru seemed to be wavering. Then the old wall of suspicion again arose. Its re-erection was greatly assisted by the recalcitrance of London opinion. Birkenhead had asked the House of Lords to treat the Viceroy's offer as 'an irrelevance': Simon was what counted. The crucial and depressing day in Delhi was December 23rd, 1929. Irwin returned that morning from a tour of South India. Three miles out of Delhi station a bomb blew up the dining car of the Vice-regal train. The Viceroy however arrived unhurt and unshaken. He took possession for the first time of the new Lutyens palace. Then in the afternoon he saw a deputation of five, including Gandhi and Jinnah. Gandhi demanded conditions, including immediate self-government, which he knew were impossible. After $2\frac{1}{2}$ hours the prospect of Congress participation in London was dead. The Party immediately conferred at Lahore, and non-participation and the demand for immediate independence were there ratified in the governing committee by a vote of 114 to 77. Irwin probably got a little more satisfaction from the size of the minority on this occasion than from the size of the majority when a motion congratulating him on his escape, advocated by Gandhi, squeezed through the full conference by 935 to 897.

Civil Disobedience then became the order of the day. On March 4th, 1930, Gandhi sent Irwin a letter, beginning 'Dear Friend', in which he informed him of the form which it would take and the date on which it would begin. A week later he proposed to begin a 1,000-mile pilgrimage to the Gujerati coast, where he would make a ritual defiance of the salt laws. On April 6th he duly arrived and to the cry of 'Hail Deliverer!' committed his symbolic act. India immediately exploded into widespread and violent disturbance. His example could command defiance but not non-violence. Irwin, who had been greatly criticised for weakness since Lahore, at last felt compelled to retaliate. Gandhi was arrested on the Bombay express in May. The other Congress leaders joined him in captivity. Motilal Nehru died as a result. The sub-continent settled into sullen *impasse*.

In these circumstances the First Round Table Conference opened bleakly. The Indian Liberals and moderates who came to London, together with a selection of Princes, did not represent much beyond their own considerable talents. But it nonetheless achieved a success of a sort. It opened the avenue of advance towards federation and provided an alternative to the sterility of Simon. It had a favourable impact in India and provided some part of the conditions for a resumption of discussions with Congress. The other essential part was the release from prison of Gandhi and his principal associates.

This was the decision which Irwin had to take. He knew that he could only do so against the feeling of the majority of his Council and to the accompaniment of a howl of execration from a substantial body of opinion in England. But he did it, and went on, in February, 1931 to an unprecedented series of bilateral meetings with Gandhi. They were unprecedented because they were close to a negotiation of equals between the head of the Raj and the leading Indian. This was exactly the point which Churchill seized upon in one of his most memorable passages of invective. He excoriated 'the nauseating and humiliating spectacle of this one-time Inner Temple lawyer, now seditious fakir, striding half-naked up the steps of the Viceroy's Palace, there to negotiate and to parley on equal terms with the representative of the King-Emperor'. Rothermere's abuse was more generalised. The *Daily Mail* attacked Irwin as a 'weak, sentimental and obstinate man [appointed] to a post of supreme Imperial importance for which he [is] totally unsuited by temperament and experience'.

The meetings were also dramatic. They were spread over two weeks, but were numerous and intensive. Gandhi assisted the drama by always walking to and from them, five miles from the house in which he was staying, alone with his stave. They led not merely to expressions of goodwill, but to a semi-formal treaty, the 'Delhi Pact', by which Gandhi called off Civil Disobedience and agreed to participate in the Second Round Table Conference, and Irwin made concessions in the Salt Tax, the release of political prisoners and the non-collection of fines. Gandhi's major demands went unfulfilled. But the real concession was the fact of negotiation in this form. The Conference achieved little, and within a year, under Irwin's successor, Gandhi was back in gaol. But the Raj could never again be put back on its pedestal. Henceforward it had to negotiate with the Indian nationalists, not decide for itself what was right for India, and in 16 years independence was the inevitable consequence.

The Pact also almost enabled Irwin to end his viceroyalty, in April, 1931, two days after his fiftieth birthday, in a glow of accommodation. But not quite: he had in the interval to appease official opinion and to execute Bhagat Singh, the murderer of a British police officer. Another burst of violence was the inevitable result. But he nonetheless arrived back in England with a great watershed behind him and to a chorus of praise from moderate Conservative opinion. He had, in the percipient insight of one of his biographers, governed India as a real *Viceroy*, almost exactly as King George V would have done. He was rewarded with the Garter, which he accepted, and the offer of an earldom, which he refused, for the characteristic reason that it would have given him a rank higher than his father. For a little more than a year he returned to a well-earned period of Yorkshire squiredom.

In July, 1932, he was pressed to join the National Government, and after an habitual 24 hours of hesitation became for the second time the titular head of the Board of Education. He remained in this office for nearly three years but, if anything, his relations with the department and the world of state education were still more remote that they had been in 1923. Even within the ambit of his governmental work much of his time was devoted to India, to the Third Round Table Conference, to the Joint Select Committee of both Houses which took 18 months to consider the White Paper, and to the piloting of the consequent Bill through the House of Lords. And the non-political events of this period were more central to his life than any educational advances or setbacks. Two months before resuming office he had become Master of the Middleton Hounds. Then, in December, 1933, he was elected to the Chancellorship of the University of Oxford, following the death of Edward Grey. This ceremonial office, which had attracted and eluded Asquith, became his without a contest. The next month his father died, only a little short of his 95th birthday, and he at last assumed the name of Halifax by which he was to be known to history.

In June, 1935, with an election clearly on the horizon, MacDonald resigned, and Baldwin, always the lynch-pin of the Government, became Prime Minister. Halifax was moved, as a stop-gap arrangement, to the War Office. He preferred generals to school-teachers, but he had little time to become more acquainted with their problems (although he retained an abiding impression of Britain's military weakness) before the post-election re-shuffle gave him a more permanent appointment as Lord Privy Seal and Leader of the House of Lords. He then had no departmental duties, which suited him, but it was understood that he would exercise his senior experience by assisting in the conduct of foreign affairs. When, within another month, Hoare had slipped on the ice of his pact with Laval, and Eden, expert, hopeful, but only 38, had taken over as Foreign Secretary, this vague assignment assumed greater importance. Halifax was intended half to assist and half to supervise, leaving the Prime Minister even freer of foreign affairs than had been his habit.

While Baldwin remained Prime Minister the arrangement worked surprisingly well. Halifax had great tact; Eden liked him; and found him something of a guard-dog as well as a watch-dog. He was an antidote to the Prime Minister's discouraging disinterest, and he gave the Foreign Secretary some Cabinet protection against the machinations of his two jealous predecessors, Simon and Hoare. When Chamberlain replaced Baldwin in June, 1937, this changed. (So did Halifax's office, but not his role; he became Lord President.) Eden then became the victim not of indifference but of excessive interference from 10, Downing Street. He found it increasingly necessary to defend the prerogatives of the Foreign Office. And, although personal relations held, he found Halifax too much the agent of the new Prime Minister and of his policy of resolute retreat.

The main event of this phase, and Halifax's first excursion into independent European diplomacy, was his visit to Germany in November, 1937. It began with an invitation, conveyed through Goering and the editor of the *Field* to visit a Hunting Exhibition in Berlin, and shoot some foxes in East Prussia while he was about it. It ended as a major political visit, complete with a pilgrimage to Berchtesgaden to see the Führer and great ceremonial banquets in Berlin. Eden was weak in not offering resolute opposition at an early stage. He became increasingly unhappy as the build-up unfolded itself; it led to his first bitter interview with Chamberlain, which the Prime Minister concluded by complacently telling him to go home and take an aspirin.

Halifax was a bland and uncomprehending visitor. He thought he was dealing with a European Gandhi, and was patronisingly sympathetic. He recovered only in the nick of time from mistaking Hitler for a footman and then conducted the interview with a stiff weakness. His major task should have been to warn Hitler against adventures in Austria and Czechoslovakia. Instead he spoke about 'possible alterations in the European order which might be destined to come about with the passage of time'. The Führer struck him as 'very sincere', although he realised that they had not begun to understand each other. Nor had Halifax begun to understand the true horror of Nazism. He had Goebbels to tea and recorded: 'I expected to dislike him intensely, but didn't. I suppose it must be some moral defect in me, but the fact remains.' Goering he found 'frankly attractive: like a great schoolboy, full of life and pride in what he was doing ... producing on me a composite impression of film-star, gangster, great landlord interested in his property, Prime Minister, party manager, head gamekeeper at Chatsworth.' He was better at understanding the subtleties of the East than the evils of the West.

Altogether the German visit was a near-disaster, although its effect was not immediately apparent. It fortified the Nazi view of the effeteness of England. It gave Halifax the quite false impression that he had an understanding of Germany and a special interest in the fostering of good relations. It pushed him firmly into the appeasement camp. 'I am amazed that Halifax with all his High Church principles is not more shocked at Hitler's proceedings', his private secretary wrote four months later, 'but he is always trying to understand Germans. He easily blinds himself to unpleasant facts and is ingenious and even jesuitical in rounding awkward corners in his mind'. And the visit also helped to set in train a pattern of relationships and a mood of personal unease which led otherwise containable disputes about the handling of relations with Mussolini on the one hand, and Roosevelt on the other, to provoke Eden's resignation in February, 1938.

Halifax was far from welcoming the resignation. He was not self-seeking, and he liked accommodation not confrontation. After the crucial Cabinet meeting he went with Oliver Stanley to Eden's room in the Foreign Office, and, although a little censorious about the 'rather restless atmosphere of whiskies and sodas, and cigarettes', and combative supporters, tried hard to persuade him to stay. He did so with perfect goodwill but without real sympathy. He could not understand what all the fuss was about. A few days later he was prevented with difficulty from saying in the House of Lords that 'the Cabinet were unaware of any threat except that of the Foreign Secretary's resignation'.

On the issue he was completely on Chamberlain's side, and for this and other reasons he was the natural successor. His prestige was high, and his appointment even received a cautious welcome from Churchill. His hesitations were less than usual, and he merely asked to be re-assured that he need not do as much work as Eden had done. This attitude was a further advantage to Chamberlain. Halifax never got too deeply embroiled with the private world of the Foreign Office. He believed that politicians should be very different from officials. He was much closer to the Prime Minister than to his Permanent Under-Secretary. He worked distantly but satisfactorily for two years with his inherited private secretary (Oliver Harvey), whose main object, during at least the first half of this period, was to make Anthony Eden Prime Minister. And when Harvey, at last despairing of this and always looking for an alternative to Chamberlain, urged Halifax's own claims in the spring of 1939, Halifax's reply was to tell him that he had been just as much responsible for the policy of appeasement as had the Prime Minister.

Altogether he was the perfect partner for Chamberlain. He softened some of his asperities. He was loyal, impressive and acquiescent. He did not have the same relationship of affection and understanding with him that he had had with Baldwin, but this made him more and not less accommodating. He was usually available, but never too obtrusive or demanding. He was ready to stay at home when the Prime Minister went on his series of Czech crisis visits to Germany, and to see him off with an uncomplaining wave of his bowler hat. He was equally willing to accompany him on the Roman extravaganza four months later and to look (to his credit) as ill-matched with Ciano as Chamberlain did with Mussolini. He lent dignity to a squalid policy.

* *

Faithful accomplice of appeasement though he was, Halifax was nonetheless more than an adjunct to Chamberlain. His reputation held up very much better than that of the Prime Minister. He did not invite or inspire the same animosity. This, combined with the circumstances of his accession to the Foreign Office, gave him a position, should he choose to use it, of singular strength: the Prime Minister could not have survived the loss of a second Foreign Secretary, particularly one of Halifax's standing. But mostly he did not so choose. He thought it his duty to go along.

Yet he had more reservations than the Prime Minister. He believed the policy was right. He did not believe it was glorious. And he was constantly urging Chamberlain to broaden the basis of his Government. By the time of Munich he had shed most of his 1937 illusions about Hitler. '(He) now regards him as a criminal lunatic', Harvey recorded on September 29th, 1938. 'He loathes Nazism'. But his loathing produced an uneven reaction. When Chamberlain brought back the brutal Godesberg terms he was at first whole-heartedly in favour of acceptance. This led to a journey of altercation with his Permanent Under-Secretary between the Foreign Office and Eaton Square and to one of his very few sleepless nights. Then he stiffened and drew a pained note from the Prime Minister: 'Your complete change of view since I saw you last night is a horrible blow to me. . . .' But the stiffening was short-lived. Much influenced by thoughts of Britain's inevitable weakness and by the non-cooperative reports of the Dominion High Commissioners, he had little difficulty in accepting the cosmetic improvements of the Munich settlement. But he did have the grace to call it 'a horrible and wretched business—but the lesser of two evils'.

His next and more important clash with the Prime Minister was in March, 1939. He refrained from indulging in the egregious optimism with which Chamberlain and Hoare presaged the German occupation of Prague and the destruction of any vestige of respectability for the Munich Agreement. Two days after this humiliating event Chamberlain was to address his constituents in Birmingham. His intention was to be complaining but compliant. Halifax said plainly that enough was enough, and had a decisive influence upon the strengthening of the speech. But, curiously and characteristically, he accompanied this by a very weak speech of his own in the House of Lords. Nor did he follow up the stiffening of Chamberlain by any determined diplomatic action during the early summer of 1939. He was as responsible as anyone for the fatal dilatoriness in negotiations with Russia.

He showed no special strength in the 48 hours of bewildering delay which followed the German invasion of Poland on September 1st. He had the excuse of being in the closest touch with the hesitations of the French ministers. After making a holding statement in the Lords on the Saturday evening he went home to Eaton Square and changed for dinner, unaware of any great problem until he was hurriedly summoned to Downing Street by an agitated Prime Minister who said he could no longer hold the House of Commons. The ultimatum to expire at 11.00 the next morning was then drafted. Thus ended the world of the 'thirties.

During the eight months of 'phoney war' Halifax's role became less central. He occupied himself with lofty but somewhat cloudy speeches about the purposes of the war and with attempts to cajole the neutrals, notably Italy and Turkey. But, amazingly as it now appears, neither the facts of the situation nor any foreshadow of his future occupation caused him to overcome the ingrained European orientation of the Foreign Office and devote any significant time or attention to relations with Roosevelt. That was left largely to the private enterprise of Churchill.

Nevertheless his strangely indestructible reputation held up, not least with the Labour Party. When, after the Norwegian *debâcle*, it became obvious that Chamberlain could not continue, Dalton, apparently with strong support from Morrison and others, was canvassing actively on Halifax's behalf. And he was clearly the Prime Minister's own favourite: Chamberlain thought he could serve under him much more easily than under Churchill. Halifax was not his own candidate. The possibility filled him with gloom and foreboding, or, as he more prosaically put it, gave him 'a stomach ache'. He had the sense to see that he was not the man to rally the nation for a desperate and ruthless struggle. To Chamberlain, who had little understanding of the need for such qualities, he conveyed it more in terms of the barrier of the House of Lords. He did not convince him. The crucial confrontation of the candidates, the one eager the other apprehensive, took place at 11.00 on the morning of May 10th. Chamberlain was present and expressed doubts as to whether

Churchill could secure the adherence of the Labour Party. Churchill described the occasion in his *Second World War*:

> I have had many important interviews in my public life and this was certainly the most important. Usually I talk a great deal but on this occasion I was silent ... a very long pause ensued. It certainly seemed longer than the two minutes which one observes on the commemoration of Armistice Day. Then at length Halifax spoke. ... He spoke for some minutes ... and by the time he had finished it became clear that the duty would fall upon me—had in fact fallen upon me.

So the issue was settled. There seems little doubt, incredible though it appears in retrospect, that Halifax, had he striven, could have been Prime Minister. But it was not by his own wish that he came so near, at such a time of crisis, to the supreme office. How long he would have lasted, or indeed whether Britain would have survived, is another matter.

Before the end of the year, he was not allowed, this time with no self-effacement, to survive as Foreign Secretary. In May Churchill pressed him to stay on. By December, when the sudden death of Lord Lothian left the Washington Embassy vacant, he was determined that he should go. In the meantime there had been two developments. First, Churchill and Halifax had found it difficult to work together: not because of policy divergence or memories of old disputes, but because of deep-seated differences of temperament and habits of life. Halifax had none of Churchill's exuberance and flamboyance. He disapproved of these qualities and reacted strongly against the conduct of business in an atmosphere of late-night conviviality. Second, his public reputation, which had for so very long seemed invulnerable, had at last begun to crack. Indeed, having for years escaped blame for matters in which he was at fault, he now began to attract it for those in which he was not. These ranged from the closing of the Burma Road, which he had opposed in the War Cabinet, but which was seen as his old appeasement influence (this time towards Japan) again rearing its ugly head, to the provision for himself (at Churchill's insistence) of a special flat in the Foreign Office.

He had ceased to be a political advantage to the Government; and he had certainly not become a crony of the Prime Minister's. Of course the offer of the change was wrapped up in flattering references to the vital nature of the Washington post. But Churchill did not regard the Embassy as vital. Otherwise he would not have kept on Lothian, skilfull as he was, but steeped in appeasement. He thought he could do the vital work through his own relations with Roosevelt, and through a proliferation of specialised British missions. He thought that Halifax would be an adequate and dignified ambassador. And he wanted Eden in his place as Foreign Secretary. Halifax was not at all pleased. He tried to persuade Eden to accept a reverse arrangement, and he took his wife to Downing Street to deploy a long case against the change. Churchill was polite but adamant. Two days before Christmas Halifax said a sad farewell to the Foreign Office.

On January 14th, 1941, he set out for Washington. The new arrangements secure, Churchill paid him every possible attention. He sent him across the Atlantic in *King George V*, the newest battleship, and escorted him himself to embarcation at Scapa Flow. The reception in America was even more impressive. Roosevelt sailed down the Potomac to meet him in Chesapeake Bay. After tea on the presidential yacht Halifax recorded his first impression with a detached friendliness:

I liked him awfully—very easy, jolly and generous. A bit optimistic I should guess about political difficulties, and curiously like Winston in some ways with his brushing aside things which he did not wish to recognise as difficult, and the broad brush with which he touched matters he discussed. But a very likeable fellow.

That evening Halifax was installed in a Lutyens palace for the second time in his life. He found the inconvenient grandeur distinctly familiar. His less immediate surroundings were not so. He had been in the United States only once before, and that nearly forty years previously. He had to accommodate himself to an entirely new rôle. Hitherto he had thrived on detachment. Now he had to make an impact on a nation which set little store by that quality. He was resolved to try. There was no suggestion of sulking over his demotion. He saw himself as a willing servant of the State, and in his third and last major post there was to be no faltering in his service.

Despite the auspicious beginning, his relations with Roosevelt were never intimate. They never approached the closeness of those between Kennedy and Lord Harlech, or indeed those of Churchill with Winant and other war-time American emissaries such as Hopkins and Harriman. But they were always adequate, as with other members of the Administration. He was assiduous and courteous, although there was some suspicion of his past. Both aspects emerge from the diary entry of Harold Ickes, the irascible, radical and long-standing Secretary of the Interior, for January 30th:

The new British Ambassador made an official call on me. . . . Some newly appointed ministers and ambassadors make these calls on members of the Cabinet, but more do not. . . . Either Lord Halifax has a good memory or he was well posted, because he recalled, in flattering detail, our former meeting in his office and even what I said on that occasion. . . . He is certainly grave and courteous, and I am convinced, a perfectly sincere man. Of course it still sticks in my craw that he was one of Chamberlain's most assiduous appeasers, but I can see that this appeared to be the most reasonable and logical course to follow at that time although I saw through different eyes even then.

It was, however, not with official opinion but with the general public that his real task lay, and where his major triumph was achieved. And here, *per contra*, he began inauspiciously. American opinion was delicately poised during the early part of 1941. The issue between isolationists and interventionists was still unresolved, and muddied by the fact that while the isolationists were at least clear in their resistance, many of the interventionists, from Roosevelt downwards, were attempting to move with finesse, half a step backwards for every step forwards. The Lend-Lease Bill was still with the Congress. In addition, Halifax had the difficult task of following Lothian, who, appeaser though he was, had been a brilliant personal success, relaxed with the press, gently persuasive with the public. Halifax began with an unhappy blend of grandeur and over-persuasiveness. He called on the chairman of the House Foreign Relations Committee at the wrong moment. He made an adversely publicised fox-hunting expedition. He was much too slow in calling those who wished to be friendly by their first names. He reacted chillily to the familiarities of the press. After a few months it was reported that his popularity had risen from zero to freezing point.

It is said that he then recovered by following his wife's prescription of 'being himself.' This seems to me an unconvincing explanation. He was certainly being himself when he rode to hounds in Virginia. He was not being so when, at the height of his popularity, he allowed himself to be photographed in Texas on a small pony, wearing a cowboy hat and with his feet hanging down to the ground. He was himself when he bemoaned Churchill's arrival because of the late night dinner parties and the listening to exuberant monologues which this involved; and not so when he went on speaking tours to every state in the Union, stood endlessly at innumerable cocktail parties, and spent many of his 'free' evenings in informal question and answer sessions with a selection of Congressmen. But it was this devoted distortion of his normal pattern of life which earned him his eventual and complete success. He hardly paused, even when his second son was killed and his third lost both his legs.

Of course he had great qualities of his own which it was worth exhibiting. He had charm, simplicity, humility, honesty and curiosity. And he had skill both in exposition and in negotiation. Otherwise the unnatural process of self-exhibition would have been self-defeating. And his wife, despite her false prescription, was a great and unfailing asset to him and to the Embassy. She never failed to ease any difficulty. By October, 1941, his early difficulties were over, and for the remaining $4\frac{1}{2}$ years of his mission he sustained the British cause with an unparalleled and almost uninterrupted success. To most of those Americans who had any awareness of the outside world he became the second most distinguished Englishman.

He never really understood their political system. He regarded much of it as a mixture of the squalid and the incomprehensible. Walter Lippmann recorded that 'every time an election took place he had to have the whole thing explained to him all over again'. Yet in a deeper sense he did come to understand America, both the habits of mind of a wide range of its citizens and the sweep and potential of the country. He probably understood it better than he had anything other than a very small segment of England. He was better with the Mayor of Des Moines than he would have been with the Mayor of Doncaster, and he even got into the habit of giving chance lifts in the embassy Rolls-Royce.

Inevitably (and he was far from alone in this) his principal friends were the strictest members of the Eastern Establishment—Stimson, John McCloy, Harriman, Lamont, Acheson. But even here there were exceptions. He established a close and invaluable relationship with Harry Hopkins, who was far from being within this category. And his broad political judgements, even if not his detailed psephological understanding, were often highly perceptive. When Roosevelt died he wrote: 'I think Truman will be a pretty good President ... he'll be honest, painstaking, sensible, fair, friendly to us all with the right international ideas. Maybe he'll turn out very good.'

Within his own Embassy he preserved more of his traditional attitude. He had his own small 'official family', mostly non-Foreign Office, and used them effectively and intimately. To the main body of professional diplomats he was remote. He rarely entered the Chancery. But to the household staff, doormen, footmen, chauffeurs, and valets, he was graciously friendly. He was their favourite ambassador. His Yorkshire feudalism lived on, and expressed itself, with a degree of self-mockery, at Miramor, the old Langhorne Virginian estate (Nancy Astor's girlhood home) which he used for some week-ends:

I regret there are no slaves. This would be my hour for visiting my slaves. I would talk affably with them. I should visit the sick and the aged and read the

Bible to them, and when gross impropriety or misconduct demanded it, I would correct them, and every now and then I should bend to pat a little head. Finally, I should have them all sing spirituals to me.

But this was fantasy. He knew it had nothing to do with the real America, or with the real England to which he was increasingly anxious to return. He stayed on and served the post-war Labour Government for its first 10 months. He sustained and complemented Keynes throughout the difficult negotiations for the American Loan, and received the reward of being a major factor in the conversion of that astringent erstwhile iconoclast to the virtues of aristocracy. At the same time he did another of his glides towards the centre, and, complaining bitterly of Conservative failure to support the Loan Agreement, wrote: 'I have never felt more humiliated by the Party to which I am supposed to belong, and which I should find it very difficult today to support.'

In May, 1946, he came back to England, departing from Washington to an accompaniment of almost universal praise. He was 65, and he had thirteen and a half years of life left. He spent by far the greater part of them in Yorkshire, although he travelled a good deal, to the scenes both of his triumphs and his vicissitudes, India, America, and even Germany, as well as to other places he had not previously visited. He spoke quite often in the House of Lords, a little equivocally as always, but mostly espousing moderate causes: the withdrawal from India, opposition to commercial television, even a cautious criticism of the Suez adventure, with its damage to Anglo-American relations. It could be said that he paid off a few old scores against Churchill and Eden. He liked to compare himself to an elephant which always tested the ground before venturing upon it. Perhaps, also, he never forgot. But a more charitable and likely explanation is that he was still, as always, seeking the maximum degree of accommodation. He never wanted the world to change, but if it had to, he wanted it done as gently and with as much agreement as possible.

He died in December, 1959, 19 years to the day after he had been prised out of the Foreign Office, the end of the one disastrous phase of his career, the only one, including the last period of retirement, which he had left reluctantly, without any sense of fulfilment.

HUGH GAITSKELL

Hugh Gaitskell

Hugh Gaitskell died in January, 1963. With his death a light went out of British politics which has never since returned. Like Adlai Stevenson, he inspired a generation. But he was a tougher man than Stevenson, and there were fewer doubts about his executive capacity. Stevenson had been the great candidate. Gaitskell, more people felt, would be the great head of a government. His death was not therefore merely poignant. It was the snatching away of a nation's opportunity, as well as his own. He left, in the title of John Strachey's obituary, 'the unreaped harvest'.

His inspirational qualities developed only gradually. Within a small circle they had been felt immediately before the war. He had been a rock around which those with good instincts but sometimes fluctuating minds could cluster. This, however, had been an essentially private exercise; he had influenced perhaps 20 people. There then began his 'technocratic' period. He became slightly intoxicated with administration. As a temporary civil servant he was almost totally absorbed with his varying tasks, and, whether they were central to the war or not, he worked with all the excessive dedication of a convert to a new way of life. When he became a member of Parliament in 1945, and was left without even junior office for 10 months, he felt and behaved like a fish out of water. He had no taste then for being a politician at large. Once in the Government, he rose inexorably. He was Chancellor of the Exchequer four years after his maiden speech. But it looked very much like the rise of a man who owed almost everything to his expertise within the machine. It was his performance, as seen by those on the inside, rather than his public reputation, which drove him forward. And not even all of those on the inside were equally enthusiastic. Aneurin Bevan, whose life was to be fluctuatingly interwoven with Gaitskell's throughout the 'fifties, the crucial political decade for both of them, was asked in 1949 why he always attempted to treat so disdainfully such a considerable member of the Government. 'Considerable?', Bevan replied, 'but he's nothing, nothing, *nothing*.' So easily can great contemporaries underestimate each other.

Bevan would have given a different answer either five years later when he was moving towards defeat after a long battle with Gaitskell, or 10 years later when he was working in surprisingly harmonious alliance with him. The strange fact was that Gaitskell, the civil servant turned politician, needed Opposition to free himself from the bureaucratic embrace and show his full stature. Even in his last office, when he was the third man in the Government, and became internally renowned for 'will like a dividing spear', he was still an inside figure. If the Treasury found a fault with him it was that he was too anxious to do the detailed work which he should have left to others.

Once out of the Government he moved, paradoxically, from moderate success to a commanding pre-eminence. When Attlee retired, at the end of 1955, he succeeded to the leadership, not without a battle, but with overwhelming support. It swept aside both Bevan and Morrison. He became not only the youngest party leader since Rosebery, but also the one who, in the whole of British party history, had achieved this position after the shortest parliamentary apprenticeship.

There then began his period of major impact upon public opinion. His leadership was always an adventurous one. He believed that a leader should point the way and not merely follow bursts of transient opinion, whether they came from inside or outside the Labour Party. This caused upheaval, with the public over Suez, with the party about his over-rational attempt to re-write Clause 4 of the Labour Party constitution and, more importantly, over unilateral nuclear disarmament. But at the end of the day it left him the best known and the most respected of all Leaders of the Opposition who had never been Prime Minister.

But, alas, it was the end of the day. He had worn himself out in the struggles in which he had chosen to engage. They had wrenched, not his personality, for that would have been impossible, but the pattern of his life, from a privately-orientated to a publicly-orientated mould. He had an over riding public purpose, which was to lead both his party and his country towards the rational, responsible and philosophically coherent social democracy in which he passionately believed. But he also believed, more quietly but equally strongly, in friendship and pleasure. He gave a high place to personal relationships. He did not hate, but he often condemned, not in accordance with some abstract moral law, but because he thought people did not behave as whole men, but applied one standard in public and another in private. This applied both to his party opponents, and to semi-allies, who could have been useful to him.

Perhaps he set himself too exacting standards and too demanding a goal. He would not stoop to conquer. He did not stoop. He almost conquered. He seemed poised to do so. But then the ultimate victory was snatched away. Perhaps it was merely the cruellest of ill-chance. Perhaps it was because he had demanded too much of himself. Whatever the answer, he left a great legacy: a Labour Party poised for victory; a tradition of welcoming not evading the most difficult issues; and a memory which shows that honest speech and a warm heart are no obstacles to success in politics.

Gaitskell was born in the spring of 1906. His family had Cumberland origins and was firmly established in the less wealthy ranks of the upper middle-class. His father was a member of the Indian Civil Service, who died young and who does not appear to have exercised any very powerful influence on Hugh's life. This, indeed, was to some extent true of all his family. With his mother, who married again and lived on until 1956, as with his elder brother, a distinguished third world expert, and his sister, who married a Conservative MP, he was always on good and easy terms. But he was never much encompassed in a close-knit and deeply-rooted family atmosphere. He brought fame to his family name rather than took strength from it.

His childhood was spent partly in a large South Kensington house in Onslow Gardens and partly in Burma, the highly untypical part of the Indian Empire in which his father did all his service. He went first to the Dragon School at Oxford, where he formed a life-long friendship with John Betjeman, and then to Winchester. He was a much less successful Wykehamist than either of his Labour Party contemporaries, Richard Crossman or Douglas Jay, and retained no great feeling for either its man-made Gothic austerities or the natural lushness of the Itchen meadows. He was much happier at Oxford, where, although he went to New College, few of his friends were Wykehamists. He branched out in new directions, both of friendship and of scholarship. He was probably closest to Evan Durbin, with whom his life ran closely parallel (and to whose judgement, exceptionally, he sometimes deferred) until Durbin, then a junior minister, was drowned in the summer of 1948. He was also much in the company of Betjeman, Wystan Auden, John Sparrow and Frank Pakenham. He had a certain tendency, which remained in later life, to keep his friends in separate compartments, to form his own private channel with each, rather than to bring them together into a single group. This was also true of the two dons who most influenced him: Maurice Bowra and G. D. H. Cole. There was no conflict between them, but there was a great difference. Cole was for the detailed, dedicated application to a chosen subject, by which Gaitskell always set great store. Bowra was for the opening of windows on to a wider, less well-known world, for epigram and gaiety, for culture and pleasure.

Gaitskell read the then new school of Philosophy, Politics and Economics. He concentrated upon the more utilitarian aspects of it. Epistemology never meant much to him. Nor, at this stage, did the refinements of recent political or diplomatic history or even the careful comparison of different governmental systems. He was essentially an economist. (In my view he persisted in attaching too great an importance to the disciplines of that somewhat inexact science. At the height of his political powers he could dismiss a fellow politician with the curiously irrelevant comment that 'he was not a very good economist'). And he buttressed his economics with a special study of Cole's subject, the history of Labour movements. He got a good first.

The General Strike came towards the end of his second year at Oxford. It had an important effect upon the development of his outlook and affiliations. It did not make him a socialist. This event occurred, with a definable abruptness, over ten years before, when he was at the Dragon School and suddenly became aware of poverty in the midst of comfort in the streets of North Oxford. Nor, intellectually, was he fully in favour of the Strike. He could see both its constitutional danger and its tactical weakness. But he felt a great emotional pull towards the cause of the miners and those who supported them. He drove a car for the local strike committee, joined the Labour Party, and developed a new commitment to progressive politics. This did not make him an undergraduate politician. Half of him was too much of an Oxford aesthete for this, and the other half was too engrossed in his work. He never spoke in the Union, he stood for no office in the Labour Club. More importantly, it made him feel that the future course of his life should be within the Labour movement.

With this thought in his mind he went for his first job to Nottingham, as an extra-mural tutor attached to the University there. He taught adult classes, mainly in the surrounding coalfield. He stayed only one year, but the work and life made a deep and continuing impression upon him. Then he came to London, as a junior lecturer in the newly-formed economics department of University College. With a break of a year in 1933-4, which he spent in the Vienna of the February civil war and the suppression of Austrian socialism, he remained at University College until 1939, rising to a readership but not to a professorship (they were rarer in those days). He published a number of small books and economic essays, mainly on 'money'. He was a good teacher, a competent administrator and a lucid expositor, but his writing was not unusually sophisticated or original.

During this period he lived what can perhaps best be described in a 'low Bloomsbury' manner. Old 'high Bloomsbury' had been largely dispersed by then, but there were many differences between it and Gaitskell's life. It was a much richer world of private entertaining with windows on to the *beau monde*; with lavish buying of books and pictures; with endless discussion, but with politics, even in Keynes's case, relegated well below the arts; with an international outlook which, even if not very strong, was essentially Francophile. Gaitskell's world gave primacy to politics, although interlacing it with some more general interest. It was a world, too, of continuing discussion, of tube journeys to and from the meetings of informal groups, often in the upstairs rooms of the cheaper Soho restaurants. The international situation, unemployment at home, the development of economics, the relevance of scientific method were the dominating themes. The arts took a secondary place, although Gaitskell did at one stage help to found a small gallery, but for the sale of reproductions, not of original paintings. The international orientation, aided by a strong admixture of refugees, was central European rather than French.

Gaitskell's continuing political position became fairly settled during these years. He had never been deeply imbued with Marxism, although in the early 'thirties he used the language of class conflict with freedom and even extremism. But by the middle of the decade he decided that Marxism was wrong both in theory and in practice. He told Professor Michael Postan that he found 'the whole system of dialectical notions hollow and boring'. He spoke of Marxism as one of the afflictions of German and Austrian socialism. And he decided, on the basis both of his reading of history and of his hopes for the future, that social democracy in Britain would need a class base far wider than that provided by the traditional Marxist analysis.

At the same time there was nothing of the Christian Socialist in him. He turned away from religion early in his life, and it never again meant anything to him; nor did he ever seek to pretend otherwise. He once sought advice from Stafford Cripps, and was disenchanted with the advice, and temporarily with the man, when all that statesman could offer, in the course of a somewhat hurried taxi-cab interview, was the recipe that the Labour movement should be reorientated on Christian principles.

The essence of Gaitskell's socialism was the search for more equality and a fairer society. He hated poverty and injustice. He wanted to make people happier: there was always a strong strand of unselfish hedonism in his political philosophy. Towards these purposes he was, and remained, uncompromisingly radical. In all his enterprises he was a 'whole-hogger'. But it was ends and not means which made him uncompromising. He was in favour of the extension of public ownership, and probably over-estimated, then and for many years thereafter, the improvement in efficiency which state ownership or government intervention could bring. But already, by the late 'thirties, he explicitly rejected the identification of socialism with nationalisation.

He was the most determined anti-appeaser of all those amongst whom he moved. He had a strong view about Britain's obligation in the world, and a contempt for those who sought to shut their eyes to what was happening outside. Yet his internationalism was shot through with many English streaks. He was not a natural cosmopolitan. He was not uncomfortable 'abroad', as were his contemporaries Evan Durbin and Douglas Jay, but he liked English ways, and thought that political problems were more likely to be solved in this island than anywhere else. He was warmly friendly towards foreigners, but he instinctively believed in the Englishman's burden.

In 1937 he married. His wife was Dora Creditor, the daughter of a Lithuanian Jewish doctor who had come to London in 1903. She had been married before, to another doctor, and had one son. The romance was exciting and absorbing. Lady Gaitskell (as she is to-day) was as sparkling and refreshing a figure throughout the 25 years of her Gaitskell marriage as she now is in the House of Lords.

When the war started, Gaitskell was 33. He had fought Chatham in 1935, and, in common with three-quarters of the other Labour candidates at that dismal election, had been roundly defeated. Two years later, following the somewhat reluctant agreement of the sitting member to retire, he was adopted as candidate for South Leeds, one of the hundred or so safest Labour seats in the country. There had been several patrons, most notably Hugh Dalton, to urge his candidature, but the decisive influence was the impact which he made upon this solidly working-class constituency during the several vetting visits which he paid prior to his selection. Neither he nor the local committee (nor indeed the reluctantly retiring member) apprehended that it would be eight years before the seat could again be contested. Throughout this long wait he took his candidature immensely seriously, speaking frequently to the largely converted electorate until the war, and then, when his civil servant status made this impossible, paying private visits and maintaining a weekly correspondence with his agent. He established a close *rapport*, which was of continuing and growing value throughout the remainder of his life. Whatever his national controversies, South Leeds was an impregnable bastion.

Within a week of the outbreak of war he left University College and joined the Ministry of Economic Warfare in a junior and temporary post. When Dalton became Minister, eight months later, Gaitskell became his private secretary, and then went with him, in early 1942, to the Board of Trade. He later achieved a more independent administrative role of his own, and finished the war as a principal assistant secretary in charge of price control, retail trade and the film industry. It was an upper middle rank which has since been abolished. In military terms it was equivalent to a temporary officer becoming a brigadier.

What is perhaps strange is that he never appears to have considered whether he should join the Army. This was certainly not due to any lack of support for the war effort or desire for self-preservation. His commitment was total, and no one can survey his whole career without believing that he had moral courage of the highest order. Nor were physical manifestations lacking. He treated the blitz with indifference. And he taxed his future health far more heavily than he would have been likely to do in the services. In the spring of 1945 overwork brought on a major thrombosis, and he hovered on the brink of incapacity for several weeks. It was simply that his over-rational mind never allowed the problem to pose itself. He could be of more use where he was. The fact that his form of service might be a political disadvantage to him in the future was not worth consideration.

His severe illness almost made his long drawn-out candidature abortive. There was grave doubt as to whether he could fight the 1945 election. Eventually he was allowed a semi-invalid campaign. This did not prevent his being returned with a majority of more than 10,000. At 39, not very young, but with a solid record of administrative achievement behind him, he was a member of Parliament.

* *

The 1945 House of Commons was a new world. It contained well over three hundred new members. The length of the preceding parliament and the size of the Labour majority combined to produce the massive and almost unprecedented turn-over. Some thought it heralded a new paradise, based on the permanent decline of the Conservative Party. Gaitskell was enthusiastic but not euphoric.

Unlike some other new members—Harold Wilson, Hartley Shawcross, Frank Soskice, Hilary Marquand—he was not immediately included in the Government. Although Attlee subsequently remained silent on the point, this was probably due only to his health. Over the next few months this improved steadily, and in May, 1946, he became parliamentary secretary to the Ministry of Fuel and Power. His appointment was greeted with some growling, for the miners, still the strongest trades union group in the House of Commons, resented the replacement of one of their own by such a quintessential middle-class intellectual. This resentment was short-lived. The National Union of Mineworkers quickly became one of Gaitskell's most important and reliable bases of support.

Shinwell was Gaitskell's Minister. Whether they ever worked well together is unclear. Gaitskell certainly foresaw the forthcoming fuel crisis more clearly than did his superior. It would have been a grave criticism of his economic training had he not done so. But his signals of alarm were muted by loyalty to his Minister. The only act of disloyalty he committed was the single but unforgiveable one of being manifestly more efficient and being chosen by the Prime Minister as a replacement when, following a decent interval after the disaster of February, 1947, it was decided that a change must be made.

Gaitskell became a full minister, with heavy responsibilities but without the advantage of Cabinet membership, at the age of 41. A few days earlier, Harold Wilson, 10 years his junior, had achieved the higher status as President of the Board of Trade. Gaitskell remained Minister of Fuel and Power for nearly two and a half years. He was a thoroughly competent middle-rank minister. He impressed his officials. He husbanded coal stocks with efficiency and realism. He was statistically magisterial in the House of Commons, where he carried the Gas Nationalisation Bill against a marathon Conservative filibuster. Within the Government he stood up vigorously for his clutch of public industries, successfully challenging on one occasion the right of Cripps, then in the plenitude of his power, to fix their investment programmes. Douglas Jay, a Treasury junior minister at the time, regarded this incident as crucial to Gaitskell's Whitehall emergence as a figure of independent strength.

With the public he was less successful. He did not incur the same notorious obloquy as Strachey, who as Minister of Food occupied an even more exposed position of similar rank. Gaitskell was not nearly so well-known; and his public impact, which as it was, gave an impression of uncertainty, even of instability. For some time his most remembered utterance was a recommendation that people should save fuel by not bathing too often. 'Personally, I have never had a great many baths', he added. It was a sound Wykehamical sentiment, but the attempt at jocularity was not altogether happy. On another occasion, when addressing a conference of the South Wales Miners, he was overcome by the emotion of the occasion and of his appeal, and choked himself for a few moments with his own tears. The incident showed a side of his character very different from the 'desiccated calculating machine' label which Aneurin Bevan later and inappropriately attempted to pin on him. But it did not seem a wholly suitable behaviour for a departmental minister. Churchill could get away with it, but he could not.

He was sensitive about these failures of public relations. During this period he went one evening with his wife to the film premiere at a West End cinema (he treasured his old Board of Trade film contacts), and was deeply dismayed when a newsreel shot of himself attracted a chorus of derisive booing. The audience was no doubt both Tory and indifferent to Crippsian-style national appeals for fuel economy, but this thought did not greatly assuage Gaitskell's wounded feelings. He never liked derision —who does?—but it had not previously occurred to him that he could arouse hatred either. He later achieved a thicker skin against such manifestations.

Inside the Government his reputation was much higher. In Cripps's absence at his Swiss clinic, Gaitskell played a crucial part in the devaluation decisions of the summer of 1949. Normally, an economic minister in his position would not have been consulted at all on a matter of such sensitivity. By contrast, he became central to the whole operation. He was the trusted man who always knew what to do. After the election of 1950 he was somewhat curiously rewarded for this by a move which was almost a demotion. He became Minister of State for Economic Affairs, working within the Treasury. His nominal status was the same as it had been before. But he had lost his independent command. On the other hand he had become the second man in the central department, under a Chancellor whose health was weakening. Cripps, however, had defeated ill-health before. There was no certainty that he would go soon. His hold on his office seemed at least as strong as, with its overall majority of five, was the Government's hold on life. Nor was there any approach to a bargain that, if the Exchequer fell vacant, Gaitskell would necessarily succeed. That was not the way that Attlee did things.

However, Cripps went and Gaitskell did succeed. He became the youngest Chancellor since Austen Chamberlain in 1903. He had been in effective charge of the Treasury for several preceding weeks, and Attlee felt that the shaky Government needed as much continuity as it could be given. He also felt that Gaitskell would make by far the best Chancellor. But with a longer prospect of office ahead he might have wished to weigh this view against wider political considerations. Aneurin Bevan was not pleased with Gaitskell's promotion. He had fulfilled his purpose and his usefulness at the Ministry of Health. On the ground both of his record there, at once distinguished and easy-going, and of his influence in the Labour Party, he was entitled to a major office. Furthermore, he had been much subject to Cripps's influence, and the removal of this, combined with the completion of his creative work on the National Health Service, was likely to leave him increasingly unanchored.

Attlee, decided that this risk was a price worth paying for Gaitskell's expertise. Five months later he compounded the risk by again passing over Bevan and giving Morrison the Foreign Office in place of the exhausted Ernest Bevin. This second snub, particularly as Bevan was more suited to the Foreign Office than the Treasury, was more decisive than the first. It was a substantial contributory factor towards Bevan's resignation, which took place six weeks later and presaged the end of the Government. Nevertheless, Bevan was more resentful of Gaitskell than of Morrison. He had been used to quarreling with Morrison. Gaitskell was the new man, suddenly injected into a position of commanding prominence. Furthermore, he was competent at his new job, which was a great deal more than could be said of Morrison.

Gaitskell needed all his competence to face the massive problems of the Treasury in the last year of the Labour Government's life. It was not that he received a bad inheritance from Cripps. The economy had responded well to devaluation, and 1950 was a year of surplus, of gold inflow, and of surprisingly stable prices. We were able to renounce Marshall Aid a year ahead of schedule. But the cloud, much bigger than a man's hand, had appeared at mid-summer. The Korean War had started, and with it the prospect of substantially increased defence expenditure, even above the very high level which we had been carrying throughout the post-war years.

Gaitskell was enthusiastically in favour of this additional burden. His commitment to Western defence far outweighted any cancellerian caution. Even before he succeeded Cripps he had announced a three year programme for a 50% increase in defence expenditure. In itself this might just have been temporarily bearable. But when its early stages were accompanied, as was less clearly foreseen, by an unprecedented rise in world commodity prices and a consequent deterioration in Britain's terms of trade, it became unsustainable. With the benefit of hindsight I believe it would have been right to have told the Americans that we could not both contain the effects of their stockbuilding and mount our own rearmament programme. Gaitskell did not do this. Instead he accepted in February the prospect of a heavy balance of payments deficit for 1951 and prepared for a disagreeable Budget. He was too loyal to Britain's allies, too frightened by a repetition of the weakness of the 'thirties.

In fact the Budget, by the most stringent standards both of the past and the future, was not draconian. There were increases in income tax, profits tax and purchase tax, but there was also a significant rise in old-age pensions. The nub was the imposition of charges on National Health Service teeth and spectacles. The amount of money involved was not large—£13 million in the first year, and £25 million thereafter. More important, in Gaitskell's eyes, were his determination, first that the health service, the costs of which had vastly exceeded estimates, should not be immune from the discipline which applied to other forms of public expenditure, and second, that when there was a Cabinet disagreement, the view of a majority of 18 should not be subordinated to that of a minority of two. Attlee, who was in hospital but fully consulted, gave him firm support. So did the rest of the Cabinet. Had he retreated, they would have thought the new Chancellor a busted flush, and have re-acted accordingly. He did not do so. Bevan and Mr Wilson resigned, although quickly widening the issue in a way which made it clear that they had been looking for an occasion to be free. The price was heavy. But Gaitskell emerged as a strong and uncompromising man, the only one in the dying days of the Government who had the force of Bevin or Cripps.

The election of October, 1951, resulted in a narrow Conservative victory. Gaitskell had for the first time to accommodate himself to a life of Opposition. He could no longer depend upon success in administration and the fully-earned patronage of the Prime Minister. He had either to establish himself as a tribune of the Labour Party or sink back into relative obscurity. There were four 'constituencies' to which he could appeal. The first was the Parliamentary Labour Party. The second was the trade union leadership. The third was the party organisation in the six hundred or so parliamentary divisions. The fourth was uncommitted but Labour-inclined public opinion.

Gaitskell's position was strong with the first. Throughout the 1951 Parliament he never had any difficulty in being elected to the Shadow Cabinet in one of the top three places. And his House of Commons performance as Shadow Chancellor was almost unfailingly good. For the first time he learnt, not merely to hold the House of Commons at bay, but to play upon it as a sensitive instrument. The second was relatively easy. Deakin, Williamson and Lawther, the three principal trade union leaders, all wanted a tough, moderate political figure in whom they could place their trust. Gaitskell filled the bill. The third was much more difficult, almost impossible. The constituency parties were then strongly Bevanite and left-wing, much more so than in recent years. Mostly they did not command the votes at the Conference, except for the constituency section of the National Executive, for which Gaitskell had twice to stand and accept defeat, but they provided much of the spirit. The fourth was less important. It was a time of strongly entrenched party warfare, with votes fluctuating much less freely than to-day. For what it was worth, Gaitskell had it.

He therefore had about a $2\frac{1}{2}$ to 1 superiority over his long-term rival, Bevan. It was a margin which made total defeat impossible, but which did not make victory certain. The minority was much more articulate than the majority. Moreover, the majority, some of it aggressive, some of it cautious, had to be kept together. This involved working closely with allies, not the least of whom was Herbert Morrison, always resentful of Attlee's leadership and determined to be his successor. Gaitskell's relationship with Morrison was close. He regarded him as a valiant ally for the causes of sense and righteousness. He glossed over the fact that his own parliamentary performances were infinitely superior. He shared Morrison's view that Morrison ought to succeed. When, following defeat at the 1955 election, it became obvious that Attlee would not for long wish to continue, Gaitskell was not his own candidate. He wanted the job ultimately, but not at that stage. It was only with the greatest difficulty that he was persuaded that Morrison might well be a loser, and, even if not so, a played-out and inadequate leader. He liked being ruthless about ideas or towards enemies, real or supposed. He hated being so towards friends. Eventually, in the late summer of 1955, he was convinced. He agreed that he would tell Morrison that, in the event of Attlee's retirement he himself would have to be a candidate.

Characteristically, he chose a private luncheon, hardly the easiest of occasions, for the imparting of the information. Morrison took it remarkably well. Either he was being very charitable or very complacent. He encouraged Gaitskell to 'have a go'. The opportunity for the 'go' came less than six months later. It was devastating to Morrison's hopes. On the first and only ballot he got only 40 votes, with Bevan obtaining 70 and Gaitskell 157, nearly 60% of the full strength of the Parliamentary

Labour Party. It was a decisive victory, secured only 10 years after his entry into the House of Commons, and one which deemed to give him the fairest prospect which any man under 50 had then attained in British politics throughout the century. He had achieved it relatively easily, although by a great display of courage and determination, and also with luck playing its normal part. But the tests of the past were to be as nothing compared with those of the future. It was a bed of nails, even more than a glorious opportunity, to which he had succeeded.

* *

Gaitskell was 49. He had another seven years of life ahead of him, and he did not change much during this period, except that he became more battle-hardened and, ultimately, more tired. Through the strains of the previous few years he had retained, and indeed developed, his warm friendly and relaxed personality. This was not universally appreciated. Some thought that his circle was too exclusive. In the sense that he only liked people of a certain type or origin or background, this was simply not so. He had a very wide range of friendship, and was always anxious, almost naïvely so, to extend it. He always wanted to meet people of worlds different from his own. He saw friendship as an ideal, not exclusive but with constantly expanding frontiers, but not to be confused with chance occupational relations. His conversation, like that of all those who make it well without indulging in monologue, was closely moulded to the person to whom he was talking. To have pretended that he was equally at ease with everyone would have seemed to him a denial of any special quality of individual relationship.

From those who were both friends and allies he expected—and gave—a very high degree of loyalty. I remember once rather pompously telling him, after a disagreement, that I would always support him when he was right. He reacted strongly: 'Anybody can do that. I want people who'll support me when I'm wrong!' Yet he was not vain. He never minded argument, or even mockery. If there was an underlying link he would quickly forgive those who did not meet his full expectation of support.

From 1939 to 1951 he had worked immensely hard. His mind had been continuously and closely applied to problems of administration or government. His achievement had been greater but his range had become narrower than in the 'twenties or 'thirties. Gaiety had diminished. He had spent too many evenings returning to his papers following a hurried domestic supper. After 1951, and still more after his leadership election in 1955, there was a reaction against this. The nervous strain of politics became greater than ever, but the hours of stodgy work became less. He had a curious feeling, a revival of the old hedonism, that he had not enjoyed his life enough. He must be more adventurous in his 'fifties than he had been in his 'forties. The result was no neglect of duty. He continued to work harder at politics than was really sensible. And he superimposed on this, by conscious choice, an immensely active, wide-ranging social life.

He adored dancing. He enjoyed it at Oxford Commem. Balls in the 'twenties, at the Hammersmith *Palais de Danse* and in Viennese *tanzlocalen* in the 'thirties, at Labour Party social evenings and mayors' receptions, as well as in private houses, and even occasionally in a night-club, in the 'fifties. No small party of which he was the centre, whether in his own house or in someone else's was complete without a gramophone and a small dance-floor. He was demanding about the activity but not about the conditions. It did not matter if the carpet could not be removed. It did matter if the gramophone broke down. All this, combined with his grinding political life, involved a good deal of candle-burning at both ends.

The early test of his leadership was Suez. His first speech on the issue, at the beginning of August 1956, was as hostile to Nasser and the seizure of the Canal as was that of Eden. He saw the Egyptians at this stage as the disrupters of international law, and his disapproval was unmitigated by any instinctive pro-Nasser feeling. On Middle Eastern affairs his natural sympathy was with the Israelis. But he had a wider and stronger view in favour of the rule of law. This was consistent with his outlook over twenty years or more. At first he thought Nasser was the transgressor. But when Eden reacted to this with the reckless folly of a military action violently opposed by nearly all Britain's allies, let alone the United Nations generally, Gaitskell regarded this as a far worse sin. He felt himself personally deceived by Eden. He also felt a sense of national humiliation. He was horrified by the fact and consequence of our being branded as an aggressor at the UN. He had a high respect for the institution and world opinion. He had always been ready to stand against an aggressor, and he was revolted by the fact that we had become one ourselves. Equally, he had been inclined to favour a bi-partisan foreign policy, and was the more resentful of Lord Avon for shattering the basis of this than were others who, believing the Tories were always wrong, had no store of reserve indignation to use against them.

Suez was a watershed in many different ways. For Britain it was the last imperial adventure, and led to ten years or more of cleaving closer than ever to the United States. For France, it led to ten years or more of distrust of the 'Anglo-Saxons'. It thus divided as well as defeated the two principal Western European powers. It also spread a sense of defeat and division at home. For Eden it meant the end of his premiership. For Gaitskell, who had aided this end by the vehemence of his attacks, it brought a new position at the centre of the most bitter party controversy for over 40 years. The old 'Butskellite' days seemed a long way off. Suez divided families, decimated the circulation of some newspapers, and enveloped the House of Commons in an atmosphere of chaotic bitterness.

The protagonist left politics. The antagonist remained, but not without the marks of the battle upon him. Suez impressed Gaitskell's personality, not wholly favourably, upon the nation. He rallied liberal opinion, but he offended the working class chauvinist vote. He temporarily lost his hold over the House of Commons: for several months the Government benches paid him back with mocking noise for his part in the destruction of Eden. More permanently, he acquired a new public *persona*. He finally exploded any view of himself as a mild-mannered, crossbench-thinking ex-don. Henceforward he was seen as a formidable and even ferocious controversialist, sometimes charging too haphazardly into an argument, arousing antipathy amongst his opponents no less than enthusiasm amongst his supporters. Thereafter, as a small but important example, he was never on really tolerable terms with his leading opponent: certainly not with Eden, but nor with Macmillan either.

In retrospect Mr Macmillan expresses a high view of Gaitskell, but at the time he wrote such private comments as 'he has ability without charm', which do not suggest closeness or instinctive understanding. Nor did Gaitskell ever really understand Mr Macmillan. He distrusted his flamboyance and thought he sailed too close to the political wind. His own reckless honesty, accompanied by a compulsive desire to set out every argument and every move in terms which were logically convincing—but sometimes emotionally provocative—made him disdainful of Macmillan's fondness for doing everything behind a smoke-screen.

During the period between Suez and the 1959 General Election, by contrast, Gaitskell showed very considerable skill at getting on with his own principal colleagues. He could not persuade Morrison to stay as deputy leader, but he helped to secure the election in his place of James Griffiths, loyal, highly respected and perfectly complementary. This election meant another defeat for Bevan, but it led to no real revival of the old pre-1955 animus. Harold Wilson immediately took over the new leader's previous role as Shadow Chancellor, and in 1967 Bevan became

Shadow Foreign Secretary. From there forward Gaitskell and Bevan worked together remarkably well. Particularly during their joint Russian visit of the summer of 1959 there was in Gaitskell's view even some approach to real friendship. If true, it was at once a tribute to Bevan's magnanimity and to Gaitskell's ability to harness the verve of Bevan's personality without hiding himself beneath its shadow.

There was therefore little of the weakness of disunity in the Labour Party approach to the 1959 election. Insofar as a major party, and particularly a left-wing one, can ever be united, the Labour Party was so in that year. There were as always differences of emphasis, style and, at the fringes, fundamental belief. But all the leading figures were in harmonious harness. There is no support here for the view that Gaitskell's leadership was naturally disruptive.

Nevertheless, he lost the election, and lost it decisively. The result was the biggest Conservative majority since the War. Why did this happen? Gaitskell fought neither a flat nor a foolish campaign. On the whole he was skilful, although he made one significant mistake, for which he was bitterly critical of himself, and which Macmillan fully exploited. He gave a promise that there would be no increase in income tax in order to finance the Labour programme. It put him on the defensive—always a bad position for the 'outside' candidate. He had to explain rather than challenge. But it was the only clear error, and he more than balanced it by sustaining throughout a note which was a mixture of high principle and practical concern. Meetings were good, workers were adequate and much of the Press was friendly. He both enthused the faithful and excited the uncommitted.

But the hidden mood of the country was against him. There was a strong latent satisfaction with the new affluence of the past few years. People did not parade this satisfaction much, but it was there, and was well exploited by the deft materialism of Mr Macmillan's campaign. In the circumstances no radical leader could have won. Gaitskell did at least as well as anyone else could have done. But he was bitterly disappointed. He had started the campaign with a realistic view of the difficulties. As it went on he convinced himself, and not merely for public purposes, that he was winning. On the Sunday evening before the poll he wrote out his Cabinet list. Four days later, in the Leeds City Hall, and with the television cameras frequently upon him, this brave hope died. As the Conservative gains mounted, previously damned-up waves of tiredness rolled over him, and as they did so he faced the prospect, not of the period of constructive power for which he was perfectly poised, but of the inevitable bickering of a three-times defeated party. He conceded defeat with quiet grace and a slow, rather sad smile. Then he allowed himself barely 48 hours of recuperation before facing the dismal prospect which lay ahead.

Dispute within the Labour Party was unavoidable. Gaitskell's instinct and decision was to meet it head on, to leave no one in any doubt where he stood, to accept the risk that he might well lose the leadership and retire into failure, with all the bright hopes of 1955 having ended with defeat at the polls and rejection by his own followers. On the other hand, if he won he would emerge as a strong leader, in command of a responsible party, which had got over its fevers early in the Parliament and could face the next election with conviction and confidence.

His strategy was as good as it was courageous. And it showed every sign of working. By the time of his death his position inside and outside the party was commanding. He deserved victory and there was a clear prospect that, in 1964, he would secure it. But his tactics (enthusiastically supported by me) had been appalling. He believed so much in attack rather than in supine retreat that he picked the first quarrel himself. At the Blackpool Conference, six weeks after the election, so far from applying balm he gave the party a tough, provocative analysis of where it had gone wrong. And he proposed his own remedy, the re-writing of that part of the constitution—Clause 4—which made a ritualistic rather than a practical statement of basic aims. Looking back, this was clearly a mistake. There was not much to be gained, and a lot of energy and goodwill to be wasted. It was the wrong war in the wrong place, fought at the best to an unsatisfactory draw.

After the stalemate came the counter attack. It was on another front, that of unilateralism and neutralism *versus* the commitment to the Atlantic alliance and the defence policy which this entailed. But basically it was the same issue—whether the Labour Party was to be a broad-based, responsible party of power, or a much narrower inward-looking group, compensating for its own defeats by the virulence with which it blamed others for having brought them about. During the spring and summer of 1960 the unilateralist forces built up with frightening speed. Union after union toppled almost casually into their camp. Gaitskell's position became more exposed than that of any party leader since Baldwin in 1930.

At the Scarborough Conference that autumn the almost unthinkable and hitherto unprecedented occurred. On the central policy issue of the year the leader was defeated. It had almost—but no quite—happened to Attlee in 1954, and it had then been assumed that, had the narrow result gone the other way, it would have destroyed his leadership. Gaitskell in

1960 fully realised that this was a possible, even a likely outcome. But he was determined not to go down without a fight. There were three theoretical possibilities open to him. He could have accepted the temporary instructions of conference, and tried to lead the Parliamentary Party along a course in which he did not believe, and where every milestone would make a mockery of his previous words. Or he could have resigned. Or he could hold on, for a year at least, and wage a desperate battle to change the decision. In the most memorable speech of his life, a few minutes before the vote which he knew must go against him, he rejected the two earlier choices, the first with contumely, and committed himself to the fight:

Supposing all of us, like well behaved sheep were to follow the policies of unilateralism and neutralism, what kind of an impression would that make upon the British people? ... I do not believe that the Labour members of Parliament are prepared to act as time servers. I do not believe they will do this, and I will tell you why—because they are men of conscience and honour. People of the so-called Right and so-called Centre have every justification for having a conscience, as well as people of the so-called Left. I do not think they will do this because they are honest men, loyal men, steadfast men, experienced men, with a lifetime of service to the Labour Movement.

.... What sort of people do you think we are? Do you think we can simply accept a decision of this kind? Do you think we can become overnight the pacifists, unilateralists and fellow-travellers that other people are? How wrong can you be? As wrong as you are about the attitude of the British people. ...

We may lose the vote today, the result may deal this party a grave blow. There will be many of us who will not accept that the blow must be mortal, who will not believe that such an end is inevitable. There are some of us who will fight and fight and fight again to save the party we love. We will fight and fight and fight again to bring back sanity and honesty and dignity, so that our party with its great past may retain its glory and its greatness.

This course he laid down for himself, difficult and hazardous in any circumstances, was only possible if his old bastion of the Parliamentary Labour Party would hold firm. It did. When Harold Wilson hesitantly decided to run against him for the leadership he was defeated by a more than two-to-one majority. But this was only the beginning of Gaitskell's battle. Throughout the coming winter he 'fought, fought and fought again' on innumerable platforms up and down the country. Often much of his audience was hostile and bitter. But he did not waiver. One of his greatest strengths was his faith in the power of reasoned argument. The superiority of the multilateralist case was to him so overwhelming that intelligent people of goodwill must surely be convinced if he explained it clearly enough. This he untiringly did. But as late as March it looked as though it would not be enough. He envisaged the prospect of a second and final defeat, and took it sadly but calmly. Then, with bewildering and inspiring rapidity, the whole outlook changed. The unions followed each other back into the Gaitskell camp as quickly as the year before, they had moved the other way. Many of the constituency parties did the same. The victory which this made certain was ratified at Blackpool in October, 1961. It left Gaitskell in a far stronger position than he had been before Scarborough. He was dominant in the Labour Party and he had impressed the public outside as a leader of force, courage and wisdom. The future seemed to lie open before him.

In fact he had only another 15 months left. During this period his problems were considerably diminished but by no means over. The first was the Common Market. He became highly critical towards Britain's first application. This attitude offended many of his closest supporters. It is a subject about which I find it peculiarly difficult to write objectively. I can only record, as I did much nearer the time, that while his attitude seemed to me not wholly consistent with his previous general outlook on world affairs, it was certainly not reached by a sudden tactical lurch. Like all his political positions it was fixed partly by logic and partly by emotion, and the emotion arose largely from his attachment to the Commonwealth, both old and new. If any one man decisively influenced him, it was K. B. Lall, the immensely able and persuasive Indian Ambassador to the Six. When I saw Mr Lall in Delhi in 1972 and told him this, he was flattered but a little surprised, particularly as he then took a much more benevolent attitude towards British membership.

Would Gaitskell himself have changed his view had he lived on throughout the 'sixties? I think it at least possible that he would, especially as his main Commonwealth counter-argument is the one which has crumbled most rapidly over the past decade. But no-one can know, and the attribution of posthumous views is usually both unwise and unfair. What I am sure is that, if he did so at all, he would have moved slowly, and then stuck with great tenacity.

The other major problem of this twilight period was the Commonwealth Immigrants' Bill, the first measure to place any restriction on free Commonwealth entry into this country. Gaitskell opposed it with passion and vigour. He saw it as the beginning of a racialist road along which he would not take a single step. And so great then was his prestige that the whole Labour Party, only a little hesitantly, accepted this lead. It was a position to which it is now difficult to believe that he could possibly have held. As a practical democrat he would have had to move. But he would have suffered great anguish in the process.

All his struggles illustrated some blemishes as well as exceptional strength. He would not have been a perfect Prime Minister. He was stubborn, rash, and could in a paradoxical way become too emotionally committed to an over-rational position which, once he had thought it rigorously through, he believed must be the final answer. He was only a moderately good judge of people. Yet when these faults are put in the scales and weighed against his qualities they shrivel away. He had purpose and direction, courage and humanity. He was a man for raising the sights of politics. He clashed on great issues. He avoided the petty bitterness of personal jealousy. He could raise banners which men were proud to follow, but he never perverted his own leadership ability: it was infused by sense and humour, and by a desire to change the world, not for his own satisfaction, but so that people might more enjoy living in it. He was rarely obsessed either by politics or himself. He was that very rare phenomenon, a great politician who was also an unusually agreeable man.

His death on January 18th, 1963, only four weeks away from the full vigour of his activity, dismayed the nation more than any other British political death of the post-war world. The shock of sudden loss and unfulfilled promise always has about it a peculiar poignancy. But the sense of loss is usually short-lived and quickly dissolves for most people into semi-forgetfullness. With Gaitskell that is not so. For many there is a sense of long-term deprivation which, as the years go by, persists and even increases.

ADLAI STEVENSON

Adlai Stevenson

The first time I saw Adlai Stevenson was in July, 1953. After the splendid but massive failure of his 1952 campaign he had spent five months travelling, mostly in Asia. He had received world acclaim to set against his national defeat. London was the last stage of his journey. I heard him speak briefly to an all-party House of Commons tea meeting. The chairman introduced him with a somewhat self-conscious impartiality: America was indeed fortunate to have been able to choose between two candidates of the distinction of General Eisenhower and Governor Stevenson. Stevenson's reply was less heavily felicitous. I recall it as being brief, graceful, self-deprecatory, and mildly moving. It was not Olympian, but it was agreeable and satisfying. It confirmed me, then a young back-bencher with few American contacts, in a simple view that it was a tragedy he had not been elected.

I did not speak to him on that occasion. Nor did I know him until another seven or eight years had passed, and he had suffered both the further defeat of 1956, still more overwhelming than the previous one, and, with the nomination and election of John F. Kennedy in 1960, the final elimination of his presidential hopes. Then in the last four years of his life, when he was a renowned but not altogether happy ambassador to the United Nations, I saw him frequently. I spoke to him on the telephone an hour before he died. I had sent a message asking him to lunch with a few people at my house on the following day. He rang back to accept with the enthusiasm for any social engagement, particularly a small one, which he always managed to display. 'Good', he said as we concluded, 'I will see you just after one o'clock tomorrow.' He did not. Later that afternoon he collapsed and died on the pavement of Grosvenor Street.

He was 65, having been born, conveniently for reckoning his age at any stage in his career, at the beginning of 1900. He lived his life in the American equivalent of the British Victorian age. Unlike the original it was not a period of peace. But in most other respects the first 60 years of this century bore for America many of the characteristics of the long years of the reign of the old Queen. There was the same sense of steadily expanding power, the same belief that rapidly increasing material wealth contained the key to most of the problems of the nation and the world, the same conviction that the domestic political system, whatever its blemishes, was the best that history had ever seen, and that its fundamental principles, subject to a little special packaging, were suitable for export as well as for home consumption. Of course there were differences. The set-back of the American slump years was more severe than anything known in Victorian England, but in the context of the century the miseries which followed 1929 were relatively short-lived. And the disparate origins of the American people, together with the tradition of violence which sprang out of the Civil War and the settlement of the West, meant that there was always a stronger under-current of fear and tension.

Throughout Stevenson's lifetime, however, these did little more than dent the surface of American national self-confidence. His liberal voice spoke from within this framework of assurance. It was a voice which, even though it never achieved a position of full authority, helped to civilise and make more responsible this plenitude of American power. It made it more acceptable to the world. He challenged the complacency of Eisenhower and the self-righteousness of John Foster Dulles, and was a counterpoise to the roughness of Lyndon Johnson. But he was nonetheless a product, although a sensitive and unselfish one, of this period of American leadership. For him there was never a conflict between liberalism and commitment abroad. To be responsible was to be involved, from Berlin to Korea, from South-East Asia to Latin America.

This background of power was far from giving him a brash self-assurance. Brashness was about as alien to his character as demagogic bombast was to such an English product of the zenith of empire as Arthur Balfour. National self-confidence does not cure personal neuroses. Disraeli was a hypochondriac, Rosebery an ill-tempered insomniac, Kipling a misanthrope, and Leslie Stephen and Mark Pattison were tormented by religious doubt. But the troubles of these quintessential figures do not undermine the essential buoyancy of Britain's imperial heyday. Compared with their neuroses, Stevenson's self-doubt was anodyne. He merely wondered from time to time whether he was suited to the office for which he strove for a decade, and whether a public career was not inevitably corrupting of a man's private personality. But he did not question the parameters within which, had he succeeded, he would have sought to exercise the supreme power, or within which, without full success, he used the very considerable influence which his fame brought him. His self-doubt had a peculiar charm. It did not extend to the values of the nation of which, even before he was given this particular title, he was the best, but sometimes ill-regarded, ambassador.

Of what did his charm—always a somewhat gossamer-like concept—consist? First it lay in his great courtesy in private relations. He was always writing whole notes of thanks or appreciation. More importantly he nearly always turned his full concentration upon any conversation. He preferred it to be bilateral rather than general. He treated his *vis-à-vis*, whoever he or she was, very much as an individual, and shaped the tone of the interchange accordingly.

He was the direct opposite of those politicians who address everyone as though they were public meetings. His conversation was highly particularised. But his public face was also remarkably like his private face. As a result, while not lacking resonance, he came near to addressing public meetings as though they were individuals. If you admired his style, it was immensely appealing.

There is a view that Stevenson was the quintessential upper-class figure in American politics. The one unfriendly (but not unskilful) biography which he has attracted is sub-titled 'Patrician Among the Politicians'. I think this view is wrong, both in fact and in inference. Stevenson did not come from a signally upper-class background. The American aristocracy is an aristocracy of wealth, preferably old wealth, and mostly Eastern seaboard. His family were well established, but they were not Easterners and, although thoroughly comfortable, had no vast riches. He lived his life against a secure and established background, but he was much less affected by his family provenance and privileges than Franklin Roosevelt, or Nelson Rockefeller or Averell Harriman. In origin he was much more the equivalent of a Haldane or a Cripps or a Butler, than of a Salisbury or a Churchill. And as a politician his hesitancies, fastidiousness and occasional incompetences were much more the product of a complicated, rather wistful personality than of any social syndrome. He was more akin to Eugene McCarthy, the son of a small Minnesota farmer, than to Roosevelt, the last of a long line of Hudson Valley squires.

Stevenson was born in Los Angeles, later to be one of his great centres of strength, but almost by accident. It is of little more significance than the fact that Lloyd George was born in Manchester. His parents both came from Illinois. His father, Lewis Stevenson, spent about ten years in various places on the West Coast, mainly because he thought it would be good for his always somewhat ailing health. He managed Hearst newspapers and occasionally other Hearst property. In 1906 he came back to

Illinois, to Bloomington, the home town of himself and his wife and their many relations, and became a large-scale farm manager, supervising 12,000 acres on behalf of an aunt. Bloomington, 125 miles south-west of Chicago, in wide corn country, then had about 30,000 inhabitants and, was an agreeable mixture of farm centre and college town. The Stevenson forebears had been there since it became a settled community about 1850. They were all of old American stock and had come in from Pennsylvania, Kentucky and the Carolinas.

Lewis Stevenson also engaged in politics, becoming Illinois Secretary of State in 1913. He knew the great national figures of the Democratic Party, to which he had a firm hereditary affiliation, and they treated him as a man of considerable local importance. As early as 1912 Adlai was taken to visit Woodrow Wilson on the New Jersey coast. Lewis Stevenson was considered as a vice-presidential candidate in 1928, but Al Smith preferred Senator Robinson of Arkansas. He died in 1929, aged 60. His wife was the daughter of W. O. Davis, the proprietor of the Bloomington *Pantagraph*, a highly successful and well-established local daily newspaper. Davis was a traditional Republican and his newspaper lived in the glory of having been the first to suggest Lincoln for the presidency.

Lewis Stevenson's father, Adlai E. Stevenson I, was a more serious politician than he was himself. He had been appointed Assistant Postmaster General in Grover Cleveland's first administration, when the Democrats came back office-hungry after 20 years of post-Civil War deprivation. Old Adlai's particular contribution had been to remove 40,000 Republican postmasters from office and replace them with good Democrats. This brought him considerable popularity in the party. It also helped to bring him the vice-presidential nomination in 1892 when Cleveland became the only President ever to return after an interval to the White House. In 1900 he again ran for Vice-President, unsuccessfully on this occasion. For the second time the Democratic ticket was then headed by William Jennings Bryan. The Great Commoner of the Cross of Gold was a better spell binder than a vote winner. McKinley, who was to be shot at Buffalo the following summer, was re-elected without difficulty. Theodore Roosevelt, elected against Stevenson, found he had gained the presidency as well. Adlai I continued in politics, ran unsuccessfully for Governor of Illinois in 1908, and was still active in support of Wilson in 1912. He died in 1914.

This was Stevenson's family background: political, prosperous, rooted, small-town orientated. The house in which he was brought up was a ten roomed, grey-stucco, gothic gabled villa set back from an elm-lined street.

His parents owned no other house, but none the less moved about a good deal. Summers were spent at the *Pantagraph* grandfather's house on Pine Lake in Michigan. Some part of a winter was often passed at a rented house in the South. In 1911 the family went to Europe for six months.

It was an agreeable and on the whole relaxed upbringing, marred by one dreadful incident. When he was 12 he accidentally shot dead in his own house a 16-year-old girl, who was his sister's closest friend and their distant cousin. He was hardly guilty even of carelessness. The gun with which he was playing had been sent for and checked as empty of bullets by the older children. But the effect of the tragedy was temporarily devastating, and must have left some more permanent scars. It may have accounted for the fact that, although he went to school in the East, as his father had done before him, he did not go until he was 16. He then went to Choate in Connecticut for two years, and then on to Princeton.

A combination of old Southern family connection and the more recent influence of Woodrow Wilson made Princeton the choice. But Stevenson was not in a position to exercise it too disdainfully. He had some difficulty in getting in, and was never a particularly distinguished undergraduate. But he was a successful university journalist, enjoyed himself, and retained a good deal of continuing sentiment for 'Old Nassau'.

He graduated in 1922 and went on to Harvard Law School. At first he hated the transition from Princeton to the harsher, more impersonal atmosphere of Cambridge. But this initial distaste disappeared and was not the reason for his terminating the course, without his law degree, in the spring of 1924. He was wanted at home, following the death of his editor uncle, in order to try to maintain the position of his side of the family in the future direction of the *Pantagraph*. He became editor, a cousin became business manager, and a dispute about shares began to grind its way through the courts. Eventually the Stevensons were defeated. Control passed to the other branch of the family. The *Pantagraph* was made safe for Republicanism. And Adlai went back to the law. He finished off his Harvard work at Northwestern University in Chicago and was admitted to the Illinois bar in June 1926. Then, somewhat adventurously, he paid an extended summer visit to Russia. By the end of the year, less adventurously, he had established himself, by Princeton rather than nepotic influence, as a law clerk in a Chicago firm of the highest repute and the best possible financial contacts. Its name, Cutting, Moore and Sidley, was a guarantee of Anglo-Saxon respectability in that strange city of hope and harshness, sophistication and squalor, snobbery and violence. The salary, at $1,500 a year, was less impressive.

For the rest of his life Stevenson was a Chicago man. Bloomington rather faded into the background. He maintained the connection when campaigning in mid-Illinois, but not much on other occasions. It left him with a love of the Middle Western countryside, but he transferred this easily enough to the very different area around Lake Forest, the epitome of rich America's *urbs in rurem*, near where, at Libertyville, he subsequently established a permanent country house and farm.

It was his early Chicago life, more than his family and Bloomington upbringing, which put upon Stevenson something of the stamp of a Scott Fitzgerald socialite of the restless 'twenties. In fact he was not very restless, nor particularly pleasure-loving, and worked hard, with growing but not sensational success, at the law. But in those days a law clerkship in a top La Salle Street firm, combined with membership of the Chicago Harvard-Yale-Princeton Club, was a fairly close American equivalent to being a Brigade of Guards subaltern in pre-1914 London. It put him on every hostess's list, and he responded with adequate eagerness and great social success to the voracity of their boom-years appetite. He lived mostly in a small apartment on the North Shore 'Gold Coast' but spent much of the summer in a shared house at Lake Forest. So he was never far from the centre of the social scene. The culmination of this phase of his life was his marriage in December, 1928 to Ellen Borden. She was rich, pretty and barely 20, one of the most sought-after butterflies of the Chicago hedgerows. She lived in a mock renaissance château on Lake Shore Drive. Her father, rich by inheritance, both made and lost a lot of money. But in 1928, like most American men of property, he was on the upswing.

The marriage was a gradual failure. Various explanations have been offered for this, the most frequent being that Ellen resented the shift in the balance of attention, and found no compensation in her husband's mounting political success. At the beginning she was the more sought-after and he witty, charming, and easy social coinage, but superficially little more. At the end, 21 years later, he was a national figure, and the Borden fortune largely dissipated. Never having known Mrs Stevenson, I offer no view. What is certain is that the break-up was a source of deep and lasting distress to Stevenson. It is also true that, particularly in its early stages, the marriage embedded him deep in the Chicago social world. He retained many of the friendships of those early days.

Stevenson's first foray away from La Salle Street and Lake Forest came at the beginning of Roosevelt's first term. He went to Washington for 18 months as an assistant counsel in the Agricultural Assistance Administration. Then he returned to Chicago and his law practice. He became a partner in 1935, and with the reorganization and renaming of the firm in 1937 graduated to a major role and a steadily growing income. By the outbreak of the war in Europe he was making $30,000 or $40,000 a year.

During this period he also became increasingly involved in community affairs, notably the Council on Foreign Relations, but also a few charities, a cross-party clean government league, and some regular party activity at the time of Roosevelt's second term election. He was then 36 and it is doubtful if he had ever before made a straight political speech. Nor did he make more than a handful for another 12 years thereafter. But he none the less began to make for himself a considerable public name amongst a minority audience. His introductions of visiting speakers at the Council became known as models of wit and felicity. They were delivered in a throw-away manner. They were not so composed. On one occasion when he was asked to insert a new point he recoiled in horror. He could not possibly do it without at least an hour's further preparation.

In 1939 he spent the early summer in England, and returned oppressed by the shadow of the coming war. His most memorable political conversation, with a certain appropriateness, was with Harold Nicolson. They both had only one foot in politics. Soon after his return he began his first substantial political enterprise, his first attempt to mould opinion. He became chairman of the Chicago chapter of William Allen White's 'Committee to Defend America by Aiding the Allies'. The length of the title was made necessary by an ambiguity of approach. The aim was to produce an Allied victory while keeping America at peace. Eventually the committee broke on the ambiguity. White said that a suitable motto might be 'The Yanks Are Not Coming'. Others, including Stevenson, were shocked. But by then a lot of vital work had been done. Chicago was a key segment of the ideological battle line. Isolationist sentiment was strong there. Colonel McCormick had the big gun of the *Tribune*. Stevenson had to stand up to a lot of abuse, both public and private. He greatly disliked it, but his controversial nerves improved under the bombardment. He organized and presided over one meeting of 16,000 people.

In July, 1941, he again took a job in Washington, this time as personal assistant to Frank Knox, the Republican proprietor of the *Chicago Daily News*, who had run for the vice-presidency in 1936, but whom Roosevelt had recently appointed Secretary of the Navy. Later that year he began to be attracted by elective office, and contemplated the possibility of running for the U.S. Senate. But American entry into the war turned his thoughts away from that. He stayed with Knox until 1943, and was then sent to try to organise civil administration in Italy. At the end of the war and in early 1946 he was occupied with the creation of the United Nations. He spent several months in London as the principal U.S. representative on the Preparatory Commission. He had become well-known in allied diplomatic circles, but not to the public, either at home or abroad.

A year after the end of war in Europe he was once more back in his Chicago law office. He was 46. He had refused an embassy. He had a good record of public service. He had developed a feel for diplomatic negotiation and some rather ill-directed sense of ambition. Not for the first or last time in his life he was uncertain what he wanted to do.

* *

By the summer of 1947, after little more than a year back in Chicago, Stevenson began to be tentatively, mock-reluctantly, interested in elective office. A presidential year was on the horizon. Truman's stock was low, and the likelihood of his defeat was strong. On the other hand the possibility of a Democrat of Stevenson's stamp securing nomination in Illinois had improved. The old Kelly-Nash machine had been beaten in Chicago. Colonel Jacob Arvey, a diminutive Jewish lawyer of humble origins and considerable political skill, had taken over as head of the Cook County Democratic organisation. Maurice Kennelly, a successful Irish businessman with a 'reform' reputation and a broader appeal, had triumphantly replaced Kelly as mayor. Richard Daley, later to have his revenge, had suffered with most of the rest of the old guard, and been beaten for Sheriff.

What attracted Stevenson was the United States Senate. If nominated, he could run against an isolationist, McCormick-sponsored incumbant who was an old enemy. If elected, he could pursue his main foreign policy interests. A trio of influential Chicago gentlemen with little direct political involvement began to canvass actively on his behalf. There were also recommendations from Mrs Roosevelt and Secretary Byrnes. Arvey was half-impressed. Mayor Kennelly's success, and his own predilections, made him open to the idea of candidates with an appeal to middle opinion. But he was not sure about either Stevenson or his associates. He thought they might be too detached from the realities even of reformed Illinois politics. He made enquiries, he carried out a visit of inspection to Libertyville, he gratefully received an assurance from Stevenson that, contrary to rumour, he had not been at Oxford, and 'not even Eton'. Eventually, he gave them half of what they wanted. He preferred Paul Douglas, then a professor at the University of Chicago, for the Senate nomination, but

Stevenson could run for Governor. A thirty-man committee would make the formal decision, but Arvey had made up his mind.

Stevenson had more difficulty in making up his. He brooded over a long snow-bound weekend at Libertyville. He took his indecision with him back to Chicago. He finally gave a rather miserable positive answer five minutes before the deadline which Arvey had calmly set him. There were quite good objective reasons for his doubt. It was federal not state politics which interested him. It was to Washington not Springfield that he wished to go, and the fact that Ellen Stevenson preferred Springfield did not greatly weigh. But there were probably subjective factors too. He always liked to be pressed to do a job rather than to seek it. To accept a bone which he had been tossed was not easily compatible with this stance.

Nevertheless it was, of course, a sizeable bone. Illinois was a great state, and the governorship, with its tradition of Altgeld, a great office. In the past, at least, it had counted for more than the Senate. It took him back to his family roots. And as the campaign wore on he became captivated by the power and personality of a state which was almost a country. 'I've seen Illinois in a capsule', he wrote in a private letter, '—the beauty of the south, the fruit belt, the coalfields, the oilfields, the great industrial area around East St Louis—and everywhere the rich, black fecund earth stretching away and away ... But I'm getting a little lyrical for a practical politician.'

In either case the nomination was far from equivalent to election. Arvey indeed, thought that both Stevenson and Douglas were likely to be defeated, dragged down by Truman's unpopularity. He was choosing candidates who could put up the best losing performance. But Arvey was much too disillusioned with Truman. He had joined in a move, supported by Douglas, to try to draft Eisenhower as Democratic candidate in his place. Stevenson stood firmly aside, and at the Philadelphia Convention in July, in alliance, paradoxically, with ex-Mayor Kelly, expressed complete and early confidence in the President's ability to win.

Stevenson's opponent was Dwight H. Green, who had been Governor since 1940. He had started as a reformer, but he and his administration had deteriorated into a lethargy and corruption which were epitomized by the Centralia colliery disaster, in which 111 miners had been killed after repeated complaints of lax safety which had been ignored by Green's inspectors who were more concerned with soliciting campaign contributions from the owners. Green was nevertheless a considerable figure who, right up to the Republican Convention, was a real possibility for either position on his party's national ticket. His defensive position looked reasonably strong. There had only been three Democratic Governors in the history of Illinois, and 1948 did not seem likely to be a year in which this small score would be increased.

Stevenson's campaign ran well but not easily. The machine, having tossed him the nomination, left him very much on his own until the last few weeks. His amateurs were enthusiastic but not very efficient. And his rich friends proved less forthcoming with their money than they had earlier suggested. He was occasionally down almost to his own resources. His speaking was at first rather hesitant and over-prepared. Later the over-preparation did not show through, but it continued to occupy a great deal of his time and meant that his set-piece speeches could not be as thickly surrounded by hand-shaking expeditions as his supporters wished. But he seemed to be making an impact upon the voters. His favourite campaign phrase was: 'I am not a politician, I am a citizen.' He had the support of a strong 'Republicans for Stevenson' group, and many Illinois newspapers urged the electors to vote for Dewey for President and for Stevenson for Governor. By the eve of the election his prospects had clearly advanced well beyond the ten to one chance which was all he had been allowed in the summer. But his supporters were far less confident than he himself. In the event he won by a landslide victory, with a record plurality of over half a million. The great bulk of it, as was natural with any Democratic candidate, came from Chicago, but he also had a narrow and unprecedented lead in the rest of the state. He ran ahead of Douglas, and even further ahead of the unexpectedly successful Truman, whose Illinois majority was only 33,000.

Stevenson had thus established himself as a remarkable vote-getter in a key state. It remained to be seen what he would make of the governorship of that state. The next four years gave him the only opportunity of his life for the exercise of major executive responsibility. They are therefore important in any evaluation of how good a President he would have made. He worked extremely hard. In part this was a reaction to the break-up of his marriage after nine months at Springfield. This left him somewhat lonely in the Executive Mansion, oversized in its pre-Civil War gingerbread style. Yet he was not alone. His sister and her retired diplomat husband soon moved in. He had a lot of friends, whom he saw frequently there or at Libertyville. And he was surrounded by a devoted staff, mostly of young Chicago lawyers, with whom he was on easy and intimate terms. It was not absolute loneliness but more a desire to prove himself by public success to compensate for private failure which drove him to heroically long hours. 'I have failed as a husband. I have failed as a father. I will succeed as a governor,' he rather over-dramatically told his sister when late one night she tried to drag him away from his office.

Yet the keynote of his administration was certainly not demonic. It was far too urbane for that. He rarely lost his temper. He was confronted with a difficult legislature: a bare and fairly corrupt Democratic majority in the House, a Republican one in the State Senate. In contrast with President Truman's contemporary methods in Washington he did not abuse those who stood in his way. He treated them with a distant courtesy. He eschewed deals, sometimes quite respectable ones, but maintained relations with all who could help him, and resorted to occasional polite but moderately effective public admonition. He got two-thirds of his legislative programme through, but the last third contained many of the most important measures.

If the legislature frustrated some of his bills, so he frustrated some of theirs. He was one of the most elegant drafters of veto messages in the history of American executive office. This elegance reflected itself in his speaking style, which became fairly established during these years. It was self-deprecatory, evocative, literary and raised the sights of most of his audiences without disappearing over their horizons. He did not hold them by flashing eye or stirring populism; he caressed them with a persuasive high-mindedness without in most instances causing a deep unease. If there was a fault of form it was a lack of a hard structure of logical argument. He shone shafts of light and wit into most subjects, but he did not relentlessly take the subjects apart and then put them together again in his own mould. His speeches were isolated works of art rather than stations on a line along which he wished to travel. He half acknowledged this when, at the end of his political career he was introducing John Kennedy in California: 'Do you remember', he said, 'that in classical times when Cicero had finished speaking, the people said "How well he spoke", but when Demosthenes had finished speaking, they said "Let us march".'

Stevenson's reputation increased steadily throughout his period as Governor. It probably rose faster than his level of accomplishment, although this was considerable. He gave the state better government in a rather non-ideological way. He took the highway police and some other agencies out of politics. He got better men to accept public appointments. He vastly improved the provision for mental health. He ran up against his own fair share of scandals, including another mine disaster and the corruption of two of his close associates, but his personal reputation was such that he had no difficulty in keeping this from damaging the core of his administration.

Despite his private troubles, he much enjoyed his period as Governor. During it he almost epitomised Gladstone's maxim that a man should never lose a night's sleep over any purely *public* event. Despite his long hours, he conducted his government in a fairly relaxed way. He was far from being an impeccable administrator. He concentrated too much on detail. He was much too inclined to give the same job, rather in Roosevelt's way, to two different men. But, unlike Roosevelt, he did it to ease personal difficulties rather than to create the tension of conflict. His associates enjoyed working with him, both because they liked his company and felt they had hitched their wagons to a star. As his term went on his national publicity grew into a favourable flood. He was clearly of presidential calibre.

Yet he did not want to be a candidate in 1952. He wanted to go on as Governor. This was partly out of shrewdness and partly out of modesty. Once he realised that Eisenhower was likely to be the Republican candidate, he did not believe that, with 20 years of office round their necks, the Democrats could win. He also had some genuine doubts about his own fitness for the supreme office; and to these he added a special fastidiousness about taking the plunge into full and lasting fame. 'I can't face the possibility of never really being alone again', he told a friend, 'of never, as long as I live, being unidentified, of never again being a private person.'

Accordingly, when Truman summoned Stevenson to Washington in January 1952, and offered him presidential support for the nomination, Stevenson said 'No'. Truman was not pleased. He had wanted, and expected, his accolade to be received with gratitude. But he explained the rebuff by assuming that Stevenson was unprepared for the offer. This was not so. And Truman could not maintain this view when Stevenson again refused in March. The President then used a public dinner to announce his own refusal to seek another term. Stevenson was present. The attention immediately focussed upon him. He remained elusive. The next day, in a television interview famous for his comment that 'flattery hurts no-one—that is if he doesn't inhale,' he remained obdurate: 'I want to run for Governor. I seek no other office. I have no other ambition.'

As the spring and summer went on, Truman became impatient and transferred his support to Vice-President Barkley. But the Stevenson boom continued to grow. The other possible candidates were Senator Kefauver of Tennessee, Senator Russell of Georgia, Senator Kerr of

Oklahoma and Averell Harriman. None of them generated much ground swell, although Kefauver won a few primaries. The Convention met in Chicago in mid-July. On the Sunday Stevenson met the Illinois delegation and reiterated his reluctance: 'I ask ... that you all abide by my wishes not to nominate me, nor to vote for me if I should be nominated.' On the Monday he went some way to neutralize this by a welcoming speech, which as Governor of the home state it naturally fell to him to make, and which was perfectly phrased to arouse the delegates to a high pitch of enthusiasm. One act of self-discipline which he could not impose upon himself was to make a bad speech.

That evening he refused an invitation to dine with Truman. On the Thursday his name was placed in nomination by the Governor of Indiana. On the Friday the balloting began. On the first ballot Stevenson was second to Kefauver, and only a shade ahead of Russell. On the second he was still second. On the third he surged ahead. He was quickly pushed over the required total. It was the only draft in American history apart from that of Garfield in 1880, and that was on the 36th ballot. But even Stevenson's took a little time. When it had happened, but only then, he accepted Truman's sponsorship. He entered the convention hall with the President and was presented to the delegates by him. His acceptance speech contained some notable passages, both of phrase and of substance, although, oddly, the style in places now sounds a little florid:

I accept your nomination and your programme. I should have preferred to have heard these words uttered by a stronger, a wiser, a better man than myself. . . . I have not sought the honour you have done me. . . . I have asked the Merciful Father of us all to let this cup pass from me. But from such dread responsibility one does not shrink in fear, in self-interest, or in false humility. So, 'If this cup may not pass from me, except I drink it, thy will be done' . . . And now that you have made your decision, I will fight to win . . . with all my heart and soul. . . . [But] more important than winning the election is governing the nation. When the tumult and the shouting die, when the bands are gone and the lights are dimmed, there is the stark reality of responsibility in an hour of history haunted with those gaunt, grim spectres of strife, dissension and materialism at home, and ruthless inscrutable and hostile power abroad. . . .

Let's talk sense to the American people. Let's tell them the truth, that there are no gains without pains . . . The people are wise—wiser than the Republicans think. And the Democratic Party is the people's party, not the labour party, not the farmers' party, not the employers' party—it is the party of no-one because it is the party of everyone. That, I think, is our ancient mission. Where we have deserted it, we have failed. With your help there will be no desertion now. Better we lose the election than mislead the people; better we lose than misgovern the people.

Stevenson had set his own style for the campaign, except that there were no jokes on this occasion. He would make a high-minded, non-partisan appeal, stressing America's world role and world duty. It would be an appeal to commitment not to an easy life. His reluctance right to the last moment was no doubt genuine. Had it been a calculated cloak for a relentless, unvarying ambition, it would have required not merely a degree of self-deceit which was alien to his character but also a monumental nerve and self-confidence which were equally unlike him. At the same time there was an element of a two-way bet about his behaviour. If it led to another candidate, well and good. He could continue in Springfield, where he was happy. Maybe he was not equipped for the presidency. In any event, '56 might be a better year. But if he was to be the candidate in '52, he had to be on his own terms. He had to be free of at least some part of Truman's legacy. He had to fight, not as an heir, but as someone who would introduce a new spirit into Washington. His reluctance lost him Truman's friendship, but gave him as much of this freedom as it was possible for any Democrat to achieve.

It did not give him victory. Eisenhower was ahead at the beginning, and remained so throughout. Stevenson succeeded in narrowing the lead a little, but never looked really likely to do more. Probably it could not have been otherwise. Eisenhower was as near to unbeatable as it was possible to be. His combination of folksiness and re-assurance was immensely appealing to middle America. It made him impervious to Stevenson's higher-minded, more articulate campaign. Against Taft it might have worked. Against a national hero who said comfortable things it could not work.

Eisenhower would 'lead a crusade' (he had led *one* already, he stressed) this time to 'clear up the mess in Washington'. He would be hard on corruption and communism. Still more important for vote-winning was his 'I shall go to Korea' statement at Detroit on October 24th. The war there hung heavily over the nation throughout the campaign. It had cost America more casualties than World War I. Although far more creditable and successful than its successor in Vietnam it was nonetheless almost as unpopular, although less frenetically so. Eisenhower's promise to go there came as a shaft of light. Most Americans did not ask what he would do when he arrived. The General would surely find a way out.

Stevenson responded with a clearly-argued but defensive anti-appeasement statement. It was less appealing that the hopeful ambiguity of his opponent. Ironically, Stevenson had already decided to go to Korea himself if elected. But he had not announced it for fear of raising false hopes.

It was an exchange which was typical of the campaign. Stevenson's speeches were more responsible, better phrased, better delivered, enlivened by a wit which was wholly lacking in Eisenhower ('I offer my opponents a bargain: if they will stop telling falsehoods about us, I will stop telling the truth about them'), and better received by the immediate audiences. But they made less impact across the nation, partly because they were less well reported by an overwhelmingly Republican press, and partly because their message was less simple. Stevenson spread his effort across too wide and diffuse a range of subjects.

Eisenhower's campaign had some seamy edges. He did not disavow McCarthyism, and indeed appeared with the Senator in Wisconsin, cutting out of his speech there a passage of praise for General George Marshall, whom McCarthy had viciously attacked, and which had been in the original draft. This aroused Stevenson's particular contempt. 'Crusade indeed', was his comment. Marshall was 'General Eisenhower's greatest benefactor'. Yet the General had given his hand to those, not only McCarthy but also Senator Jenner of Indiana, who had traduced him. This was a break from Stevenson's habit of courteous, almost over-courteous, treatment of his opponent. He reserved most of his acerbic remarks for the then Senator Nixon, second man on the Republican ticket, who specialized in suggesting that the Democratic candidate was steeped in the Acheson-inspired conspiracy to hand over the United States to communism. Stevenson called him 'the brash and patronising young man who aspires to be Vice-President', and forcibly defended his own position in terms of classical liberalism.

Stevenson wound up his campaign in Chicago, where it had started, and awaited the returns in Springfield. At nine in the evening he was told what the result would be, and accepted it calmly. It was a disappointment (he had earlier thought he would win comfortably with 381 electoral votes) but it could be accommodated within his reiterated view that 'I don't *have* to be President'. He carried only nine states, all in or on the edge of the South, but Eisenhower's proportionate victory was not as great as those of Roosevelt in 1932 and 1936, or that of Hoover in 1928 or that of Harding in 1920. A few hours later he went across to his local hotel headquarters and conceded graciously. He added, spontaneously it seemed, that someone had once asked a fellow townsman—Lincoln—how it felt to lose: 'He said that it felt like a little boy who had stubbed his toe in the dark. He said that he was too old to cry, but it hurt too much to laugh'. He was as urbane in defeat, as he had been, four years before, in victory.

* *

Defeat left Stevenson with a lasting fame, both at home and abroad; dedicated minority support, particularly amongst the educated young, balanced by a strong current of criticism from others about the way in which he had conducted the campaign; and no very clear political role. His ardent supporters felt that he had widened their horizons and given them a purpose and commitment in politics which they had never before experienced. His detractors pointed out, with some justification, that he had been aloof, not very good on television, above the heads of much of his audience, sometimes elegantly flippant when he ought to have been stolidly earnest, and rather ill-organised. His lack of a clear future role was endemic in the American system. He automatically remained the titular head of his party. But he had no forum in which to exercise his leadership; and 1956 was a long way off, with a second attempt for a defeated candidate nearer to the exception than the rule.

He did not return to the law until 1954. The substantial office which he set up in Chicago was for the practice of politics. He had heavy campaign debts, but was not short of money. He travelled a lot, he wrote a lot, he spoke a lot. He remained in the news. His speeches were at first directed mainly to foreign affairs, and were a little bland. They achieved more effect when he turned to a hard domestic issue. His attack on McCarthyism at Miami Beach in March, 1954, made a significant contribution to the turning back of that malign tide. This was followed by a notably successful part in the mid-term elections of the following autumn. In six weeks he spoke in 34 states, and his speeches had more bite than in 1952. The Democrats regained control of both Houses of Congress. It was a considerable victory and improved both Democratic morale and Stevenson's stock.

But it did not mean that Eisenhower was dangerously vulnerable for 1956. He was always able to ride above the misfortunes of his party as well as the mistakes of his administration. And the collapse of McCarthy closed a Republican flank. If Stevenson had reason to be hesitant about 1952, he had still more reason for hesitancy in 1956. There were obvious attractions in missing a turn and waiting to run against a new Republican in 1960. He was unlikely to be forgotten.

To these attractions he was impervious. He did not push himself hard or prematurely, but by 1955 he made it obvious that he wanted the nomination. Until Eisenhower's heart attack in September of that year it looked as though he could have it for the asking. Then others, beckoned by a more encouraging prospect, entered the field. Kefauver began a vigorous campaign. Averell Harriman, at that time Governor of New

York and backed by Truman, who was getting his own back for 1952, switched his support from Stevenson to himself.

They both campaigned from a more hard-line Northern liberal point of view than did Stevenson. He was trying to breathe new life into the old Roosevelt coalition. They wrote off the South. He was for conciliation by means of steady but not precipitate or troop-enforced progress on Negro integration. But it soon became obvious that a 'unite the party' ticket would not enable him to avoid primary campaigning. He approached the task with repugnance, but also with confidence. The confidence was misplaced. He was badly beaten by Kefauver in Minnesota in March.

He might have been expected to recoil with dismay from such a setback. Curiously it had the opposite effect upon him. He held a press conference the next morning and said 'I feel simply that I have failed to communicate and must try harder'. Asked whether this meant more hand-shaking he smilingly acknowledged that a certain identity did seem to be established between a shaker and a shakee. Thereafter he shook a lot of hands. He ran, in his own words, 'like a singed cat'. He even wore an occasional fancy costume. He avenged Minnesota in Florida and swamped Kefauver in California.

At the convention, again in Chicago, he was comfortably nominated on the first ballot. But he paid a price for this. The primaries left him tired before the real campaign began. And they also left him a little shop-soiled. There was a new tendency to say 'He's just another politician'. Altogether the 1956 campaign, although in some ways more professional, lacked something of both the sparkle and the inspiration of 1952. It was intended to be domestically orientated. The theme was to be the *New America* to carry on the tradition of Wilson's *New Freedom*, Roosevelt's *New Deal* and Truman's *Fair Deal*. There was also to be a determined attempt to show Stevenson as a vigorous yet experienced challenger to a President who had been at best half-time, and was now manifestly not up to the job.

The strategy failed to work. Eisenhower was so brilliantly packaged and presented that whenever he got to a television studio he looked much fitter than his rushed and tired opponent. Stevenson's attack also got diverted, perhaps by a natural predilection, on to foreign and defence policy issues. He demanded an end to H-bomb tests and the replacement of the draft by a professional army. He was almost certainly right on both points, but he totally failed to convince ordinary American opinion that he could be more expert on either than the great General.

Then, in the last days of the campaign, the Suez War obtruded sharply. The strength of the Democrats was that people instinctively associated the Republicans with big business and neglect of the small man at home. The strength of the Republicans was that people instinctively feared that the Democrats were the war party. The diversion of strategy reduced the first strength and increased the second. It helped to produce a victory for Eisenhower still more decisive than that of 1952. His popular majority was $9\frac{1}{2}$ million. Stevenson carried only seven states. He won Missouri, where he had failed in 1952, but he dropped West Virginia, Louisiana and Kentucky. In neither campaign had he carried any of the big northern states, not even Illinois.

This second defeat was much worse for Stevenson than the first. On the former occasion he had greatly enhanced his reputation. He started the campaign as a successful Governor. He ended it as a world figure. And he could husband this reputation and live to fight another day. In 1956 he had gained nothing and on any likely prognosis was at the end of the road. Only Clay and Bryan in American history had been allowed third attempts, and Bryan's were not consecutive.

A month after the election Stevenson issued a formal statement of withdrawal. He would continue to work for the Democratic party, and to warn the American people 'against complacency and a false sense of security', but he would not again be a candidate. This governed his behaviour over the next four years. He was active. He continued to speak, to write and to travel the world. He was always treated as a major statesman. In 1958 he had a $2\frac{1}{2}$ hour dialogue with Krushchev in the Kremlin. He was kept at arm's length by the Southern Democratic leadership in the Congress. But so, indeed, were all the other possible future candidates. Johnson, leader in the Senate, and Rayburn, leader in the House, were playing a congressional not a presidential game.

Stevenson, however, was able to keep his imprint on Democratic policy through an advisory council on which he collected all the main figures of the past and the future: Truman, Harriman, Mrs Roosevelt, Kefauver, Humphrey and later Symington and Kennedy. His stamp remained that of anti-complacency at home and deep commitment abroad. He became increasingly concerned with the problems of the underdeveloped world, and sought to arouse America and NATO as a whole to the need for a sustained and massive forty-year programme to raise up the poor countries. He was against any rash adventures in support of Chiang Kai-Shek, and in favour of the admission of Peking to the United Nations. But he was also in favour of a strong and expensive defence posture, which indeed led on to the Kennedy/McNamara doctrine of flexible response.

There is also little doubt that, as the 1960 election came nearer, so he became in favour of a third try. He would hardly have been human had he felt otherwise. He had devoted some of his best years to fighting when it was not possible to win. For 1960 the prospect looked quite different. Nixon seemed to be emerging as the most likely successor. Stevenson viewed him with strong disapproval verging upon contempt. He was certain he could beat him. Moreover, he was constantly told, everywhere he went in the world, that he was the man to whom humanity was looking for the reburnishment of America's leadership.

He therefore determined on a compromise course. If he was offered the nomination he would accept it, but he would do nothing to seek it. It probably gave him the worst of both worlds. It brought tantalization followed by chagrin at the Los Angeles convention. It did not give him the reward, and it weakened his position with the new President. Right up to the end he appeared to be hovering on the brink of a more positive move. In the late winter he went on a long tour of Latin America. The enthusiasm was not only remarkable in itself, but was in sharp contrast with the rather cool welcome which the President received there at about the same time. He was back in the United States for the fiasco of the Paris Summit, which Krushchev aborted because of the U-2 incident.

Stevenson responded to this by making one of the most powerful and controversial speeches of his life. The main fault was Krushchev's: 'But we handed Krushchev the crow-bar and the sledgehammer to wreck the meeting. Without our series of blunders, Mr Krushchev would not have had a pretext for making his impossible demand and wild charges'. The words do not sound particularly inflammatory, but America was in a bruised mood with a strong tendency to rally round an humiliated President. As a result there was a howl of execration such as Stevenson's speeches rarely provoked. He got more letters—from both sides—than almost ever before. He also got more appeals, from Mrs Roosevelt, from Senator Humphrey, from a host of others, to declare himself a candidate.

There was a strong 'stop Kennedy' element in this. That 'bright and able young man', too unseasoned and brash for the Presidency, as Stevenson saw him, had just trounced Humphrey in West Virginia. And the Kennedy forces were at that stage using rough tactics against those who stood in their way. Stevenson was indirectly warned that he would not even be considered for Secretary of State if he continued to do so. He neither got out of the way nor responded to Mrs Roosevelt and the others. He continued to be available but undeclared. And this was still his status when he arrived at the Los Angeles convention. His supporters had been there before him, working hard. There was no doubt that they were running him as a candidate whatever he was doing himself. The Kennedy bandwagon was rolling hard, but it was still short of a first ballot victory, and it was at that stage arousing more professional admiration than popular enthusiasm. Many thought that if Stevenson would give a clear lead and set alight the latent flames of nostalgic affection and respect which were smouldering in the hearts of many delegates, the convention could still be turned.

There were a number of occasions when he might have done this. He refused them all. There was the moment of his arrival in the convention hall. He was greeted by a demonstration of frenzied enthusiasm. It took him 12 minutes to get through it. He had to make a response from the rostrum. He could so easily have summoned up all his qualities of evocative eloquence. Instead he replied with three rather flat sentences. He met the Minnesota delegation. They greeted him with a standing ovation. They were waiting for a sign. Instead he delivered a conventional attack on the Eisenhower administration. There was no standing ovation when he left.

Later that same day he met an important group of New York delegates. They too were expectant. He was still more elusive. He excused his early departure by quoting Robert Frost:

>But I have promises to keep
>And miles to go before I sleep.

The more optimistic among his hearers thought that this meant he was going to spend the rest of the night rallying support. They were wrong. A few minutes later he was in his pyjamas.

Yet he allowed his name to be placed in nomination. Indeed he actually suggested the proposer, Senator Eugene McCarthy of Minnesota. It was an excellent choice—but for what purpose?—and produced the greatest oratorical feat of the week. 'Do not turn away from this man', McCarthy said. . . . 'Do not reject this man who has made us all proud to be Democrats.' There was another tremendous demonstration, but it came even more from the galleries than from the floor.

Meanwhile Stevenson had already started work on a speech introducing John Kennedy to a post-convention rally. Altogether it was a most mystifying week's performance. It was certainly not calculated to endear him to the Kennedy camp. He had taken too much of the gilt off their gingerbread. Nor did he make it easy for his friends. Yet they did not revolt or even complain. Their springs of loyalty and affection were too deep. 'We would not have had him otherwise', George Ball said.

This was the last week of his political career. It had lasted 12½ years. Thereafter everything was, not bathos, but anti-climax. He was not offered the Secretaryship of State. The obscure Dean Rusk, as unknown to Kennedy as he was to the nation, got that. Stevenson accepted the ambassadorship to the United Nations, sweetened by the rather meaningless prestige symbol of Cabinet membership. And his associates nearly all got good jobs. He was as loyal to them as they had been to him.

For Kennedy Stevenson's was a brilliant appointment. Stevenson discharged his duties with flair and imagination. It was no longer his own standard, but that of an administration with which he was not wholly in sympathy, which he carried. But he did it with most of his old distinction. He continued to foster world respect for the United States. But he again paid a price. He was under instructions. He defended causes in which he did not believe. He was no longer his own man. He lived in luxury and esteem at the top of the Waldorf Tower. He used his eloquence. He was warmly welcoming to the delegates of the emergent nations. He saw his old friends, and went to too many parties. He thought of resigning and trying to run for the Senate, but did not do so. And then it all ended on a July afternoon in a Mayfair street. It was certainly not the happiest period of his life.

Stevenson, with the possible exception of Bryan, was the most famous unsuccessful candidate in American history. By definition, therefore, he was a failure in his central purpose. But he inspired a generation. And he influenced the world view of the United States more than any other politician who never handled the levers of full power.

ROBERT KENNEDY

Robert Kennedy

The last time I saw Robert Kennedy was at the funeral of Martin Luther King in April, 1968, eight weeks before his own death. It was not merely a polite encounter, with the muttered exchange of a few words, such as might take place outside Westminster Abbey after a memorial service. The occasion did not lend itself to that. It was a long day of emotional and physical exhaustion with grief and guilt and fear all strongly present amongst the 50,000 participants and the several hundred thousand more who lined the streets of Atlanta.

After the charged, revivalist atmosphere of the suffocatingly packed service at Ebenezer Baptist Church there was a chaotic five mile march to the campus of Morehouse College, on the other side of the city, for a vast and final ceremony. The march took four and a half hours. It was not made less exhausting by the slowness of the progress. The long waits, interspersed with brisk periods of movement until the route jammed again, all took place under a relentlessly hot sun. Spring had come early and fiercely to Georgia that year. There was no shelter, no support for aching backs, no food (a serious matter as the afternoon wore on for those who had left New York or Washington soon after six in the morning) and water or Coca-Cola only as an exceptional offering from those who stood in the streets in front of their houses.

There was no order or precedence about the procession. Anyone could walk where or with whom he wished. And in the uneven movement of the turgid crowd it was easy to find oneself first with one group and then with another. Over some stretches I walked with a liberal Republican column, headed by Governor Rockefeller and a number of senators and congressmen. They made some attempt to turn the shambling mass into a march. They held their heads up, linked arms, and burst into 'We Shall Overcome' whenever the opportunity presented itself.

Walking with Robert Kennedy was quite different. He was accompanied by no notables but by a large group of adherents. He did not link arms or sing—he sang very badly—or even hold his head up. He walked when he could with a slightly slovenly speed, rather like a boy kicking a can along a gutter and recalling to mind the well-known photograph with his dog at an Oregon airport taken a few days before Los Angeles. His only attempt at introducing order into the column was occasionally to look back a few rows and say, half bantering, half challenging: 'Can't you keep up, Ethel?' After a time he took his coat off. Some people said he should not have done so. It showed lack of respect. I do not think the crowd minded. Particularly in the Negro districts it was he and his party which got most of the badly needed offers of water and Coca-Cola.

As we entered downtown Atlanta through a security man's nightmare, with high buildings lining and facing the route and thin rows of people standing on top of most of them, he was complaining that a simple lack of physical courage had kept President Johnson away. It may have been a prejudiced and foolish remark. But there was no bravado about it. In a longer term sense he felt very exposed but I do not think he had any immediate sense of his own danger although it must at that moment have been very considerable.

I talked to him again after the end of the march. I noticed with a certain satisfaction that he looked at least as exhausted as I did and that Ethel had 'kept up' as well as he had done. The prospect may have been straining him as much as the day. He went back to the Indiana primary campaign the next morning and then to Nebraska and Oregon and California. At that stage the prospect was depressing as well as exhausting. Indiana was proving an unrewarding state and he thought he saw the nomination slipping away from him. By the end of the Californian campaign, despite the fact that in Oregon he had been the first Kennedy ever to lose a public election of any sort, the outlook was immensely brighter. But only for an hour or so. Then there was another funeral.

It is peculiarly difficult to appraise Robert Kennedy as a politician. Inevitably the nature of his death still casts a film of distortion—of roseate distortion, some would say—over the recollection of his life. Perspective is made still more difficult by the relationship of his own tragedy to that of his brother. Almost the whole of his own independent contribution to politics was made in the four and a half year twilight between the assassination at Dallas and the assassination at Los Angeles. In the haze of that twilight it is sometimes difficult—at least from this side of the Atlantic—to distinguish clearly between the two principal characters. After his brother's death Robert Kennedy changed and matured greatly. But was he maturing into the likeness of John Kennedy or into something else? Was it the phoenix rising again from the ashes, or some quite new creature? Had he won the Presidency in 1968, would it have brought a restoration to Washington or the beginning of a new régime?

The answer remains elusive. Robert Kennedy was very much a part of his family, even more so perhaps than John Kennedy. His father was a self-made man. His brother was a self-made politician. But he was above all an heir. His name was an immense advantage to him. His early political career was almost all spent in the service of his brother. His reverence for him never diminished. Almost the only streak of slight pomposity in his very unpompous character was that, from 1963 onwards, he never referred to him except as 'President Kennedy' and looked rather askance at those who did otherwise, 'Jack' or even 'your brother' he regarded as an approach to *lèse-majesté*. But it was not respect for the office as such; Lyndon Johnson got no title from him.

Yet it was more complicated than that. There were a lot of ideological fights which went on over Robert Kennedy's body and probably within his mind too. When the first hostile bumper stickers proclaiming 'Bobby ain't Jack' appeared during the 1964 Senate contest in New York—and came out again during the Indiana and Oregon primaries—a lot of his closest confidants and supporters were delighted. They thought it was a different world from 1960 and they wanted a different, more radical, less Whiggish candidate. Their pleasure at the stickers did not result in their exclusion from his inner circle.

For 35 of his 42 years, Robert Kennedy was hardly a radical. He was the seventh of nine children. He was the smallest, shyest, least physically co-ordinated of the four boys. He was also the most closely tied to his origin, the most Catholic, the most Boston-Irish, superficially the most conservative. He was born in late 1925. He was still a boy during his father's embassy to London and for most of the war years. He missed the full impact both of England and of service in the United States forces. He disliked the episcopalian New Hampshire preparatory school to which he was first sent and was quickly removed to a Catholic seminary in Rhode Island. At Harvard he rather kept away from the urbane metropolitan set in which his brothers had moved. From there he went to the Virginia Law School, and then into the Department of Justice. He soon found himself working as an investigator for the Hoover Commission, with his own father as one of the members, enquiring into the organization of the Internal Revenue Service and the Reconstruction Finance Corporation. It was a somewhat nepotic job. It was also a needling one, requiring qualities of relentless tenacity rather than broad human sympathy. You kept at people until you had driven them into a corner. You did not let them go, even when they had broken down. He continued to do jobs of this type for a full 10 years.

In 1950 he married Ethel Skakel, of Greenwich, Connecticut, the daughter of a family less rich but even more devoutly Catholic than the Kennedys. They immediately acquired Hickory Hill, near the Virginia end of the Chain Bridge over the Potomac, eight or nine miles from downtown Washington. More slowly they began to acquire the 11 children (the last he never saw) who subsequently filled the house.

From 1946 John Kennedy had been a congressman from a highly Democratic, machine-organised Boston-Irish district. In 1952, he decided to run for the Senate. It was a fairly hazardous adventure. Massachusetts had no firm tradition of electing Democratic senators. The machine was good at running Boston but much less effective over the state as a whole. Worse still, Ambassador Joseph Kennedy mistakenly thought he could control Massachusetts politics. He had hardly been there for 20 years. The campaign got off to a start of near disaster. Then Bobby, rather against his will, was called in. Once there he had one desire, and only one—to get his brother elected a United States senator. To this end he worked nearly 24 hours a day, he politely but firmly pushed his father into the background, took over the organisation from the 'pros', lashed the volunteers into activity and never once wavered in the relentless search for votes. That was the object, not to discuss issues or to let politicians enjoy themselves. He succeeded. In a strongly Republican year, with Eisenhower at the head of the ticket, John Kennedy had made a decisive break into national politics. Robert Kennedy had given himself an occasional but indispensable role as his brother's campaign manager. He was then 26.

He was to perform this role again in 1956 (when John Kennedy was narrowly beaten for the Democratic vice-presidential nomination), in 1958 (when he needed and secured a landslide re-election to the Senate), and above all in 1960, both in the primaries and in the presidential contest itself. But he had to fill in the years without campaigns. Ambassador Kennedy did not believe in letting his sons do nothing but spend his money. On the night of the Senate victory, perhaps getting a little of his own back for the discipline to which he had been subjected during the campaign, he told Bobby: 'You'd better go out and get a job'. Bobby did, but unfortunately one of those which he acquired was working for Senator Joseph McCarthy's notorious committee of investigation.

Robert Kennedy was only lightly touched with the McCarthy brush. He worked directly for him only for a few months, and then became counsel for the increasingly hostile Democratic minority group on the committee. He had come to disapprove of the methods of McCarthy's investigations but he did not disapprove of their general purpose and as a man he rather liked the Senator without admiring him. He did not recoil from him after his downfall. In 1957 he flew out to Wisconsin to attend his funeral.

When the party control of the Senate changed in 1956, Kennedy became majority counsel on the McClennan Committee on Improper Activities in the Labour and Management Field. This so-called Rackets Committee had with three exceptions a highly conservative membership and became focused on union affairs, with James Hoffa, the monumentally corrupt boss of the Teamsters' Union, fixed firmly in their sights. Kennedy came to regard Hoffa as the embodiment of evil. He pursued him as relentlessly as he had pursued votes in the Massachusetts Senate contest. People who saw a lot of him at this time remembered a narrow, repetitive intensity and found him chiefly notable for his energy, his loyalty to his brother and his obsession with Hoffa.

From this not very encouraging background he launched himself in late 1959 into the campaign to make his brother President. There were incidents during the next year which showed, in retrospect at any rate, the beginning of a broader, more liberal, more sympathetic outlook. But the reputation which came through to the public, who were of course much more interested in Robert Kennedy than they had ever been before, was still that of a singleminded operator, a man who got things done but who spent little time reflecting on either his methods or his basic purpose. He was hard, rough, and effective.

He had no patience with anyone who got in his way. He threatened Hubert Humphrey outrageously at the Los Angeles Convention when he thought he was working for Johnson. He had no sympathy to spare for Adlai Stevenson, or for the old Stevensonian liberals who were uneasily poised between nostalgia and realism. But on the whole he won votes rather than lost them. He directed all the efforts that he could control at the crucial points and not at the easy ones. He never accepted the soft answer. J. K. Galbraith noted that, unlike most politicians, he was interested only in the effect of interventions, not merely that they had taken place. He never asked an intermediary 'Did you talk with X?', but always 'Did you get him?' As a result, his tally of delegate votes was accurate and not merely optimistic.

His tactical advice was mostly good, and his brother mostly took it. His one major set-back was the nomination of Lyndon Johnson as vice-presidential candidate. He would have preferred one of the northern candidates, Orville Freeman, Stuart Symington or 'Scoop' Jackson. This was partly on personal and partly on ideological grounds. He did not believe a southerner and a Capitol Hill fixer was necessary or desirable. On electoral need he was probably wrong. But he was willing to do a little fixing himself. In the Chicago studios for the first and crucial Kennedy-Nixon debate, Robert Kennedy looked at the then Vice-President in the television monitor and was appalled by the picture presented of him. Nixon saw him looking and asked if he should change anything. 'Dick, you look great' was the reply. To ask Robert Kennedy's advice when he was not on your side was at that stage unwise.

His role in 1960 cannot be properly understood in isolation, however. Everything he said and did had meaning only in relation to the position of John Kennedy. Bobby was the self-appointed lightning conductor. He would be rough in order that his brother might be urbane. He would fight bitter battles in order that J.F.K. might rise above them. He eschewed ideology because that was Jack's business and not his. He sought victory and not repute. An inevitable result of this was that, with victory achieved (by the narrowest of margins), the determination of the new President to have him in the Cabinet, and his decision that this should be as Attorney-General, aroused the most widespread lack of enthusiasm.

Robert Kennedy's legal qualifications were somewhat exiguous. He had never appeared in a court room. He had never been a member of a legal firm of repute. But more serious than that was the fact that, as it appeared, a rather narrow-minded hatchet man had been appointed the youngest holder for over 150 years of an office (roughly analogous in this country to the Home Secretaryship as well as the Attorney-Generalship, with a little of the Lord Chancellorship thrown in also) which required breadth and balance of judgement as well as the ability to administer a department of 30,000 persons.

After he took office there was a rapid but uneven dissipation of some of the worst fears aroused by his appointment. He secured good assistants. Within the department he rushed round energetically, finding out what everybody did, brushing cobwebs out of remote corners. But this was in accordance with his reputation. No one doubted his energy. Somewhat more impressively he argued a major case—in favour of the equal apportionment of Congressional districts—before the Supreme Court, and at least did it without disaster. But he made several bad judicial appointments in the South. He tried hard to control J. Edgar Hoover of the F.B.I., who was becoming incompetent as well as reactionary and insubordinate, but fell well short of full success. His attempt was stronger than that of any Attorney-General before or afterwards, but so with his special relationship with the President it ought to have been. Although closely informed, he offered no advice against the ill-fated Bay of Pigs venture. And, in spite of a good if recent relationship with Martin Luther King, he gave an impression not of illiberalism but of insensitivity in his approach to the problem of relations with the blacks.

At this stage he saw the problem in terms of a rather sterile liberalism, of an abstract legal equality of rights. He thought of it as just one aspect of the general problem of a melting-pot society. 'My brother is President of the United States, the grandson of an immigrant', he said to a black group on one occasion. It was not an understanding remark. For one thing they were not the children of recent immigrants. Most of their forebears had been there much longer than the Kennedys. They had always been part of the country, but the wrong part. Continuing poverty and a lack for so many of opportunity to escape from it made them deaf to the 'fellow immigrants' appeal.

It was an odd blind spot for Robert Kennedy, for he later became more aware of what poverty meant in hard practical terms, certainly more angered by it, particularly as it affected children, than any American politician of his generation. As a very rich man, he often found it difficult to appreciate the limitations on time and freedom which the problems of having to earn their own livings and organize their own lives imposed on those of his associates who had ordinary middle-class incomes. But he found it much easier to understand what it meant for a child to have a face scarred by the gnawing of rats in Bedford-Stuyvesant or to be pot-bellied from hunger in the Mississippi delta.

But when he became Attorney-General he had seen little of this, and his mind worked in a specific, almost tactile way. What he knew from his experience affected him much more than what he was told by others. And at this stage he had known very few blacks. 'I didn't think about them much', he said later with a characteristic flat honesty. 'I didn't know about all the injustice.'

It took him some time to learn, although the tensions of Mississippi and Alabama in the next two summers, the Freedom Rides, the admission of James Meredith as the one black student at an all-white state university, soon began to teach him that he was up against something more than the integration of the Kennedy forebears into Brahmin-dominated Boston. As late as June, 1963, Robert Kennedy could signally fail to make contact with a handpicked group of leading 'unofficial' blacks whom the novelist James Baldwin had assembled to meet him in New York. 'Bobby didn't understand what we were trying to tell him', Baldwin said; 'He didn't understand our urgency.' And in that same month Cardinal Cushing, almost the family chaplain of the Kennedys, told me in Rome that both John and Robert Kennedy were inhibited from 'solving' (an optimistic word) the race problem in the United States by a coldness of heart and manner. To Ambassador Kennedy and to Senator Edward Kennedy he attributed a much greater warmth. It was a remarkable conversation for him to hold with a stranger. But what is quite certain is that he could not possibly have said these words of Robert Kennedy a few years later. Indeed they were already somewhat out-of-date by June, 1963.

The stubborn arrogance of the Southern whites had already aroused his anger. His visits to the worst parts of the South in the next year were to arouse his understanding and compassion. He had started on the road that was to make him by 1968 by far the best-loved white politician in any black district of the United States.

* *

By the time of his brother's death, Robert Kennedy had convinced most people that his appointment as Attorney-General was justified on grounds other than nepotism. He was showing considerable skill in striking the delicate balance between public order and private liberty which is the major task of his office. He had won the strong approval of at least two men, one of whom was probably his most distinguished living predecessor, the other as yet his most considerable successor. Francis Biddle, who was Roosevelt's Attorney-General throughout the war, thought that Kennedy was 'certainly the finest Attorney-General in the last 20 years, probably the best in this century'; and Ramsey Clark thought that although 'he could have been a disaster', he had completely destroyed 'all that doubt and resentment' associated with his arrival at the Justice Department.

But he had to be judged by more than his performance in the Department of Justice. He was also the unofficial Assistant President—far more so than Vice-President Johnson. He was the one person in the government who could be certain of access to his brother on every issue. This gave him great power but also exposed him to every wind of Washington jealousy and criticism. Even John Kennedy, when he saw a *Time* cover story nominating Bobby as the second most important man in Washington, jocularly told him: 'Well, that means there's only one way for you to go, and it ain't up.' Joking and jealousy apart, however, Robert Kennedy's special position meant that he was bound to be judged by his general impact upon government and not merely by his administration of his own department.

In this broader field he decisively vindicated himself in the Cuban missile crisis of October, 1962. He emerged as a man of calm and humane judgement with a capacity to persuade others, older, more experienced, in some cases more detached than himself, not by needling their minds or twisting their arms but by the force and sweep of his arguments. He was decisive in swinging opinion in the Executive Committee of the National Security Council (the so-called Excom) against Dean Acheson's case for destroying the missile sites with an unannounced American air strike.

Mr Acheson had one of the most formidable and incisive forensic minds in the United States. His arguments were presented with the sharpness and clarity of diamonds and sustained by his own conviction of their value. I saw him in 1970, then near his eightieth year, make an adversary as distinguished as Senator Muskie look like a flabby whale stranded on an unfamiliar shore. Robert Kennedy had none of Acheson's verbal dexterity. But he convinced the majority of those present that such a pre-emptive strike would be against the American tradition, a Pearl Harbor in reverse, an unnecessary threat to world peace. Douglas Dillon, then Secretary of the Treasury and a man of very different style from the Attorney-General, has recorded: 'He spoke with an intense but quiet passion. As he spoke, I felt that I was at a real turning point in history.... With only one or two possible exceptions, all the members of the Excom were convinced by Bob's argument.'

His role in this second Cuban crisis showed his capacity to learn from experience and his ability to see the world in much less simple, narrow, categoric, black-and-white terms than had been his habit as an investigating Senate counsel. But it did not at this stage change his appearance or his manner. The first time I ever talked to him at length was almost exactly a year later, when we squatted one golden October afternoon on the steps leading down to the garden from the terrace of the British Embassy in Washington and discussed the crisis events of the previous autumn.

'Discussed' is probably the wrong word. It is too leisurely. I wanted his views on exactly what had happened the year before, and up to a point he was prepared to be very informative. But his conversational style was not much suited to reflective reminiscence. It was staccato, often inarticulate, more interested in the future than in the past, more given to asking questions than to providing answers. He appeared much less rounded, much less widely informed, much less at ease with the world than his brother. He had a magnetism, certainly, but it was that of energy allied with power rather than of profundity. His hair was still aggressively short (as it was to remain until 1965 or 1966), and his eyes and face were bright but occasionally hard. He had no look of someone who had been 'to the mountain top' and seen great visions. He was still a terrier who knew what he was doing and enjoyed it, who was sometimes impatient that events did not move faster, but not with the framework in which he was operating.

He had no need to be. The benevolent sun of the Indian summer shone on Kennedy Washington, and there was little reason to think it would not do so for at least five years to come. The city was the capital of the world in a way that it had never been before. Cuba had been a triumph for cool liberalism. There were only about 10,000 United States troops in Vietnam. The economy was expanding without inflation. The problem of the blacks looked menacing, but no more so than many other problems which America had faced and overcome in the past. The country was confident and glittering. Robert Kennedy still had a brother to serve. It was six weeks before Dallas.

I next saw Robert Kennedy at dinner in London two months after the assassination. He was on his way back from a mission to Indonesia, which was almost his first attempt at a return to work. I cannot recall what the mission was about. I hope it was not very important, for I cannot believe that it was well done. He was still completely disorientated, vastly changed from October, but changing into what it was still impossible to say. Perhaps merely into someone null and finished.

Thereafter I saw him two or three times a year, sometimes in London, sometimes in Washington or New York, until the final meeting in Atlanta. Over this period he did not recover his old balance, but he achieved a new one. He became more contemplative, perhaps more patient in spite of his new sense of time running fast against him, certainly less brittle both in appearance and in character. He left the Cabinet. He became Senator for New York. He broke with President Johnson. A little reluctantly, he came out against the Vietnam war. He moved well to the left in American internal politics. He became the hero of the dispossessed, and established a contact with alienated minority groups comparable with, although different from, Roosevelt's relationship with the 'forgotten man' of the 'thirties.

In direct contradiction of Cardinal Cushing's judgement of 1963, he looked the one man who might heal the most dangerous schism of all in American society, that between the blacks and the 'blue-collar' ethnic groups, the Poles, the Italians, the Irish, and would do it, if he did, much more by personality than by policy. He became a presidential candidate for 1968, timing his entry into the race with almost incredible ineptitude, but nevertheless acquiring sufficient momentum for it to be a wide open question at the time of his death whether he would have won the nomination at the Chicago Convention, and whether, if chosen, he would have beaten Mr Nixon.

What caused these developments in Robert Kennedy? Ambition, his enemies would have answered without hesitation, hard, ruthless, driving ambition, which became still less restrained when his brother's death meant that it was no longer vicarious. And he had enough enemies for their voices to amount to a mighty chorus. If he aroused passionate support he also aroused violent antipathy, and not only in country clubs and corporation boardrooms. Many of Senator Eugene McCarthy's liberal supporters (including perhaps the Senator himself) disliked him far more than they disliked Vice-President Humphrey, although the Vice-President was much further away from them on policy issues. Although he could arouse great enthusiasm Robert Kennedy could also arouse great antipathy. He was probably the most hated man in American politics since the death of Roosevelt.

The judgement of those who hate is rarely good, and it would therefore be a great mistake to accept the view that Robert Kennedy was blown here and there by opportunistic winds of ambition and by little else. Of course, once he had decided to compete, he wanted success, and he wanted it at the highest level. He had been taught from his earliest childhood the harsh Kennedy doctrine that the important thing in life was to win. Coming second or third did not count. And he accepted also the hubristic family view that, just as when the eldest son was killed in the war, the need to strive for the Presidency devolved on Jack, so with Jack dead the sword of Kennedy endeavour was automatically handed on to him. But even had he not thought this it would have been difficult for him to sink into obscurity. There were so many people pushing him on. He was at once a symbol of the most poignant nostalgia and the brightest hope for the future. And even those who were not pushing were speculating about his intentions. 'What will Bobby do?' asked a lot of headlines in the spring of 1964.

What he wanted to do, somewhat surprisingly, was to become Lyndon Johnson's vice-presidential candidate. But it must be remembered that it was still very much John Kennedy's Administration in which he wanted to become Vice-President. Until Senator Goldwater was nominated as

Republican candidate it seemed an attractive proposition all round. Then President Johnson had no need of him—he was so far ahead on the polls—and did not want his victory to be diluted by a Kennedy name on the ticket. This was a perfectly reasonable decision for him to make and he told Kennedy of it directly and immediately. But he tried to assuage the blow by two very doubtful moves. First he said he would accept anyone else whom Kennedy cared to name (an offer which was wisely declined) and then he announced that he was ruling out all Cabinet members from consideration. Bobby responded to this with a typical Kennedy joke, announcing at a luncheon that he had telegraphed his Cabinet colleagues saying 'I am sorry I had to take so many of you nice fellows over the side with me'. The President further responded by spreading a highly disobliging account of how badly Kennedy had taken the news. The downward spiral in their relationship was gathering momentum.

Robert Kennedy then decided to contest the Senate seat in New York. It offered the prospect of a major political base, but the hazards, first of trying to make sense out of the perpetually feuding New York Democratic Party, which has the distinction of always possessing more registered votes than the Republicans and practically never winning any state-wide elections; and second, of running in a state of which he was not thought to be a genuine resident. Technically he was qualified, but he sounded and seemed like a Massachusetts man, which indeed he was. This enabled his liberal Republican opponent, the incumbent Senator Keating, to exploit both the 'ruthless opportunism' charge and the 'Bobby ain't Jack' theme. 'And the man (the Democrats) are promoting', he said in his acceptance speech, 'comes before our people not to ask what he can do for New York, but what New York can do for him.'

It was not a glorious campaign. Sometimes there was wild enthusiasm, but there was also a lot of opposition, some of it from liberals. Kennedy fought mainly on the record of his brother's administration, but it was the flood-tide of Lyndon Johnson's popularity, and in the last weeks the original bills proclaiming 'Let's put Robert Kennedy to work for New York' were replaced by 'Get with the Johnson-Humphrey-Kennedy Team'. However, he won. His majority was not nearly as great as the majority by which the President carried the state but it was a good performance by any normal New York Democratic standards.

* *

His entry to the Senate therefore owed a good deal to Johnson's coat-tails. But within two years these positions of relative popularity were dramatically reversed. By the autumn of 1966 Kennedy was shown by every poll to be more popular across the nation, both among Democrats and among voters generally, than the President. This was because of the appeal of his name and charisma, not because of his work in the Senate. Although he spent a lot of time on the premises, Kennedy was never a wholly committed senator. In this respect he was more akin to John Kennedy than to Edward Kennedy. But everything he did attracted immense public attention, so that he gave the impression of being more active on Capitol Hill than was in fact the case. In the 'fifties John Kennedy had to work hard for his national reputation, but Robert Kennedy's was bequeathed to him. This was not in all ways an advantage. It made it peculiarly difficult for him to move on issues, especially where he appeared to be resiling from a position for which his brother's administration bore some responsibility.

Above all this applied to Vietnam. His scepticism about the war probably began as early as 1965, but it took him several years to move into a clear position of hostility to President Johnson's policies. This was partly because of a tug-of-war around and within him. The leaders of his own Senate staff (who in total numbered no less than 43) were mostly young and strongly anti-war. They wanted him to move as far and as fast as possible. But many of those who had been closest to him in the Kennedy administration, notably Robert McNamara and General Taylor, were still committed to the war, even if far from being extreme hawks. In the words of one of his many biographers (David Halberstam):

He was at the exact median point of American idealism and American power. ... The correlation was such that his speeches could be written by young radicals like Adam Walinsky and Peter Edelman, and yet his children (were) named after Douglas Dillon and Maxwell Taylor.

It was by no means a wholly comfortable position. And it was made worse by the fact that any attempt to adjust the balance by moving from one dug-out to another had to be done in the blazing light of maximum exposure, and was usually accompanied by a concentrated barrage of artillery fire—mainly from the White House. Thus, when in early 1966 he held a press conference which did no more than put him in line with what 20 other senators, including some of the most prominent Democrats, had been saying without excitement for some time, there was a flurry of bitter response from those around the President. He came off rather badly from the exchange, as he always did in his attempts to find a position which suited his views and supporters without making too sharp a break with his past or appearing to be animated by personal hostility to President Johnson. Vietnam, right up to the end, was a damaging issue for him. He did not get on to really solid ground until a few months before his death. And then, almost immediately, his fox shot himself. President Johnson withdrew from the 1968 contest, and for a crucial few weeks the war subsided as a major political issue.

Yet I do not believe for a moment that Robert Kennedy's gradual and rather uncertain movement to opposition was part of an opportunist and ruthless search for votes. Certainly, if so, it was one of the most inept in history, and totally at variance with the skilled political traditions of the Kennedys. His prepared speeches on the subject were mostly unsatisfactory. Too many hands had been at them, attempting to reconcile too much. But his unprepared exchanges or answers to questions were notably firmer, more convinced, more convincing, more hostile to the policy of the Administration. That is not usually a sign of the calculated exploitation of an issue.

Equally unhelpful to Robert Kennedy was his handling of the question of Senator Eugene McCarthy's candidature in the winter of 1967-8. Had Kennedy himself been prepared to announce in late 1967, there would have been no McCarthy candidature. The effective dissidents, even the anti-Kennedy ones, would have been prepared to rally behind anyone who could do the most harm to Lyndon Johnson—and Kennedy could certainly do that.

But at that stage Kennedy would not move. His reluctance was perfectly understandable. Every political rule said that an incumbent President could not be denied the nomination. For a challenger as strong as Kennedy to contest it would cause sharp bitterness and do deep damage to the Democratic Party, but all without the hope of success. He would merely be destroying his chances for 1972. And by so doing he would be inflicting a wound not merely upon himself. He not only had great prospects but was the repository of great hopes. To dash them against the rock of a hopeless and premature contest would be a sign not of noble courage but of incontinent self-indulgence. These were the arguments which most of his friends—and nearly all these he had inherited from his brother—urged upon him.

Eugene McCarthy was subject to no such conflicts. He had little to lose, particularly as events have shown that he placed no value on his Senate seat. None the less his battle of the New Hampshire snows had an heroic quality about it. And it was not only heroic but also surprisingly successful. Well before the result became known it was apparent that he was eating into a significant part of Kennedy's natural constituency.

The early months of 1968 were an unquiet time for Kennedy. The arguments for and against running raged to and fro around and within him. He became less and less happy with negative advice. Eventually, in early March, he reversed his earlier decisions and made up his mind in favour of a challenge. It would be idle to pretend that the McCarthy campaign had not been a vital catalyst pushing him in this direction. But it was the sense of being left out of the struggle rather than a calculating belief that he could pick the fruit which Senator McCarthy had grown that pushed him on. He took his decision on March 5th, a week before Senator McCarthy's unexpectedly good result in New Hampshire. He toyed with the idea of announcing almost immediately, but then decided this would look as though he were trying to weaken McCarthy's momentum in the primary. So he delayed his announcement until March 16th. This gave the maximum impression of bandwagon jumping. Through intermediaries he even mishandled the timing of a private message of intention to Senator McCarthy, so that relations with his rival as well as with some of the public were unnecessarily exacerbated. The ineptitude at this stage was of epic proportions.

The President's withdrawal a fortnight later was a further blow to Kennedy. Until this happened there was a good hope that many would accept his ability to carry in stronger hands the anti-Johnson torch which Senator McCarthy had lit. But with President Johnson out of the way the stronger hands did not seem so necessary, and some of the venom which the President had previously attracted was now directed against Kennedy. Ill-luck was piled on ineptitude.

That he was able to recover from this disastrous beginning and achieve the success and arouse the enthusiasm of the next eight weeks is a remarkable tribute to the inherent strength of his position. Robert Kennedy could hold together a disparate coalition, and make different parts of it feel a little better towards each other. He could excite both the great crowds who came to see him for the first time, and achieve the enduring affection of those who worked for him every day. He could kindle men's hearts, and the resulting warmth gave him a high and unusual quality of leadership.

Such power of leadership can of course have a corrupting aspect to it. I do not think this was a danger with Robert Kennedy. He had too much sense of the ridiculous, too great a capacity for self-mockery for any messianic feeling to take hold of him. This led him on occasions to balloon-pricking jokes which most English politicians (in spite of our supposed fondness for a more ironical style than the Americans) would consider politically very rash. After his New York Senate election in which his alleged carpet-bagging pursuit of ambition had been the main and serious charge against him, he told the first Washington audience that he addressed:

First of all I want to say how delighted I am to be here representing the great state of ... er ... (long pause and simulated look at notes) ... New York. ... I have been accused of over ambition. I can assure you I have absolutely no presidential ambitions—and neither does my wife, Ethel Bird.

During the 1968 primaries he finished most of his informal open-air meetings with a Shaw quotation. 'As George Bernard Shaw once said: "Most men look at things as they are and wonder why. I dream of things that never were and ask why not?"' To the audience the mention of Shaw may have been inspiring, but to the accompanying journalists it became a sign that the end had come and they had better get back quickly to the press bus. Suddenly one wet day in Omaha, Kennedy said, 'Well, as George Bernard Shaw once said, "run for the bus",' and departed himself at some speed. The press thought it funnier than the audience.

Robert Kennedy also had the grace of honesty about himself. He was not self-righteous, or self-justificatory. While he was Attorney-General he was neutral about capital punishment, although he later became a firm abolitionist. One evening in London when I was Home Secretary for the first time I remember discussing with him the question of reprieves. He had not had to deal with many, for United States executions are mostly a matter of state law. But he particularly remembered one difficult case of a serviceman. 'What did you do?' I asked. 'I let him die,' he said in a flat, down-beat voice. It was an accurate and unembroidered use of rather unattractive words. But I can think of very few others who would not have dressed them up in a cocoon of explanation or regret.

Again when a meeting of prosperous and right-wing medical students in Indianapolis were questioning him hostilely about who would pay for the improved welfare programmes he was advocating, his answer was unconciliatory for a politician who badly needed votes. 'You will', he said. (Of course it could be said that he was after bigger blocks of support. But his support of the dispossessed was not a psephological exercise. The black vote was of immense value to him. But he also spent a great deal of time on the problems of Red Indians, who were electorally quite negligible, and of Cesar Chavez's Mexican grape-pickers.)

He had a surprising streak of modesty and patience. At least from 1963 onwards he was almost universally recognized and half idolized as well. There were always a lot of people who just wanted to touch him. Yet one day soon after he entered the Senate when he drove me to the White House for some bill-signing ceremony he was stopped by an officious security guard (Irish of all nationalities) who showed no response to his identity and made a lot of fuss about a pass. It was barely a year since the house and staff had been his brother's. But he took it all very calmly and politely. 'I'm not as well known here as I used to be,' was all he said.

Whether had he lived he would have been a President, and if a President, a great one, is impossible to say. He had a far more complex character than was generally appreciated. He had developed greatly from the rather brittle and parochial little Irish boy which he once seemed to be. His view of the world was increasingly broad and humane. His appeal to the dangerously alienated elements of American society was unique, although he was perhaps stronger in the warmth of his sympathy than in the detail of his policy for their problems. He could also inspire many of the most talented. His administration would have had some of the style of John Kennedy's. But it would have had more intensity and more urgency. It would not have failed through falling below the level of events.

Index

Abyssinia, 89
Acheson, Dean, Joseph McCarthy and, 119, 121-2; Halifax and, 156, 197, 215
Adenauer, Konrad, xi
Alexander of Hillsborough, Lord, 99
American Loan, Keynes and, 1, 24, 157; Cripps and, 101; Halifax and, 157
Anderson, Sir John, 74
Annan, Lord, 25
'Apostles, The', Keynes and, 3-6
Aristotle, 3
Arvey, Colonel Jacob, 190, 191
Asquith, H. H. (1st Earl of Oxford & Asquith), 84, 85, 98, 138, 148; Keynes and, 10, 12-13
Asquith, Margot (Countess of Oxford & Asquith), 13
Astor, Nancy, Lady, 156
Attlee, Clement Richard, 177; Bevin and, 63, 69, 70, 71, 73, 75-6, 77; Cripps and, 84, 88, 92, 99, 100-1; Churchill and, 97, 98; devaluation and, 102; Indian Statutory Commission and, 145; retirement, 162, 172; Gaitskell and, 168, 169
Auden, W. H., 163
Auriol, President Vincent, 43, 48, 52, 54
Avon, Lord, Blum and, 49; Bevin and, 64, 65, 74, 80; Halifax and, 148-50, 154, 157; Gaitskell and, 174-5

Bainville, Jacques, 47
Baldwin of Bewdley, Earl, 29, 177; Cripps and, 93; Halifax and, 135, 140, 148, 150; 1923 defeat, 139
Baldwin, James, 213-14
Balfour, Arthur (Lord Riverdale), 184
Ball, George, 202
Barkley, Vice-President Alben, 194

Barrès, Maurice, 34
Bay of Pigs, 213
Beaverbrook, 1st Lord, xi, 74, 96, 97
Beazley, J. D., 5
Bell, Clive, 12
Bell, Vanessa, 12, 15
Benn, Anthony Wedgwood, 103
Benn, William Wedgwood (Lord Stansgate), 145
Benton, William, 118, 123
Benton, William Hart, 114
Betjeman, Sir John, 163
Bevan, Aneurin, xi; Cripps and, 90, 92; Churchill and, 93; Gaitskell and, 161-2, 169-70, 171, 172, 175-6
Bevin, Ernest, ix, x, 24, 63-80, 89, 92, 100, 170, 171
Bhagat Singh, 147
Biddle, Francis, 214
Bingley, Lord, 139
Birkenhead, Lord, Halifax and, 138, 140, 141, 143, 144-6
Bismarck, 10
Bloomsbury set, Keynes and, 3, 12-13, 15
Blum, Auguste, 30-1
Blum, Léon, ix, x, 29-59, 90; *Du Mariage*, 33-4; *Stendhal et le Beylisme*, 34; *Réforme Gouvernmentale, La*, 39-40
Blum, Lise, 34, 44, 46
Blum, Thérèse, 46, 51
Blumel, André, 50
Bohlen, Charles, 123
Bonham-Carter, Lady Violet, 93
Borgo, Pozzo di, 6
Bose, Subesh Chandra, 143
Bottomley, Horatio, 114
Boulanger, General, 45
Bowra, Sir Maurice, 163-4

INDEX

Bradley, Francis Herbert, 3
Brailsford, Henry Noel, 66
Bretton Woods Agreement, 1, 2, 23–4
Briand, Aristide, 35, 43
Bright, John, 36, 114
Browning, Robert, 41
Brussels Pact, 80
Bryan, William Jennings, 186, 200, 203
Buchenwald, Blum at, 29, 57
Burge, Bishop, 86
Burner, Secretary, 190
Butler, Lord, xi, Cripps and, 83, 102; Stevenson and, 185

Cachin, Marcel, 40, 41, 42, 44, 45, 46, 47
Caillaux, Joseph, 48, 51
Cain, Senator, 123
Calhoun, Senator, 114
Cambridge University, Keynes and, 2, 3–4, 7, 9, 12, 15, 22
Campbell-Bannerman, Sir Henry, 8
Carroll, Lewis, ix
Chamberlain, Austen, 8, 169
Chamberlain, Joseph, 73
Chamberlain, Neville, 29, 91; Cripps and, 95; Halifax and, 135, 149, 150–2, 155
Chautemps, Camille, 45, 46, 49, 51, 52
Chavez, Cesar, 222
Cherwell, Lord, 16
Chiang Kai-shek, 94, 200
Christ, 3
Churchill, Sir Winston, 169, 185; Keynes and, 1, 13, 24; Blum and, 56; Avon and, 65; Bevin and, 74–5; Cripps and, 92–3, 95, 96, 98, 102–3; Halifax and, 135, 139, 145, 147, 150, 152–4, 155, 157
Ciano, Count Galeazzo, 151
Citrine, Sir Walter, 67, 69, 74, 89
Clark, Ramsey, 214
Clay, Henry, 114, 200
Clemenceau, Georges, 9, 10, 39
Cleveland, President Grover, 186
Clichy riots, 50, 51
Clive, Robert, Lord, 141
Cohn, Roy, 123, 125, 127
Cole, G. D. H., 68, 163–4
Combes, Émile, 38
Comintern 41
Common Market, (OEEC), 78, 179

Commonwealth Immigrants' Bill, 179
Cot, Pierre, 48
Cripps, Charles Alfred (Baron Parmoor), 84–5
Cripps, Dame Isobel, 85, 95
Cripps, Sir Stafford, x, 22, 71–2, 73, 83–105, 165, 168, 169, 170, 171, 185
Crossman, R. H. S., 163
Crowe, Sir Eyre, 11
Cuban missile crisis, 215–16
Curzon, Lord, 64, 83, 142; Halifax and, 135, 137, 141
Cushing, Cardinal, 214, 216

Daily Herald, 70
Daladier, Édouard, 48; Blum and, 43, 45, 46, 52, 53, 55
Daley, Richard, 190
Dalton, Hugh, xi, 83; Bevin and, 68, 69, 70, 71, 73, 74; Cripps and, 92, 100; resignation, 101; Halifax and, 152; Gaitskell and, 166, 167
Darlan, Admiral, 56
Das, C. R., 143
Davis, W. O., 186
Deakin, Arthur, 172
Déat, Marcel, 42
Debussy, Claude, 32
De Gaulle, President, xi, 56, 58
Delbos, Yvon, 48
Dever, Governor, 118
Devon, 11th Earl of, 135
Dewey, Thomas E., 120, 192
Dickinson, G. Lowes, 4
Dillon, Douglas, 215, 219
Dirksen, Senator, 129
Disraeli, Benjamin, 184
Dormoy, Marx, 52, 54
Douglas, Paul, 190, 191, 192
Doumergue, Gaston, 45, 46
Dreyfus, Captain Alfred, 36–7
Dreyfus affair, 35, 36–7, 45
Duckworth, 5
Duclos, Jacques, 44
Dulles, John Foster, 123, 124, 184
Dunkirk, Treaty of, 59, 80
Durbin, Evan, 163, 166
Dworshak, Senator, 129

Eberlain, Mike G., 111, 112
Eckermann, J. P., 32
Eddy, Loyal, 116

INDEX

Edelman, Peter, 219
Eden, Sir Anthony, *see* Avon
Eisenhower, President, 109, 119, 183, 210; Joseph McCarthy and, 122, 123, 124, 128; Stevenson and, 184, 191, 194, 196–7, 198, 199–200, 202
Elgin, Lord, 141
Elliot, Colonel Walter, 139
Ervin, Senator Samuel, 129

Faure, Paul, 51–2
Fauré, Gabriel, 34
Flanders, Senator Ralph, 118, 129
Flandin, Pierre, 46
Fonteyn, Dame Margot, 24
Forster, E. M., 12
Foxwell, Professor, 2, 4
France, Anatole, 34
Franco, General, 49
Freeman, Orville, 212
Frossard, Ludovic-Oscar, 40, 41, 52
Frost, Robert, 202
Fry, Roger, 12
Fulbright, William, 118, 125

Gaitskell, Dora, Lady, 166
Gaitskell, Hugh, x, 30, 103, 161–79
Galbraith, J. K., 211
Gamelin, General, 53, 55
Gandhi, Mahatma, 97; Cripps and, 99–100; Halifax and, 143, 145, 146–7
Garfield, President, 195
Garnett, David, 9, 12
Gasperi, Alcide de, xi
General Strike, 66, 69, 164
George V, 147
Gide, André, 32
Gladstone, William Ewart, 36, 194
Goebbels, Dr Joseph, 149
Goering, Field-Marshal Hermann, 149
Goethe, 33
Goldwater, Senator Barry, 217
Grant, Duncan, 5, 9, 12, 15
Green, Dwight H., 191–2
Greenwood, Arthur, 70, 92,
Grey, Charles (2nd Earl) 136
Grey, Sir Edward (Viscount Grey of Falloden), 20, 64, 65, 148
Griffiths, James, 175
Guesde, Jules, 37, 38, 39, 42
Halberstam, David, 219
Haldane, Viscount, 185

Halifax (Edward Wood) 1st Earl, ix, x, xi, 58, 93, 94, 135–57; *The Great Opportunity*, 139
Halifax (Charles Wood), 1st Viscount, 136
Halifax (Charles Lindley Wood), 2nd Viscount, 136, 148
Halifax, Dorothy, Lady, 137, 154, 155, 156
Hallam, Arthur, 3
Harding, President, 197
Harlech, Lord, 139, 154
Harriman, Averell, 185, 195; Churchill and, 154; Halifax and, 156; Stevenson and, 198–9, 200
Harris, Seymour, 19
Harrod, Sir Roy, 14
Harvey, Oliver, 150, 151
Heath, Edward, 64
Henderson, Arthur, 69, 89
Herr, Lucien, 35
Herriot, Édouard, Blum and, 30, 43, 46, 48, 49, 52
Hiss, Alger, 119
Hitler, 11, 29, 84, 130; Blum and, 49, 50, 53, 56; Halifax and, 135, 149, 150, 151
Hoare, Sir Samuel, 139, 149, 151
Hobson, John Atkinson, 16
Hoffa, James, 211
Holroyd, Michael, 4
Hoover, President Herbert, 197
Hoover, J. Edgar, 212
Hopkins, Harry, 154
Hull, Cordell, 65
Humphrey, Hubert, 217; Stevenson and, 200, 201; Robert Kennedy and, 211, 218
Hyndman, Henry Mayers, 66

Ickes, Harold, 154–5
India, Cripps and, 94, 97, 99–100; Halifax and, 135, 141–8, 157; Indian Independence Act, 100
International Monetary Fund, 23, 25

Jackson, Senator, 125, 127, 212
Jaurès, Jean, 44; Blum and, 30, 33, 35–6, 37–9, 40, 52, 53, 58
Jay, Douglas, 163, 166, 168
Jenner, Senator, 123, 126,197
Jessup, Philip, 121

INDEX

Jinnah, Mohammed Ali, 97, 145, 146
Johnson, President, 200, 214;
  Stevenson and, 184; Robert Kennedy
  and, 208, 209, 211, 216, 217–18, 219,
  220, 221
Jowitt, Earl, 87

Kahn, Lord, 17, 68
Kaldor, Nicholas, 68
Kean, Senator, 123
Keating, Senator, 218
Keble, John, 137
Kefauver, Senator, 194, 195, 198, 199, 200
Kelly, Mayor, 190, 191
Kennedy, Edward, 214, 219
Kennedy, Ethel, 208, 210
Kennedy, President John F., Harlech
  and, 154; Stevenson and, 183, 193,
  200, 202–3; Robert Kennedy and,
  208–10, 212–14, 216, 218, 219, 223;
  death, 217
Kennedy, Joseph, 209, 210, 214
Kennedy, Robert, ix, x, xi, 207–23
Kennelly, Maurice, 190
Kerr, Senator, 194
Keynes, x, 1–25, 58, 67–8, 91, 93, 157,
  165; 'Agenda for the President', 20;
  Indian Currency and Finance, 8;
  Economic Consequences of the Peace,
  10–11, 14; *Essays in Biography*, 10–11;
  *General Theory of Employment, Interest
  and Money*, 16–21; *How to Pay for the
  War*, 19; *Revision of the Treaty*, 16;
  Tract on Monetary Reform, 16;
  Treatise on Probability, 16
Keynes, Lydia, 15, 21
Keynes, Florence Ada, 2, 25
King, Martin Luther, 207, 213
King's College, Cambridge, Keynes and,
  2, 3, 7, 14, 15, 25
Knowland, Senator, 120, 123
Knox, Frank, 189
Korean War, 103, 119, 120, 128, 170, 196
Krushchev, Nikita, 200, 201

Labour Party, British, xi, 35; Keynes
  and, 13, 14; Blum at Bournemouth
  Conference, 52; Bevin and, 66, 69,
  70–1, 76–7, 79; Cripps and, 71–2,
  83–4, 86, 89, 90–3, 98–9, 165;
Gaitskell and, 162–3, 164, 166, 171, 176–9
La Fallette, Robert M. (Snr), 111, 114, 130
La Fallette, Robert M. (Jnr), 111–12, 114, 116
Lall, K. B., 179
Lamont, Thomas W., 156
Landon, Alfred Mossman, 120
Lansbury, George, 70, 88, 89; Bevin and, 72–3
Lansdowne, Marquis of, 64, 135, 138, 141
Laski, Harold, 16, 90
Lassalle, Ferdinand, 30
Lattimore, Owen, 121
Laval, Pierre, 46, 53, 57, 148
Law, Bonar, 9, 138, 139
Lawther, Will, 172
League of Nations, 89
Legge, Lady Dorothy, 137
Lehmann, Senator, 118
Lend-Lease, 24, 155
Lenin, 42
Le Troquer, 55
Lincoln, Abraham, 197
Lippmann, Walter, 156
Lloyd George, Earl, 64, 98, 185;
  Keynes and, 9, 10–11, 13; Blum and,
  36; Cripps and, 85; Halifax and, 138
Lodge, Senator, 118
Longuet, Jean, 40, 41, 42
Lothian, Lord, 153, 155
Lucas, Scott, 120–1

MacArthur, General Douglas, 119, 121
MacCarthy, Desmond, 4, 5, 12
McCarthy, Eugene J., 110; Stevenson
  and, 185, 202; Robert Kennedy and,
  217, 220–1
McCarthy, Jean, 124, 131
McCarthy, Joseph, x, 109–31, 197, 198, 210
McCloy, John, 156
McCormick, Colonel, 124, 189
MacDonald, Ramsay, Blum and, 41;
  Bevin and, 67, 69, 71, 75; Cripps
  and, 87; Halifax and, 140, 145;
  resigns, 148
McKenna, Reginald, 8
McKinley, President, 186
McLellan, Senator, 125, 129

INDEX

McLeod, Scott, 123
Macmillan, Harold, 175, 176
Macmillan Committee, 67–8
McNamara, Robert, 200, 219
McTaggart, J. M. E., 4
Maisky, I., 96
Malines Conversations, 136
Mallarmé, Stéphane, 32
Mandel, Georges, 52, 53, 54, 56
Mansfield, Senator, 131
Mantoux, Étienne, 11
Mao Tse-tung, 115
Marie, André, 59
Marquand, Hilary, 168
Marquet, 43
Marshall, Alfred, 1, 7, 16
Marshall, General George, 119; Bevin and, 77; Joseph McCarthy and, 109, 121; Eisenhower and, 122, 197
Marshall Plan, 64, 170; Bevin and, 77–8; Cripps and, 101
Marx, Karl, 35, 40
Maurice, Frederick Denison, 3
Mayer, Daniel, 58, 59
Mercier, Cardinal, 136
Meredith, James, 213
Miller, Mrs, 124
Millerand, Alexandre, 35, 37, 43
Moch, Jules, 54, 57
Mollet, Guy, 58
Molotov, Viacheslav, 94, 96
Mond, Sir Alfred, 13
Mond-Turner talks, 67
Moore, G. E., 3, 4, 6, 12
Morell, Lady Ottoline, 12
Morrison, Herbert (Lord Morrison of Lambeth), xi, 69; Bevin and, 70, 71, 74; Persian oil crisis, 76; Cripps and, 96, 92, 100, 101; Halifax and, 152; Gaitskell and, 162, 170, 172, 175
Mortimer, Raymond, 12
Moyne, Lord, 139
Mundt, Senator, 129
Munich Agreement, 52, 151
Muskie, Senator, 215
Mussolini, 29; Abyssinia and, 89; Halifax and, 135, 150

Nasser, President, 174
NATO, 200; Bevin and, 64, 80
Nazi-Soviet Pact, 52
Negro problem in U.S.A., 213, 216

Nehru, Jawaharlal, xi; Cripps and, 94, 97; Civil Disobedience and, 143; Halifax and, 144, 145
Nehru, Motilal, 143, 145, 146
Newman, Cardinal, 136
Nicolson, Sir Harold, 189
Nixon, President, 109; Joseph McCarthy and, 120, 122, 124, 129; Stevenson and, 197, 201; Robert Kennedy and, 212, 217
Norman, Montagu, 21

OEEC, 78, 179
Onslow, 4th Earl of, 137

Painlevé, Paul, 43
Pakenham, Frank (Lord Longford), 163
Palestine, Bevin and, 79
Palmerston, Lord, 136
Partridge, Ralph, 12
Patel, Vallabpbhavi, 143, 144
Patel, Vittnalbhai, 143
Pattison, Mark, 184
Paul-Boncour, Joseph, 43
Peace Conference, Keynes and, 9–10
Pericles, 10
Pétain, Marshal, 53, 54–5, 56
Pethick-Lawrence, Lord, 99
Pigou, Arthur Cecil, 7, 17, 20
Plowden, Lord, 101, 104
Populaire, Le, 43; Blum and, 31, 32, 57, 59
Porto-Riche, Georges de, 33
Postan, Michael, 165
Potsdam Conference, 76, 77, 99
Potter, Senator, 129
Proust, Marcel, 32

Ramsay, Sir William, 85
Ravel, 34
Rayburn, Senator, 200
Reading, Marquess of, 143–4, 145
Rees-Mogg, William, ix
Reichenbach, Jeanne, 57
Renard, Jules, 33
Renaudel, 43
Reparation Commission, 9
Renaud, Paul, 51, 52, 54
Ricardo, David, 1, 16
Riom trials, 29, 55
Robbins, Lord, 23–4
Robertson, Sir Dennis Holme, 16, 17

INDEX

Robinson, Senator, 186
Rockefeller, Governor Nelson, 185, 207
Roosevelt, Mrs Eleanor, xii, 190, 200, 201
Roosevelt, President Franklin Delano, x, 29, 47, 77, 118–19, 155, 197, 214; Keynes and, 20–1; Blum and, 49, 56; Cripps and, 91; Joseph McCarthy and, 111; Halifax and, 150, 152, 153, 154; Stevenson and, 185, 188, 189, 194, 199; Robert Kennedy and, 216, 217
Roosevelt, President Theodore, 186
Rosebery, Lord, 162
Rothermere, Lord, 95, 145, 147
Rovere, Richard, 109, 130
Runciman, Sir Stephen, 5
Rusk, Dean, 203
Russell, Bertrand, xii, 1, 4, 5, 6
Russell, Lord John, 136
Russell, Senator, 194, 195
Rylands, Dadie, 12

Salengro, Roger, 48, 50
Salisbury, Lord, 185
Sankey, Lord, 87
Sarraut, Albert, 46
Schacht, Dr Hjalmar, 22
Schine, David, 123, 125, 127–8
Schuman Plan, 80
Selburne, Lord, 139
Sembat, Marcel, 39, 42
SFIO, Blum and, 38
Shaw, Bernard, 19, 222
Shawcross, Lord, 168
Sheppard, J. T., 4
Shinwell, Lord, 168
Shove, Gerald, 12
Sidgwick, Henry, 3
Simon, Sir John, 143, 145, 146, 149
Sinclair, Sir Archibald, 93
Smith, Adam, 1, 16
Smith, Governor Al, 70, 186
Smith, Margaret Chase, 118
Snowden, Viscount, 69, 83
Socialist League, 68, 90, 92
Soskice, Sir Frank, 168
Spanish Civil War, 49, 90
Sparrow, John, 163
Spears, General, 53
Spencer, Herbert, 3
Stalin, 115, 123; Cripps and, 94, 95, 96

Stanley, Colonel Oliver, 93, 150
Stassen, Harold, 124
Stavisky scandal, 45
Stendhal, 32, 34
Stephen, Adrian, 12
Stephen, Sir Leslie, 184
Stephen, Thoby, 12
Stephen, Virginia, 12
Stevenson, Adlai Ewing I, 186
Stevenson, Adlai Ewing, x, 109, 122, 161, 183–203, 211
Stevenson, Ellen, 188, 191
Stevenson, Lewis, 185–6
Stimson, Henry Lewis, 156
Strachey, James, 9, 12
Strachey, John, 161, 168
Strachey, Lytton, 12, Keynes and, 3–6, 9, 15, 25
Strachey, Oliver, 12
Strauss, George, 90, 92
Suez, 157, 199; Gaitskell and, 162, 174–5
Swinton, Lord, 139
Swithinbank, B. W., 5
Symington, Senator Stuart, 125, 129, 200, 212

Taft, Robert Alphonso, 117, 121, 123, 196
Tawney, R. H., 86
Taylor, General Maxwell, 219
Tennyson, Lord, 3
Thomas, Albert, 42
Thomas, J. H., 66, 69, 70
Thorez, Maurice, 44, 51
Tillett, Ben, 72, 73
Torrès, Henri, 57
Transport and General Workers' Union, 170, 172
Trevelyan, G. M., 7
Trollope, Anthony, 32
Truman, President, 125, 190, 199; Bevin and, 77, 79; Joseph McCarthy and, 109, 119, 121, 122; Stevenson and, 190, 191, 193, 194, 195, 196, 200
TUC, Bevin and, 64, 66, 70–2, 74; Cripps and, 87
Tydings, Millard, 118, 119, 120–1

UN, Bevin at, 77, 79; Suez and, 174; Stevenson and, 183, 190, 200, 203

UNESCO, 58
USSR, Bevin and, 76–7; Cripps and, 94–7

Vaillant, Edouard, 37
Vandenberg, Senator, 120
Van Susteran, Urban P., 116
Verlaine, Paul, 32, 33
Vietnam War, 196, 216, 219, 220
Vinson, Fred, 25
Viviani, René, 35, 37, 39, 43

Walinsky, Adam, 219
Waverley, Lord (Sir John Anderson), 74
Wayne, Senator, 131
Webb, Beatrice, xii, 84
Webb, Sidney, 86
Webster, Senator, 114
Wechsler, James A., 125–7
Wellesley, Arthur (Duke of Wellington), 141
Werner, Judge, 112
White, Harry Dexter, 23
White, William Allen, 189
Whitehead, Alfred North, 4, 7
Wicksell, Knut, 17
Wiley, Alexander, 112, 114, 115, 131

Wilkie, Wendell, 120
Wilkinson, Ellen, 90
Williams, Francis (Lord Francis-Williams), 70
Williams, Robert, 72, 73
Williamson, Tom, 172
Wilson, Geoffrey, 94
Wilson, Harold, Parl. Sec. to Min. of Works, 64; in 1945 Government, 168; resignation, 171; Shadow Chancellor, 175; leadership challenge to Gaitskell defeated, 178
Wilson, President Woodrow, 9, 18, 199; Keynes and, 20; Stevenson and, 186, 187
Winant, John G., 154
Winterton, Earl, 139
Wood, Sir Kingsley, 93
Woolf, Leonard, 3, 12
Woolf, Virginia (Virginia Stephen), 12
World Bank, Keynes and, 23, 25

Yalta Conference, 77

Zinoviev, Grigori, 42
Zola, Émile, 37
Zwicker, General, 124